What People Are Saying About
A Teen's Guide to Living Drug-Free ...

"Read this book.... It'll be all you ever need to know to make a choice to never use drugs. It's not about being scared to use (although you should be!); it's about respecting the power of chemicals. If you're already using, this book will help you break free."

Brad Schaffer, 15

"After being chemically addicted for three years, I am now clean and sober. When I was 'partying,' I used drugs with many other friends my age. To this day I feel that the drug-related death of one of my friends is my fault. I also feel responsible for many other people's addictions. Even though I can't change what has happened or directly make amends to my friend, I can change my life for the better and help reduce the tragedies that may lie ahead for myself and others if I don't change. It's a choice I have to make each and every day. So when I hear other teens say that as long as you don't use drugs or drink *all the time*—that it's okay to use once in a while—I know they're really kidding themselves, because it's your body or brain that decides, not you. And when you're hooked, your own private chaos, pain and hell begins. I consider *A Teen's Guide to Living Drug-Free* a book that can help me and other teens learn the real truth about drugs—a truth I don't ever remember being told before."

Lauren Hellerman, 17

"*A Teen's Guide to Living Drug-Free* speaks to teens in all stages of drug and alcohol experience: those who have never used, those who are now using, and those who have stopped using and are working to stay clean and sober. This excellent book offers a practical guide for parents and teens either needing information or faced with substance-abuse problems. I highly recommend this book; it will prove to be a welcome addition to the growing concern of chemical dependency in our youth."

Marsha Mathews, M.A., M.F.T.
program manager, Mental Health Systems, Inc.,
Options for Recovery and Family Treatment Center

"I know a lot of teens who are using and who know they're running into a problem, but they don't know how to *stop* using. I had a drug problem two years ago, and not knowing what to do and where to turn for help (in the beginning, I didn't want to tell my parents or teachers), my problem went on for a lot longer than it would have otherwise. This book would have given me the direction I needed to help myself. As it was, it took me nearly two years to stumble around until finally I hit a bottom so low that at last I got the help I needed—but it took three months in a jail cell first. That doesn't have to be the case. This book is going to help a lot of people."

Juanita Hill, 16

"As I reviewed *A Teen's Guide to Living Drug-Free* with my son, I also gained a wealth of insight. I'm thoroughly convinced that helping my son make it through adolescence without succumbing to drugs is one of the most important—and critical—jobs I face. This book is going to be a big help with that job."

Christopher Briley
parent of teen and school-board member

"In my work in juvenile corrections, I'm confronted with the fact that drug use and abuse among teens lead to serious and heartbreaking conse-quences. *A Teen's Guide to Living Drug-Free* helps keep teens from ever hav-ing to face such disastrous outcomes by providing them with the information they need to say no to using drugs and alcohol—as well as tools for staying clean and sober and building their recovery. This comprehensive and much-needed book is deserving of a place in every public and school library, cor-rection centers of all types, and most especially, homes everywhere."

Loretta Taylor, M.A.
supervisor, Riverside County Juvenile Detention Facility

"I appreciated the honest, open approach in this book. Especially helpful is learning what you can do to get off drugs, and then what it takes to stay clean and sober—that's information that's not really a part of the 'just say no' campaign you always hear about. Every teen—and maybe fifth- and sixth-graders, too—should read this book, whether they've never used or are already deep into using."

Maria Selene Rios, 15

"Learning what it takes to get free of drugs was all the information I needed to make me clear on my decision not to try them—ever."

Leticia Murose, 13

"No matter what their age, children look to their parents as a reliable source of information on the serious issues that affect their lives—certainly drug use is one of those issues. I believe all parents should consider adding this book to their teen's library. The stories from the teens themselves are sure to lend the lessons even greater weight with other teen readers. This is a book I can feel good about recommending to all parents of teens."

Marta Hemmeter
educator, Wilson Middle School

"I've used for a couple of years and have done some really awful things to get drugs. Some people don't understand that using changes your life to the point where you just feel hopeless, and like you can never again be what you were. So you end up feeling like a 'lowlife.' Although I'm hooked—an addict—I don't want to be. Reading this book was like a ray of hope. I am a person who is chemically dependent—but I can, with help, break free of my addiction. I've wanted to for nearly a year—and now I know how to begin. I also have a realistic view of how hard I will have to work to reclaim my life. But I am going to do whatever it takes to make it."

Samile Watts, 15

"Sadly, adolescents are one of the most under-addressed populations in the field of recovery. *A Teen's Guide to Living Drug-Free* helps fill this void, first by providing teens with solid information and resources for where to go when they or a friend or family member needs help with getting clean and sober, as well as offering really useful solutions for teens to strengthen their recovery and live life drug-free. The potential effects of getting this information to teens is far-reaching: If just one teen is spared the suffering of addiction and gets his life together, it could in turn impact many other teens—by that teen's not affecting peers in a negative direction."

Mark S. Carpenter, C.A.S. (Certified Addictions Specialist)
systems administrator, Mental Health Systems

"A lot of my friends are starting to 'check out' different drugs. I don't want to use, but it's difficult to know how to say 'no' like you really mean it, especially when you're curious about using. But after reading *A Teen's Guide to Living Drug-Free*, I learned about where drugs can lead just by reading the stories of teens who did use. So now I know I can handle saying, 'No thanks,' even with my friends."

Vanessa Michaels, 14

"According to the U.S. Surgeon General, one out of five young people in our country shows signs of having a mental-health problem, and half of these young people will also develop a problem with drugs. It's a well-known fact that young people with mental-health problems often turn to alcohol and street drugs to try and treat themselves, or 'self-medicate,' which often leads to drug addiction. *A Teen's Guide to Living Drug-Free* provides teens with everything they need to know to get and stay drug-free. It will also be useful in another area: to allay the fears of parents and family members. With proper treatment, people do recover from addiction disorders, resulting in improved relationships, strengthened coping skills and other behaviors that can make life better. This is a most valuable book."

David C. Mancuzzi, M.D.
director, Center for the Treatment Adolescent
and Family Addiction Issues

"I used and my life really fell apart, but now I'm in recovery. This book is great. Not only does it help kids who have never used drugs or alcohol, but it gives teens like me, who are in recovery, direction on how to stay clean—which is the biggest and most difficult challenge I've ever faced."

Tyson Eckhart, 17

"In general, people don't just naturally know how to cope with friends or family members who are using drugs or alcohol. To expect teens to come by this knowledge without help is unreasonable—and it could even be *dangerous. A Teen's Guide to Living Drug-Free* provides teens with practical direction for coping with friends or family members who are using drugs and alcohol. It goes on to be of value to *all* teens with its convincing arguments on why not to use in the first place and its tools for how to do this, as well as with its information on how to get clean and sober and its effective strategies for preventing relapse. It's encouraging to see a book of this magnitude for teens."

Debbie Corso
assistant director, Choices in Recovery,
Residential Recovery Program

"Chemical dependency is a disease, and it takes treatment to deal with it. I know because I used for three years, starting at the age of ten. Now I've been clean for two years, and it's really, really tough when you attend a school where a good 40 percent of the students use. I liked this book because, more than anything else, it gives teens 'permission' not to feel like a loser and to get on with sorting out their lives. It's the message they need—and want—to hear. Thanks for making this book happen for teens."

Jessica Black, 15

"I work 'on the streets' where I see the ill effects of drugs and crime, and the devastation they reap. I was thrilled to find *A Teen's Guide to Living Drug-Free* so thoroughly addressed the topic of substance abuse and its *real* consequences for teens. From helping teens making a choice to never use, to saying no even when confronted with peer pressure, to knowing what to do once deep in the pit of their use, this book will help."

Justin White
police officer, juvenile division

"People who are addicted aren't able to decide to just stop once they're hooked; they need help. After reading this book, I have a better understanding of how drugs work on the body and brain to make them 'addicted.' I can tell you that some of my friends use and, of those who do, some are trying to put on a good front, as if they like using when, in fact, they don't. This book is going to be big with teens. I know my friends will put a different book jacket on it so that no one sees them reading it, but it'll work its way around to teens in my school."

Kent Paulenwitz, 16

"Our teens are certain to be confronted by drugs and alcohol in some way—but pretending the problem doesn't exist could prove to be disastrous. Since they'll be faced with making a stand as to whether or not they'll say 'no,' or use but only 'a little,' it's vital that they know the truth about the effects of these chemicals. More importantly, it's crucial for them to know how to follow through with a decision to say 'no.' In spite of the popular slogan, our young people seldom feel like there is any 'just' about 'saying no' to their peers. *A Teen's Guide to Living Drug-Free* can help them learn to be resolved in saying no to using drugs and alcohol."

Katherine H. Kelly, Ph.D.
family issues counselor

"Now that I'm in recovery, I want to do everything I can to make sure I stay clean and sober. *A Teen's Guide to Living Drug-Free* can help me avoid a relapse. I learned everything from how to deal with my problems without getting high to figuring out what my own personal 'triggers' are (the people and situations that can make me want to use). After reading this book, I feel like I have some tools to fight off the feelings and physical cravings I get that make me want to use."

Terry Drake, 17

"I loved the way this book treats me, which is, that I'll understand the truth about drugs and alcohol. Now I can make my decisions based on facts. It's also cool to hear from other teens who are going through the same decisions or have already made decisions. This book wasn't afraid to say it all, and I'm grateful for that."

Lauren L. Lowe, 16

A Teen's Guide to Living Drug-Free

Bettie B. Youngs, Ph.D., Ed.D.
Jennifer Leigh Youngs

**Authors of the bestselling
Taste Berries™ for Teens series**

Tina Moreno

HCI TEENS™

**Health Communications, Inc.
Deerfield Beach, Florida**

*www.hci-online.com
www.tasteberriesforteens.com*

We would like to acknowledge the following publishers and individuals for permission to reprint the following material. (Note: The stories that were penned anonymously, that are public domain or were previously unpublished stories written by Bettie B. Youngs or Jennifer Leigh Youngs are not included in this listing. Also not included in this listing but credited within the text are those stories contributed or based upon stories by teens.)

The Twelve Steps. Reprinted by permission of NA World Services, Inc., from Narcotics Anonymous, Fifth Edition ©1988 by NA World Services, Inc. All rights reserved. Adapted from the Twelve Steps of Alcoholics Anonymous with permission of AA World Services, Inc., New York, N.Y.

Catch Me—If You Can! by Gianne Warren. Reprinted with permission by publisher Health Communications, Inc., Deerfield Beach, Florida, adapted from *Taste Berries for Teens: Inspirational Short Stories and Encouragement on Life, Love, Friendship and Tough Issues* by Bettie B. Youngs, Ph.D., Ed.D. and Jennifer Leigh Youngs. ©1999 Bettie B. Youngs, Ph.D., Ed.D. and Jennifer Leigh Youngs.

Dear Crystal . . . by Paige Olds. Reprinted with permission by publisher Health Communications, Inc., Deerfield Beach, Florida, adapted from *Taste Berries for Teens #3: Inspirational Stories and Encouragement on Life, Love, Friends and the Face in the Mirror* by Bettie B. Youngs, Ph.D., Ed.D. and Jennifer Leigh Youngs. ©2002 Bettie B. Youngs, Ph.D., Ed.D. and Jennifer Leigh Youngs.

Library of Congress Cataloging-in-Publication Data

Youngs, Bettie B.
    A teen's guide to living drug free / Bettie B. Youngs, Jennifer Leigh Youngs.
      p. cm.
    ISBN 0-7573-0041-3 (tp)
      1. Teenagers—Drug use. 2. Drug abuse. 3. Narcotic addicts—Rehabilitation I. Title: Teen's guide to living drug free. II. Youngs, Jennifer Leigh, date. III. Title.

HV5824.Y68 Y624 2003
613.'8—dc21

                2002027397

Publisher: Health Communications, Inc.
        3201 S.W. 15th Street
        Deerfield Beach, FL 33442-8190

Cover illustration and design by Andrea Perrine Brower
Inside book typesetting by Lawna Patterson Oldfield

To: _____

From: _____

Also by Bettie B. Youngs

A Taste-Berry Teen's Guide to Setting & Achieving Goals (Health Communications, Inc.)

Taste Berries for Teens #3: Inspirational Stories and Encouragement on Life, Love, Friends and the Face in the Mirror (Health Communications, Inc.)

A Taste-Berry Teen's Guide to Managing the Stress and Pressures of Life (Health Communications, Inc.)

More Taste Berries for Teens: A Second Collection of Inspirational Short Stories and Encouragement on Life, Love, Friendship and Tough Issues (Health Communications, Inc.)

Taste Berries for Teens Journal: My Thoughts on Life, Love and Making a Difference (Health Communications, Inc.)

Taste Berries for Teens: Inspirational Short Stories and Encouragement on Life, Love, Friendship and Tough Issues (Health Communications, Inc.)

Taste-Berry Tales: Stories to Lift the Spirit, Fill the Heart and Feed the Soul (Health Communications, Inc.)

A String of Pearls: Inspirational Stories Celebrating the Resiliency of the Human Spirit (Adams Media)

Gifts of the Heart: Stories That Celebrate Life's Defining Moments (Health Communications, Inc.)

Values from the Heartland: Stories of an American Farmgirl (Health Communications, Inc.)

Stress and Your Child: Helping Kids Cope with the Strains and Pressures of Life (Random House)

You and Self-Esteem: A Book for Young People—Grades 5–12 (Jalmar Press)

Safeguarding Your Teenager from the Dragons of Life: A Parent's Guide to the Adolescent Years (Health Communications, Inc.)

How to Develop Self-Esteem in Your Child: 6 Vital Ingredients (Macmillan/Ballantine)

Self-Esteem for Educators: It's Job Criteria #1 (Jalmar Press)

Keeping Our Children Safe: A Guide to Emotional, Physical, Intellectual and Spiritual Wellness (John Knox/Westminster Press)

Developing Self-Esteem in Your Students: A K–12 Curriculum (Jalmar Press)

Getting Back Together: Repairing the Love in Your Life (Adams Media)

Is Your Net-Working? A Complete Guide to Building Contacts and Career Visibility (John Wiley)

Managing Your Response to Stress: A Guide for Administrators (Jalmar Press)

Stress Management Skills for Educators (Jalmar Press)

Problem Solving Skills for Children (Jalmar Press)

Also by Jennifer Leigh Youngs

A Taste-Berry Teen's Guide to Setting & Achieving Goals (Health Communications, Inc.)

Taste Berries for Teens #3: Inspirational Stories and Encouragement on Life, Love, Friends and the Face in the Mirror (Health Communications, Inc.)

A Taste-Berry Teen's Guide to Managing the Stress and Pressures of Life (Health Communications, Inc.)

More Taste Berries for Teens: A Second Collection of Inspirational Short Stories and Encouragement on Life, Love, Friendship and Tough Issues (Health Communications, Inc.)

Feeling Great, Looking Hot & Loving Yourself! Health, Fitness and Beauty for Teens (Health Communications, Inc.)

Taste Berries for Teens Journal: My Thoughts on Life, Love and Making a Difference (Health Communications, Inc.)

Taste Berries for Teens: Inspirational Short Stories and Encouragement on Life, Love, Friendship and Tough Issues (Health Communications, Inc.)

Contents

UNIT III: YOU WANT TO STOP USING: WHAT TO DO AND HOW TO DO IT

Contents

UNIT IV: YOU'RE CLEAN AND SOBER: HOW TO STAY THAT WAY

13. **A Road to Recovery: Walking the Twelve-Step Program**

UNIT VI: YOUR PERSONAL—
AND PRIVATE—JOURNAL

20. How Journaling Can Help You Survive Your Feelings

Acknowledgments

We would like to thank those in the development of this book. First, to the many teens who were a part of this book: Thank you for so generously sharing your experiences so that other teens might better understand theirs. As always, you teach us the importance of living close to your heart and to greet each day with anticipated wonder. In working with as many teens as we do in the *Taste Berries for Teens* books, we learn firsthand of your challenges in finding your way and making your place in the world. We appreciate and respect your valor as you continue your sincere work to both fit in and find your own voice.

As always, we extend a heartfelt gratitude to our publisher, Peter Vegso, whose vision of "changing the world one book at a time" is an awesome model of bringing all that is noble about being a taste berry into the world. We'd also like to thank the talented and loyal staff at Health Communications—most especially those with whom we work most closely: Lisa Drucker, Susan Tobias, Christine Belleris, Lori Golden, Kim Weiss, Randee Feldman, Tom Sand, Larissa Henoch and Terry Burke, as well as so many others who are intricately woven into transporting our works into the hands and hearts of our readers. We also extend a very special thanks to the taste berries in our office who worked closely on this project, most especially a staff of teens whose valuable input in this book is evident throughout.

Working on this book has been a huge undertaking. The task of instilling the desire to live drug-free in teens, as well as inspiring the belief in everything that supports it, is an enormous and important one. In the course of collaborating on this book, the three of us developed a deep appreciation for what teens are up against living in a world that sends so many conflicting messages. We grew to appreciate working together as well. The synergy of our three hearts, minds, education and life experiences wove together to create a richer perspective. Each of us came away from the experience with an even deeper respect and admiration for each other.

We would also like to thank some of the very special people in our personal lives:

Bettie: Thank you Dad and guardian angel Mom, and my brothers and sisters and their families. Thank you Maria Rios; your loyal friendship and loving spirit never cease to amaze me. You make my life easier, and I thank you for that. To "my little chicken," Jennifer Youngs; you sweeten my life "just because." Always I honor the tenderness of who you are and deeply respect the privilege of watching your soul journey in this realm. You've been the most complicated and heart-tenderizing of all my life lessons, and you've been my best and most prized teacher, as well. It's because of you—and with you—that I experience my deepest joy. Let's journey together, always! And to Tina Moreno, for your "footwork" on this book, of course, but also for the gift of the years I've known you—all in which you've shown me the radiance of an angelic spirit. You are an obvious child of God, an enlightened soul and a kind heart in all the world. Always it is meaningful and sheer fun to collaborate with you. Thanks to special friends: Karen Billings, Mia Semo, Terry Edgar, Jenny Hawkins, Suzee Vlk, Cathy Schmatenberger, Genta Hawkins and "Bonkers Brian"—you all are a source of pure friendship and pure delight. Thank you for sharing my life and holding my heart in such a touchingly human way.

Jennifer: From the bottom of my heart, Mom (Bettie Youngs), thank you. I so appreciate the time we share in working together almost as much as I honor the love we have for each other. Every year I learn how special it is that in life we have one another. I am blessed. Thank you for listening to me in a way that always allows me to feel heard; it means so much to me. And thank you for all the coaching and encouragement that help me stay true to myself. Most of all, thank you for my life—and for your unrelenting diligence to see that I honor it, always. You're brilliant and beautiful—inside and out. Thank you, Dad (Dic Youngs). You are my hero! And a very special thank-you for the love and support of Genta, Fred, Tyla, Ken, Paula, Jimmy, Shari and to Joe—you're the best of the best!

Tina: I'm honored to have the opportunity to acknowledge and express my gratitude and appreciation to the following people: To my husband, Mark Carpenter, a dynamic example of integrity in both the field of recovery and in life—your love and support enhance all my endeavors in life. I both love and thank you for being the exceptional man you are. To my children, Kristi, Cory, Lena and Delia, who continue to teach me new lessons in love, humility and acceptance: Thank you for your patience and love. I want to thank my mentor in the field of recovery, Marsha Mathews, whose tireless dedication, professionalism and genuine compassion are truly inspiring (and who was a wonderful resource in the writing of this book). I'd also like to thank the esteemed addictionologist, Dr. Robert MacFarlane, who was kind enough to serve as a reference in the writing of this book—thank you, "Dr. Bob." Thank you also to the women in my twelve-step support group—especially to my sponsor and dear friend, Deb C.; words can't express my gratitude for your years of selfless love and guidance. Also Joanne L., who never fails to help me find the humor in life—thanks for making sure I never get too serious about myself. And to my favorite spiritual advisors: my friends, Rev. Alice Bandy and Katherine Economou, RScP—no matter what the professional or personal project, you are always there to lovingly remind me of the "eternal perspective," and I thank you both so much for that. Finally, to Bettie and Jennifer—how we've all watched each other grow through the years! Bettie, as our relationship has evolved, both professionally and as two souls making our journey through life, you've taught me so much; in fact, I'd dare to say you were one of the great teachers in my life. Thank you for being a "taste berry" and for all the ways you've shared your wealth of life experiences with me. Jennifer, I've had the opportunity to watch you go through some amazing changes. You have such a kind and generous heart, and I have a genuine respect for all you are doing with your life.

And from the three of us: We give glory to God, from whom all blessings flow.

Introduction

Dear Teens,

Welcome to *A Teen's Guide to Living Drug-Free*, a book for teens about one of the most important decisions you will ever make. As you are all too well-aware, drugs and alcohol have become such a presence in our society that, as Amber Hill describes below, most teens are sure to be touched by them in some way.

I went to a party with two of my best friends, Emily and Peyton. I wasn't shocked that beer turned up and that some of the kids were offering it around. But I was surprised when my friend Emily casually accepted the offer. Worse yet, she started acting so pathetic—saying things in a real exaggerated way and flirting with practically every guy there. Then she ended up in a fight with another girl over a guy she'd just met (and who, I think, may have been the boyfriend of the girl she was fighting with). I was embarrassed because everyone was egging her on. Since she'd been drinking, Emily didn't "get" that she'd become the entertainment. At least my friend Peyton kept her head about her, which I appreciated when we walked outside to get some fresh air. There stood a couple of kids who were smoking a joint and, when they saw us, they offered it up to us. "No thanks," Peyton said casually for both of us, and we walked away from them. But I noticed that Nate Breceda, a guy from our class at school, had taken them up on their offer. So, it's just inevitable that a lot of kids are going to use, because alcohol and drugs are pretty much everywhere. Still, I'm trying not to use them, and so far I've succeeded.

Amber Hill, 9th grade

Just as Amber knows, alcohol and drugs are "pretty much everywhere," so to pretend they won't come into *your* life in some way could be dangerous. Sooner or later, like Amber, you will have to make a choice about using (even if you are using now)—and be able to defend your choice. Be smart: Know the facts.

So what is your position? Where do you stand? How do you make choices about what is best for you? You know it's never as simple as "Just say no." If a friend is offering you drugs or alcohol—and everyone is "egging you on" to "try it"—you don't want to look like you "can't handle it," like you're rejecting your friends. And, of course, you do want to be "cool"—so what do you do in this situation? Even though you know drugs and alcohol aren't for you, the desire to fit in may tempt you to go ahead and try them. *Will you, or won't you?* Then again, maybe you associate using "just a little bit" of alcohol or drugs with having a good time. Maybe you hear friends say it can't hurt as long as you use "just a little" and you think maybe that's okay then. Or perhaps you've already used drugs or alcohol, and you know it's affecting you and you're thinking it's time to stop. Maybe you're having a serious problem using, and you want to stop, but you are already chemically dependent—addicted—and feel trapped. You don't know what to do or where to turn. Maybe you have a friend or a family member who has a problem, and you have no idea how to deal with it. No matter which of these situations describes your own, *A Teen's Guide to Living Drug-Free* can help.

This book is designed to be your handbook, giving you straightforward information on alcohol and drugs and their effects on your mind and body. It will also help you understand—for yourself—the ways in which "using" can alter your ambitions, change your priorities, misalign your goals and undermine your relationships—with parents and other family members, teachers, even friends. Please understand that this book is not intended to "scare" you about drugs, but rather to give you a healthy respect for the ways in which alcohol and drugs—chemicals—react within the human body, and why, how and when, chemical dependency (addiction) sets in. It will also inform you how to get free of drugs, and stay clean and sober so that you can get your goals—and life—back on track.

Again, know the facts. Don't be naïve; even if you've made the choice not to use, you'll have to defend your position so as to keep it that way. We live in a world where drugs and alcohol are readily available, and where the stigma of using has all but evaporated. The sobering reality is that 49 percent of teens will "experiment," and of those, nearly 34 percent will become "casual users." Of those, 28 percent will come to have "a problem"; in other words, they will become chemically dependent.

Don't be fooled by myths like "it won't happen to me" because "I can stop when I want" and "besides, I only use just a little." No one starts out saying, "I'd like to become chemically dependent." No one ever intends to become "an addict." Again, be smart: Understand how alcohol and drugs work. This book is intended to give you information on what you'll need to know about how alcohol and drugs work, in order to help you make the choice to be drug-free. And, if you or one of your friends or family members is already using, it will tell you what you can do and what kind of help is available. If you've quit using drugs and alcohol and want help staying drug- and alcohol-free, you'll find support and direction on how to bolster and maintain your hard-won drug-free status.

The book, divided into six units, is designed to give you:

- Clear, assertive, "cool" ways to say "no" to using drugs and alcohol when you're face-to-face with needing to take a stand—and pronto
- The plain facts about alcohol and drugs and their effects on the body and mind

- An understanding of "using" versus "chemical dependency" (addiction)
- Effective ways for "helping" friends (or family members) who are using
- Information on where to go when you (or a friend or family member) need help getting clean and sober
- Tools for staying clean and sober once you've stopped using
- Skills to prevent relapse and cope successfully with the stress and situations that "trigger" relapse
- Information and knowledge to get and stay in "recovery"— a working plan to stay clean and sober—and how to surround yourself with those who support your sobriety and help you have fun in "safe" ways so as not to relapse
- A guided journal section to use for getting your thoughts out of your head and down on paper so as to get a clearer perspective of your problems and their solutions

Doing what it takes to stay drug- and alcohol-free isn't all that easy in today's times. You'll want to be open to all the support you can get with this goal. Has someone reached out to help you when you felt overwhelmed and helped you cope with the situation? Have others shared themselves, their insights and information to help you deal with a problem or to answer some questions in your life? On some days—especially those when we're not quite so sure what to do next, or we need help doing what we know is right—we could all use such support! You can consider this book your personal handbook of support. What's more, staying drug-free can make you a supportive role model to others as you show them by example how staying drug- and alcohol-free works in your life.

We know it's not always easy being a teen. We know it takes determination and courage to meet your busy, hectic schedule and to thrive in a world that all too often doesn't support young people in all the ways they need to grow up drug-free. But you *can* do it. As so many teens tell us, the most difficult part of life is managing your feelings and emotions in relation to all that is going on. Doing this with an "audience" of peers watching, most of whom are trying to understand their own emotions and feelings as well, can make it all the more trying. But know that you *can survive* your feelings. What's more, you want to face them, "feel" them and deal with them in an open and honest way. Don't believe the myth that alcohol or drugs will help you manage your life "bigger, better, quicker." You know the *sell job:* "Drugs can alter your feelings, give you courage and self-confidence, and make your fears, stress and anxiety go away." And because it's somewhat acceptable within your peer group, "using" can even make you seem like you're "bonded" with others and therefore not "alone," and like you're one of the group, "hip," willing to be "extreme"—in a word, "cool."

Fortunately, you know better than to buy into the "sell" — because the truth is, there is a price, a toll to be paid for altering your body's chemistry via alcohol and drugs. Take the time to know exactly what that price is so that you can learn to balance the "pain and strain" of your emotions in healthy ways—without using chemicals to do it. Learning how to cope effectively with hectic and stressful—and boring and "uncool"—times in positive ways gives you confidence and the skills to handle life—real life. The more you build a storehouse of positive experiences of seeing yourself as successfully handling difficult times in positive ways, the better able you are to handle other tough times. Having said that, it's important to remind you that, while many teens can handle the day-to-day struggle of life, some stresses, strains, pressures, problems and pains—especially chemical abuse—are too much for anyone to handle alone.

No one expects you to go it alone, nor should you. If you are facing a situation or times that seem overwhelming, rather than suffer alone or resort to doing things that are self-destructive, we urge you to seek help. This is especially true in cases of physical, emotional or sexual abuse, suicidal feelings, eating disorders, depression, pregnancy and, as we said previously, drug or alcohol abuse. If you are uncertain where to go for counseling, turn to an adult (whether a parent, teacher, school guidance counselor or clergyperson) whom you feel you can trust to direct you to the proper place. Also, many schools provide peer crisis counseling, and there are any number of toll-free hotlines that offer teens valuable information and can direct you to other sources of help. Again, use this book as a handbook for direction on what to do and where to turn for help and support in living your life free from chemical dependency. Remember, you do deserve all the rewards that life has to offer, but you need to do what it takes to keep traveling the road toward acquiring them—staying drug- and alcohol-free is part of that footwork.

As always, we look forward to hearing from you! We'd love to hear about the taste berries in your lives and how you've learned to be taste berries in the lives of others. To that end, we invite your comments on how you found this book helpful and welcome your stories about how you're coping with teen life. We'd love to hear about the incredibly powerful and positive things you are doing and how staying drug- and alcohol-free has helped you achieve those things. We are now working on a new, upcoming edition of our *Taste Berries for Teens* series, so if you have a story or a poem you'd like to submit, please send it to us at:

Taste Berries for Teens
c/o Teen Team
3060 Racetrack View Drive
Del Mar, CA 92014

A Special Word from the Authors

This book is intended as a self-help and reference guide only, not as a substance-abuse treatment manual, nor a medical manual. The information provided is designed to help teens make informed decisions about their health and well-being in regards to living drug- and alcohol-free. It is not intended as a substitute for drug or alcohol treatment, or a recovery or chemical-dependency program. If you are a teen who suspects you have a substance-abuse problem, we urge you to seek the help of chemical-dependency professionals.

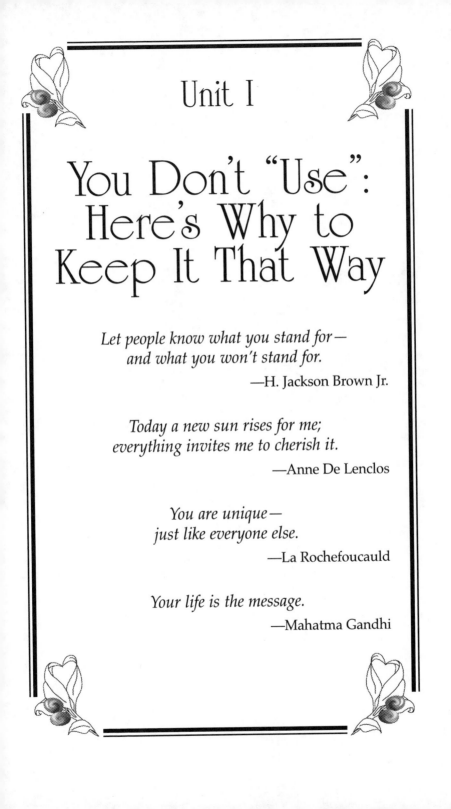

Unit I

You Don't "Use": Here's Why to Keep It That Way

Let people know what you stand for—
and what you won't stand for.

—H. Jackson Brown Jr.

Today a new sun rises for me;
everything invites me to cherish it.

—Anne De Lenclos

You are unique—
just like everyone else.

—La Rochefoucauld

Your life is the message.

—Mahatma Gandhi

Living Life Drug-Free: The Rewards Are Real—And You're Worth It!

Finally—I've Got a Life!

This year I finally have a life! I'm feeling less like a kid and more grown-up, like, finally, things are beginning to happen.

I'm in the ninth grade, so things are pretty hectic, but exciting, too! I have a lot going on. There's the typical stuff, like school and sports and all, but there are also some "goals" that are really important to me—and I'm so excited about them. For one, Habitat for Humanity has a project in our community, and I've been chosen to be on the team of teens who gets to help with building a home for a family in need—from the ground up! That's not all. I got into the photography class I wanted. The teacher is known to be the most awesome around—even has a background as a photojournalist (which is really cool, because it's what I'd love to do for a career)! But it gets even better than that. Even though I'm just a freshman, I get to be on the photography committee for the school annual. So we get to travel with the basketball team to out-of-town games to take all the pictures. Our team is really good, and they'll be going all the way to the state capital if they win—which they are expected to. So guess who'll be there, too!

3

I have other goals, as well. Like in the love department, I want Justin Holt, who is in my class, to notice me and to be my "hand-holding, walk-me-to-my-locker, sit-with-me-at-lunch, meet-me-at-ballgames-dances-and-the-movies, hugs-and-kisses boyfriend!" I'm hoping things will work out, but it's going to take a little time, I think. Justin is cute, a "serious" student, and really shy. He asked me to dance (finally) at the school dance three weeks ago, but only one dance—the last dance. Still, it was a great one dance. I don't know if it took him that long to work up the courage, or if he danced with me because his friends put him up to it. I think he's as nervous about having a girlfriend as I am about having a boyfriend, but I know all the anxiety I feel is worth it, because the idea of having a someone special in your life is a very, very good feeling. Even though it's still not a for-sure thing, the idea of having Justin be my boyfriend for this year is a really big deal for me!

Fitting in, having friends and, I'd have to say, getting along with them are probably what stresses me out most. I mean, you really have to keep track of things, and you can never quite be sure about anything. Like, I've learned that sometimes someone can be a part of a group, but it doesn't necessarily mean everyone in that circle of "friends" will be loyal to you. Some friends always like to hear that everything's going great for you, but some get jealous pretty easily. It takes some doing to always know the rules of the game—and to play the game, because you can't trust everyone. Like if Jessica Robinson knew just how much I liked Justin, she'd say things and probably screw it up for me. So I find the friendship thing tricky. Last year when Tilly Moreno, a girl in our group, told Jessica she had a crush on Charles Tamen, Jessica stood up in the cafeteria and got everyone's attention by banging on her tray. When everyone stopped talking, good old Jessica announced that we should all "clap for the two new lovebirds," and then announced their names. Well, as you can imagine, Charles's face got red, and Tilly's jaw almost dropped to the floor and she almost fainted. So though the two had never become "lovebirds" (I seriously doubt whether Charles and Tilly had talked more than a couple of times), any chance that they might end up in a boyfriend–girlfriend thing was history by the time Jessica finished her meddling that lunch hour.

While the friendship thing can be very tricky, I can't imagine not having a group of friends to hang out with. Being in the student center and library and at school assemblies would be a "brutal" experience if you were to face each situation all alone. I mean, each and every day, just walking in to a class is a total "check-you-out" experience. It can be pretty unnerving to be looked at up and down, or to have someone criticize or joke about the way you talk or the way you walk. So having a friend sort of buffers that.

Still, friends have problems of their own, and if you're a friend, you're drawn in to that, too. I have a good friend whose parents are divorcing, and it's really upsetting and scary for her. Another friend just broke off with her boyfriend of six months, and she's really heartbroken. And yet another friend has started smoking pot (because her boyfriend does), and I'm worried that the guy she likes is a real pothead, and I'm afraid she's going to get caught up in it, too. Sometimes it's tough to know just what is the best way you can help a friend make it through her own tough spots.

Another big thing going on in my life is that I'm trying to do the best I can in school. Although I'm not certain what I want to do for a career, I do know that I'd like to go to college. So, I'm working at getting good grades so I get accepted. For me, school is probably the center of my life. Everything revolves around it. My parents probably judge how well my life is going from what happens in school—grades, friends, my being excited about how I'm doing and going about things. And practically everyone in the universe says that school is the only way to your "future" so I'm just trying to do the best I can. And I do have some really good friends, and it's great being with them—and Justin goes to the same school as I do! Plus, I play on the girls' softball team. While it's a seasonal sport, it takes up a lot of time, but I love to play—and I'm pretty good at it, too.

So like I said, life is hectic. There are so many things going on, and getting everything done always seems like it's impossible. Yet you want to make it possible; you want to make it happen. I want to be cool. I mean, having it all together, feeling good about myself, liking the way I look and thinking about my future are all really important to me. I hear all the phrases, like "sky's the limit" and "go for it!" and stuff, and I want to do it all—but it takes a lot of energy. Everything is always a priority, and I seem to live in a state of "tense." I try to run my life according to goals I set for myself, but the truth is, I run according to my feelings. I am, it seems, my feelings. But all and all, I manage. A lot of really good things are happening for me. I want to "keep on keeping on" and make my life even better (which is one of many reasons I don't ever want to get involved in drugs). I don't want to mess up my life. I'm having a lot of fun—especially this year! So, I intend to stay drug-free because I know it's really worth it!

Carrie Sharritt, 16

Be Smart—Don't Mess Up;
Say "Yes!" to (Your) Life

As Carrie Sharritt's description of the things going on in her life shows, teen life is hectic, stressful—and very full and exciting, too! In fact, we might conclude that her life is very "ordinary" for teens her age, or at least for those who are living drug-free and not battling chemical addiction. The point is, adolescence is *the* time to have all of the many things Carrie had going on: a full life building positive experiences at home, at school and with friends.

The easy part is that your life is busy, filled with activities that can help you go about discovering your interests, talents and aptitudes. But as Carrie alluded to, the more difficult part is managing your feelings and emotions in relation to all that is going on—and then doing this with an "audience" of peers watching. If there is any one big "tough stuff" that resonates with most all teens, it is, as they say, to "survive my own feelings."

Surviving your feelings is about managing them. How do you sort out all that you are to "do" and "be" and come away feeling good about yourself? It's a big job, and a difficult one in a culture which all too often sends mixed signals about always needing to be "on top of your game," but "balance" life; about fitting in but staying true to yourself; and about "saying no to drugs"—but here's a (chemical) "solution" to help you feel any way you wish.

Don't fall for the lie that alcohol or drugs will make you "bigger, better, quicker." You know the "con": Drugs can alter your feelings, give you courage and self-confidence. They can relieve your fears, stress and anxiety. And, if it's somewhat acceptable within your peer group, using can help you fit in by giving you a common identity that makes you one of the group. Hopefully, you know better than to be taken in by this "con"—and can see beyond it to the "bigger picture." You must. The truth is, as in all things, there is a toll to pay for changing your body's chemistry by using alcohol and drugs.

As you—and hundreds of thousands of other teens—know, you can learn to manage the stress, strains and pressures of life in healthy ways—and without using chemicals to do it. Altering your body and mind's ability to meet the daily demands of life is sure to change your experience, and not in a positive way. When you are "present" for your life, you are able to experience your life to its fullest. You are able to experience "you" to your fullest—who you are, who you are becoming and your ever-changing, ever-growing potential.

Great Reasons to "Just Say Yes" to Life—Drug-Free

It's fairly certain that as a teen you've been taught the dire effects of drugs. You've heard how they can harm your physical and mental health. You've learned when a person becomes caught up in chemical dependency, his or her life becomes characterized by attitudes and behaviors that are sick, unhealthy and dysfunctional. Knowing all this can be a good reason to say no to drugs. But while being absolutely sure you don't want to play a part in destroying your health and life in these ways, there is an even better reason to say no to using: You have plenty of great reasons to say "yes" to life. Imagine if Carrie Sharritt didn't say "yes" to wanting to be present for all of the things she has going on in her life.

Being drug-free gives you a better chance to "show up" for your life. Like Carrie, being a teen means you have much to do. Having a life as big as you do, you know you don't want to miss it. Here are some of the many ways you "show up" for your life when you're drug-free:

- You're better able to be a loving person and to feel the love that flows to you.
- You're better able to think about what you want in relation to who you are, and to discover your talents, interests and aptitudes.
- You're better able to communicate in a straightforward and open manner with those in your life—parents, teachers, friends and others. This means that you can share your joy, express your concerns, and ask for help and support when you're facing tough times and trying situations.
- You're better able to feel that life is meaningful, and just

as you need others, you also can be of service and assistance to them.

- You're better able to be a thoughtful friend, which is a sure way to attract thoughtful friends into your life and reap the satisfaction of being in positive relationships with others.
- You're better able to decide what you want to achieve on a daily basis, as well as plan for your future.
- You're better able to handle the tough times without blowing them out of proportion, and to face your problems and cope with them effectively.
- You're better able to be a joyful person so that you might be an inspiration and encouragement to others.

You probably won't "Just Say No" if you haven't decided there's something to "Just Say Yes" to. What will you "Just Say Yes" to?

✓ Will you say "yes" to feeling healthy and taking care of your body—one that in adolescence is in a most arduous stage of growth and development?

✓ Will you say "yes" to relationships with family and friends that are really close and positive?

✓ Will you say "yes" to knowing that you're doing your best?

✓ Will you say "yes" to achieving your goals?

✓ Will you say "yes" to success in school and preparing for your life beyond high school?

✓ Will you say "yes" to a future that is filled with promise—and a past that you can be proud of?

✓ Will you say "yes" to confronting problems and challenges head-on—and looking for resolution in healthy ways?

✓ Will you say "yes" to finding the meaning and purpose of *your* life?

✓ Will you say "yes" to a life without chemical addiction?

Such rewards are excellent reasons not to use drugs and alcohol. If you think about it, the rewards are *life*—living it at its fullest or, in the words of Anne De Lenclos, "Today a new sun rises for me; everything invites me to cherish it." Believe that you are worthy of sunrises and be conscious so that you can cherish them! All it takes, really, is to say "yes" to life.

Questions to Think About

♥ What rewards for staying drug-free do you value most?
♥ What makes you feel good about yourself?
♥ How did you "show up" for life today?
♥ What rewards of staying drug-free do you see as part of your future? (What will you accomplish? What are your goals and plans for making your dreams come true?)

2

How to Say "NO!"— Even When Your Friends Are "Using"

Friendly Persuasions

"I know . . . I know—please don't lecture me again!" I would say this to my parents when they would remind me for the umpteenth time about not drinking or doing drugs when I was getting ready to go out with my friends. I hated those lectures, but I have to say this: I'm seventeen, and I don't drink or do drugs. I don't know if the lectures had anything to do with it, but I'm sure they helped. *But my reasons for not using have more to do with hanging around my friends than simply listening to my parents' advice.* In fact, I'd say that my friends have taught me all I ever need to know about drugs.

In my town, using drugs and drinking alcohol is really common—especially for teens. No one even bothers to gossip about who is using. For sure no one looks down on those who use. I know that many of the adults—parents and teachers—have no clue which teens drink and do drugs, nor the extent to which they do it. I'd go so far as to say that unless a teen is "zoned out" or drunk to the point of stumbling or falling down, most adults are likely to think, "Well, some are probably *experimenting* and *dabbling,* but that's the extent of it and that just comes with the territory of being a teen." I'd say that unless or until one of their

11

own kids gets involved with using, and then to the point of making their own life or their family life hell, they (erroneously) think kids will "outgrow" using.

So my take on it is that a lot of adults operate under some assumptions and myths about teens and drugs. One is that "good kids" don't—and won't—use, and "bad kids" do. It's not like that—there are no guarantees. I'd say that it's nearly impossible to say which of our classmates will get through high school without ever doing drugs. At my school, getting "high" is not "weird" or "terrible." It's just what most kids do with their friends; no one thinks twice about drinking at parties. Even so, I don't drink, and I don't use drugs. It's not because I'm a "goody-two-shoes" or a geek. I've simply made the choice not to drink or do drugs. Don't get me wrong—I'm tempted all the time. As a teen, you pretty much have to make up your own mind and take a hard stance about whether or not you're going to use. I have.

I hang out with a group of friends who have all made that choice, too. We've watched as other friends "experiment" and seen their lives slowly but surely change. Using seems really stupid if you think about it. I mean, as a teen, you spend so much of your time trying to convince your parents that you're "mature and grown-up" so you can get more freedom and then, if you start using, it's all swept away. You don't have to be a rocket scientist to see that the moment you're on a roll with drugs, they're in charge—and you aren't! Still, like others my age, I don't believe that using means that I'll steal my parents blind and get kicked out of the house, or that I'll become an addict and then a homeless street person. But I do know there's a price to pay for using, and I don't want to pay that price. I'm smart enough to know that being "high" won't help me accomplish the things I want to achieve. I just can't see that using is going to help me out or make my life better in any way. I don't see drugs as an answer to any of my problems: They're not going to help me get better grades; they're not going to help me be any smarter; they're not going to help me buy cool clothes, make my hair shiny or clear up my complexion. Using isn't going to help me win over a really cool guy, nor is it likely to keep a guy interested in how witty or smart I am, nor intrigued with my winning personality. I have my share of struggles with trying to be popular with my classmates. But I'm not convinced that my sharing a joint with a few friends is going to make me any more popular with anyone, including those who use on a daily basis. In spite of everything you hear about teens doing drugs to be one of the crowd, the truth is, those teens who use aren't liked any better by anyone. In fact, using doesn't make kids seem any "cooler" either. Sometimes they even have to take a lot of "razzing" to their face, being identified with names such as "Tommy Tweeker" or— even worse, "Cokehead." So, I have to ask, "What's in it for me— other than a lot of lost time?" So I hang out with about eight kids who are pretty much like me. We talk about the other groups all the time. I figure there are about ten different groups of kids in our school, and I'd say that six of them use alcohol or drugs— some more than others, of course.

The biggest reason I've stayed with my decision not to use is because of the effects drugs have on a person. I've seen what drugs do, firsthand. I have friends who use, and some have used for a long time. Some use a little; some use a lot. Sometimes you hear someone say that they used a certain drug so they could get all of their work done, or that they use a particular drug because they think it makes them more "creative." Believe me, it isn't that simple. There is no one drug that makes you smarter or better able to keep up. A couple of really good friends who use have gone from being some of the smart kids in my class to merely getting passing grades. Some have even dropped out of school because using made passing their classes totally impossible.

Not only can using change your ability to handle your school life, but it can change your personality to the point of being somebody totally different from who you are. I've seen some of my friends change to the point of scaring me enough to never want any of that to happen to me. I know one girl, once a friend of mine, who is now spaced out most of the time, but I can't tell if she's that way because she's still using, or if it's a permanent condition now because she's used for so long. I've seen friends go from being average-looking kids to looking scrawny and haggard, with gray circles under their eyes after using for a while. I even know a girl who nearly died from overdosing. I know another girl who is suicidal because of what she's using. Imagine that—I'm trying to get out of the house so I can spend more time with my friends, and she's trying to end her life so she doesn't have to be with any of us! It's crazy.

I know kids whose biggest goal of the day is getting high and then trying to act like they're not (mostly trying to hide their use from teachers and parents). I know kids whose biggest daily goal is to find their hit—it's their biggest "achievement." I think that's sad. What is even more sad is that once they get caught up in their use, their life revolves around it, and worse, they don't even see how far they've "dropped out." They're oblivious to just how much they've lost out.

My friends and I talk about all this, and we keep coming back to what we think is one of the strongest points for not ever "experimenting" or "trying just a little." Of all the friends we know who use, most of them admit that they're sorry they ever started, and they admit that we're "lucky we never got into it!"

Luck? Not! Believe me, for me (and many of my friends) luck had nothing to do with the decision not to use. It had to do with looking around and opening my eyes to seeing the effects of drugs—and yes, even for those who use "just a little." We also talk about another comment some of our "user" friends make, which is, "Why did you let me drink so much at the party?" or "Why didn't you take it [the joint] away from me?" or "Why didn't you get me out of there before I got so messed up?" We think about their comments—and talk amongst ourselves about why we don't take more of a stand for them about using. After all, we're not afraid to take a stand for ourselves. If we're at a party where drugs and alcohol suddenly start appearing, we say no and act like it's no big deal. Sometimes we make a point to leave the scene, or else we just go about having our own fun. But if it gets bad and a lot of "druggies" show up, we leave and go elsewhere. So we've decided that it's possible to stay clean and sober and still find fun. But we don't take a stand on others using. It seems easy to say, "Hey, go ahead if you want to, but I'm not going to do the stuff."

Even so, you know that lives are going to change at that party. So many of our friends have gotten in such big trouble with their parents for doing drugs or drinking because they've done stupid things, like break laws or get into fights or come home stoned or drunk—and, of course, get grounded for it. I even have a friend who got pregnant because she had unprotected sex when she was drinking. Others have gotten tickets for driving under the influence (or having drugs or open beer cans in the car)—which, as you know, is really big trouble both legally and when it comes to affording car insurance after that. I'll spare you the most horrible story about a friend who was involved in a tragic car accident—because of a stupid decision of another friend to drive while under the influence. These are all predictable outcomes. And everyone knows it. So why don't friends say, "Using is stupid, so stop"? Probably we don't because we're under the illusion that telling our friends not to use or to stop using isn't cool, or that we'd sound uncool. Probably we think that as long as we take care of ourselves and don't use—you know, to each his own—then we've done enough. And maybe we think that if we tell a principal or counselor that a particular student is using, that person will go to jail—when in fact, probably that teen would simply get some help with his or her drug use.

Still, you always hear the slogan, "Friends don't let friends drive drunk." Well that applies to using, too. And both apply to more than just being behind the wheel: They apply to just being, period. So the group of my friends who don't use are talking about this now. We know we've made the decision not to use. And now, we're talking about how to get the message across to other friends, as well.

How do you tell friends—in ways they'll understand— "Using is stupid and you need to get some help so you can quit, because if you don't, you're going to really screw up your life"? I don't have the answer, but I do know it's one of the things that is missing from the "Just say no" we teens hear all the time.

I'm not going to lecture you like my parents do me, but I'd like to put in a little friendly persuasion and tell you that drinking and doing drugs is not likely to help you get a better life any time soon. I know the choice is up to you. I've made mine. But I'm a good friend—and I would like you to consider not using, even when your friends try to persuade you otherwise.

Mandy Martinez, 17

When There's More Than "Just" About Saying "No"

Mandy, like many teens, chooses not to use even in the face of peer and social pressure that would make it easy to use. As Mandy pointed out, it's not easy living in a culture that doesn't necessarily believe (or fear) that drugs might well sweep them into an addiction that will raise havoc, even devastate their lives. With alcohol and drugs becoming more and more accepted as an "in" thing to do, and readily available to anyone who wants to use them, you need to know that, like Mandy, you *can* make the choice to live drug-free. But you will have to make that decision and vow to stay with it, just as your friends will have to make the choice for themselves. Even so, they are your friends, so by all means, you can discourage them from using, and encourage them by letting them know that you can still have fun hanging out together at clean and sober events.

Learning how to make good decisions is part of growing up. You have to be willing to stand up for yourself and not feel shy about speaking up for what you believe in. And you need to feel confident that even though you want your friends to think you're cool, there comes a time when you have to say no to them. That can take courage—but that's what "cool" is all about. Be wise: Make the choice to stay drug-free—even when you have friends trying to convince you to do otherwise.

Cool—And Persuasive— Ways to Say "No" to Using

How can you refuse the offer to "Try it, you'll like it, trust me—we're all having some," or "Oh, come on! Here, don't be such a geek!" without feeling like an outsider or as if you're losing popularity? Here's some advice from teens on how to say "No thanks" in cool, graceful and yet certain terms.

Eileen Lucas, 13: "When a friend asked me if I wanted to smoke some pot at the park with some kids from school, I said, 'No, thanks. I need to keep all the brain cells I've got!' She just kind of laughed and left me alone."

Keith Economou, 14: "If I'm out with friends and someone says, 'Want a beer?' or 'Want to smoke a joint?' I'll say, 'Nah. I don't mess around with getting high. I'm not into it. I need all my wits about me so I don't do something stupid, and I'm able to get out of the way of someone else who is about to do something stupid because *he's* in a foggy stupor.'"

Terry Corley, 13: "I've been asked a few times to drink or use drugs, and I just say, 'My parents would absolutely kill me if they ever found out. I don't want to risk it. I like living at home, and besides, I'm not ready to die.' Then I just walk away. My friends are cool enough to get it that I have my reasons for saying no—and that's exactly what I'm saying."

Joshua Salem, 16: "I had a friend who was always trying to see if I'd smoke or drink with him. He didn't get weird when I didn't, but it just irritated me that he kept on asking. Other than that, he was a good guy. Finally, I just told him, 'Hey, I really like hanging out with you, but I'm not going to get faded with you— ever.' He just said, 'Whatever, dude, that's cool.' We still hang out, but he's never again asked me to use."

Lisa Prather, 13: "When my friend Brenda started drinking and experimenting with drugs, she tried to get me to get high with her. In the beginning, I made up excuses for not using. But I got tired of finding one that sounded anything but lame. Finally I told her, 'Listen, we've been friends for a while, so I know I can trust you to understand that I just don't want to use or drink.' She never asked me to get high with her again."

Trent Lorenz, 14: "My older brother is in recovery. He started using when he was in the eighth grade. Even though he's been clean and sober for eight months now, I saw what drugs did to him and how hard he had to work to get and stay clean—to say nothing of what it put our family through. So when someone offers me a 'chance' to use, it's real easy for me to say, 'No, thanks. My brother's an addict, and I'm not taking any chance that it might run in the family—besides it didn't look like any fun at all to me.'"

Keara Coleman, 14: "I was over at my friend's house spending the night, and her parents were out. She pulled out a joint and said, 'Let's smoke this.' I shook my head and said, 'Let's not—I'm not into it. Let's find something else to do.' And that's just what we did. My saying no was no big deal, and we put on CDs and talked. It was cool. I was surprised saying no would be that easy."

Ian Branson, 16: "When I come up on any friends or acquaintances getting high, I laugh and say, 'Busted!' and then I just keep on walking and find someone else to talk to. That's what works for me, to keep it light and keep on going. It lets them know I'm not going to use, so they don't bother to offer me any."

Christopher Soto, 16: "My friend Todd kept wanting me to try whatever drug he was trying. At the time, Todd was still making it to school and doing other things besides drugs. It wasn't like he was some total loser druggy. I didn't want to lose his friendship, but there came a time when I had to say, 'Todd, you're practically one of my best friends, but that doesn't mean I have to do whatever you do.' He just shrugged and said, 'Just asking.' He still asks me from time to time, but he doesn't pressure me."

Kimberly Muir, 18: "Once a friend invited me to go with her and two of our other friends to a party. At first I said, 'Sure.' Then she told me that all of them were going to take some Ecstasy, and she asked if I wanted to take some, too. I looked at her and said, 'Are you serious? Have you heard the statistics on your chances for brain damage, psychosis, even the possibility of dying from using that? Count me out, and you really should think about what you're doing, too.' Her eyes got big, and she looked terrified and walked away. I don't think she'll ask me to use with her again! I'd like to think that she might not use, but I don't have any way of knowing. I ended up making other plans because I knew it wasn't the kind of party I'd be comfortable being at."

Suzee Vlk, 15: "I try to practice the 'thirty-second rule.' I was told that when you're being pressured, you'll want to find your way out of the sticky situation in thirty seconds or less, because after that, it's like your staying or hesitating means, 'maybe,' or even 'yes.' So I leave as fast as I can—even if it means saying, 'I've gotta go pee. Bye.'"

Kendra Frampton, 14: "Usually I don't have to say 'no.' I just have to say, 'excuse me,' turn around and leave, and go hang with a couple of different friends. They get my drift."

Benji Miller, 16: "When my friend Kyle lit up a joint when we were driving to school together one day, I said, 'I probably don't have to remind you that the secondhand smoke from that stuff is bad for my lungs, too.' He rolled his eyes, but he put it out."

Jared Nichols, 16: "When someone tries to pass me a joint or a drink, I say whatever I need to say to get away— 'I'm going to get a soda,' 'I need some fresh air,' 'I think I see someone I need to talk to over there,' and then I just walk away."

Marcie Kenton, 13: "If you come up on a group of people getting high, just walk away. Everyone I know says that after the first time, it's much easier to end up using again, even when you don't want to. So I'm not going to do it the first time."

Nelson Johnson, 14: "When someone asks me if I want a drink or a hit, I play it off like I don't hear them—but immediately start up a conversation with the person they're with. This may sound like an avoidance approach, but it's very effective because it makes the person feel small for asking—which is exactly how I feel about someone who asks if I want to put a poisonous substance in my body. Frankly, I don't care if they feel one-upped."

Kristin Balistrari, 15: "When I'm offered drugs, I think about my friend, Josie, who for nearly two years battled addiction. It was horrible. And she was a 'regular' sort of person. I just don't want to have to put myself through that. So, I say, 'Oh, no. No. For sure, no!'"

Ryan Preston, 15: "When someone offers me drugs, I quickly say 'no, thanks' and then start talking about something else. That way, everyone sort of feels that the gathering isn't about using. So whoever is using ends up feeling like he's in the wrong place for it."

Sean Grover, 17: "I don't use, but a lot of the kids I know do. So my rule for not using is that if I don't have more than one friend at a party who, like me, doesn't use, I leave. Not only do I want to avoid getting caught up in the madness of using, but I don't want to go home smelling like weed, nor do I want to be party to the very real possibility of being hauled to jail should the place get raided!"

Johnna Victor, 16: "I learned from personal experience that if your friends just won't leave you alone about using, it's probably time to look for new friends. It's just a big set-up to hang around with friends who are using. I knew for myself that if I didn't find new friends it was only a matter of time before I started using drugs, too. I've actually tried marijuana a couple of times, and I think I could like it. I just want to make sure I don't."

Lynne McTighe, 16: "Recently I agreed to study with a couple of classmates at one of their houses. As we were taking our chairs around the table in her dining room (her parents were out for dinner), she suggested that we have some 'blast-off' so as to get down to studying. 'No crystal for me,' one of the girls laughed, while another said, 'I can't sleep for days on end when I use that! No, none for me. I need my sleep.' The other girl said, 'The last thing I need is to act like a caged wild woman. I have to do well on this test tomorrow.' I was shocked that the girl offered us a drug as powerfully addictive as crystal as a study tool! Well, I would have said no to her under any conditions, but given the other girls had said no so easily, too, I just blurted out what I wanted to say, which was, 'You have got to be out of your everloving mind to use crystal!'"

What Is Your Comeback When You're Being Enticed to Use?

How about you? What do you do or say in situations where others try to entice you to use? Whether you simply say "No" or find a way to walk away from the situation, you'll want to feel confident that you can trust yourself to do that. You'll want to know exactly how to do this even if, to date, you haven't been tempted or enticed. Odds are, at some point you will be asked to use or drink. Here's something you might want to try. There's a simple little skill called role-playing, where you ask someone else to help you rehearse what you might say in a situation in which you are likely to be confronted about using. Rehearsing what to say can help build your confidence in sticking to your decision to stay drug-free when you're actually faced with the situation.

Consider it a sort of pre-planning that can lower the stress of being overwhelmed when suddenly you find yourself face-to-face in such a situation. Many teens "rehearse" what they will say with a best friend, or with one or both of their parents. Just think about who would be the best person to help you identify likely situations you might find yourself in and then what you could say that will help you stay with your decision to remain drug-and alcohol-free.

Do what you can to stay away from being tempted in the first place. Of course you don't live in a cocoon, and you can't always tell when someone is going to offer you drugs or alcohol, but you can try to avoid getting into the situation of defending yourself. Here are a couple of good suggestions for making sure you're saying what you mean—all the time!

- Don't mislead your friends into thinking that while you don't drink or do drugs at the present, that maybe you'll try them "later on." Always give the message, "I don't use, I'm not going to use, and I don't think using is the right thing to do."
- Don't wear clothing that depicts that drinking or alcohol is cool, or has pictures (or suggestions) of using, such as with a marijuana leaf or slogans that make it sound like drugs are cool with you. Doing this only sends out the message that you're open, into or okay with using, and you're sure to attract those who use.
- Make a point of developing friendships with those who have made the choice to be drug-free, and make a point of talking with your friends about how "cool" this decision is.
- Speak up about not using. Those who don't use will be encouraged and inspired that there are others who know it's

healthy, smart—and very cool—to be drug-free. You've heard the saying "You are the message"—it applies to your words, as well. By not using—and letting others know that—you are an inspiration, a taste berry, to those who are in the process of (or struggling with) making that same decision.

Questions to Think About

♥ What influenced you to make the choice to remain drug-free?

♥ Do you trust yourself to stand your ground when being pressured to use?

♥ Do you have a pat "line" you use for saying "no" if and when you are asked to drink or use, or do you say something different each time based on who offers and given the situation?

♥ If you see a friend using, or being tempted to use, would you say something to that friend? What would you say?

3

Can "Just a Little Bit" Hurt?

Back on Track—Even at the Beach

My freshman year was the best year of my life. For one, I was my school's shining star in track and field! And if I was placing first in nearly every event in every track competition as a freshman, you can only imagine how high my expectations were for where I could be as a senior. My coach and my counselor at school were all telling me that if I kept doing as well as I was, I could get a scholarship for a really good university, which was really encouraging, because my dream was to become an engineer. For that I need to go to college, and a scholarship was my ticket to college.

Life was just great! I was a somebody, and I knew it! So did the teachers: A lot of them smiled and said hi to me when they passed me in the halls. Practically all the kids at school—including some of the most important seniors—knew who I was and respected me. And Marissa Hunter noticed me—in a big way! I could tell she wanted me as her boyfriend, and I couldn't have been happier! Marissa and I became one of the most popular couples in our freshman class.

At home, things were as good as they were at school. With my doing well in sports and getting decent grades, my parents almost never badgered me anymore—like they had the year before when I was more or less just getting through my days. And they were proud of me, too. I could see it in the way their eyes filled with pride when they talked about how well I was doing. Like I said, life was practically perfect.

But that was when I was a freshman.

The summer between my freshman and sophomore year, I decided to add swimming to part of my conditioning routine, so I'd go to the lake and swim. Some of the other guys did that, and it seemed like a good idea. Pretty soon the lake became sort of a hangout for a lot of the kids—which was really fun. So I'd go for my swim and then hang out with my friends and any of the kids who were there. Maybe it was because it was a secluded place that the kids thought they could smoke and drink without anyone seeing them. Whatever the reason, the lake became a place that attracted more and more of the kids who not only smoked, but used other drugs, too. While in the beginning the kids kind of sorted themselves into two different groups, eventually we all sort of became one group. I think it's fair to say that as a result, a lot of kids started smoking cigarettes or pot and started drinking—some for the first time.

For the first few weeks when I was hanging out there, I didn't do any of it, but then one day a kid offered me a cigarette and I said, "Sure." I don't even know why—it just seemed like everyone else happened to be smoking so I thought I'd try one, too. It tasted terrible! I had to really play the part to get through that first cigarette. But then after that, I'd go ahead and take a cigarette from time to time if someone offered me one. Then, after awhile, they weren't so hard to smoke. Still, it wasn't like I'd ever go out and buy them.

Then, one day, while I was sitting with them smoking a cigarette, one of the guys offered me a can of beer. At first I refused, but the guys were teasing me about not being "a guy" and well, they're good friends, and besides, what's only one beer? So I drank it. And then one more. I guess you could say that's how my drinking and smoking got started. It was a thing to do with everyone—a bonding thing. We had a lot of fun. It was sort of how I had pictured college life—somewhere between achieving things on my own—my studies and being an athlete—and doing grown-up things with a group of friends. And it all seemed so innocent and fun. And to tell you the truth, as far as I was concerned, college was right around the corner. So I was cool with it all.

The thing is, I began to drink a lot. I tried to reason it out: I needed to get beer and bring it to the lake so at least I was "contributing" my fair share, and not always just mooching theirs. Then, because I was bringing beer, I'd feel freer to drink more. I did worry a little about how much I began to drink, because sometimes I'd drink to the point of needing to hang out a little longer so I didn't feel so "tipsy"—and so that my parents wouldn't notice that I'd been drinking. Still, it seemed like no big deal; nor did an occasional "hit" of something that was being passed around.

The summer ended, but drinking and smoking pot didn't. And that's when things really changed.

Even though I was just using a little bit, things got weird between my parents and me almost right away. They started looking at me—like they were checking out my eyes—and asking me questions all the time. They especially asked questions about my friends and why I wasn't getting up for my early morning run anymore. It got to the point where I had to start lying to them—there were just too many questions I couldn't answer honestly. Other things changed. I don't know if I can put my finger on what it was exactly; it just wasn't the way it was when I was a freshman.

Somehow, I was losing my edge. I noticed it first with my relationship with my parents—their intense scrutiny and all. And I noticed it in my performance on the track field, too. While I'd started out going to the lake to build my conditioning routine, it hadn't really turned out that way. I'd quit running early every morning, too. Although I still got in a run at some point each day, I just wasn't up to my freshman performance.

I didn't seem to have the drive. I found myself skipping practice to go hang out with the guys. I started skipping homework, too. That's when Marissa started looking at me funny and asking me a lot of questions, like my parents had during the summer. She had spent most of the summer in England on a study tour, so she hadn't been a part of the group activities at the lake. As far as I knew, she didn't even know about them. And now my parents were saying I'd better be careful or I was going to be dropped from the track team. Everyone, it seemed, was now on my back. Practically every teacher was hitting me with, "Why didn't you do your homework?" The coach went so far as looking me up in the student center and asking in front of all my friends, "Why can't you make it to practice?" Then, this was followed by the threat of his dropping me from the team if there were more absences.

Well, I did get dropped: Marissa dropped me for Tommy Burnett, a senior and also a track athlete. Then my grades dropped, which is what led to my being dropped by the track and field team—just as my parents had predicted. My father's question hit home the most: "What's happening to you, son?"

Good question. I lost my great girlfriend, and I'm not seen as a track hero by everyone at school anymore. I don't have the "good kid on his way to a bright future" status with the teachers anymore. My parents and I argue all the time. I know that they're frustrated and disappointed. But it's not like I set out to screw everything up—and it's not like I use hard drugs or anything. Still, I know this can't go on. I really do want my life back. It's been two months now since I've used pot or had a can of beer. And I need to keep it that way. I just can't be the person I want to be when I'm using, not even "a little bit." So, I'm getting back on track. It's a little hard; it's amazing how much easier things seemed when everyone thought I was cool. And I genuinely miss that. I miss Marissa so much; it just kills me to see her walking hand in hand with her new boyfriend, but I should've known she wouldn't want to be with someone who used, not even "a little." But I'm regrouping: I'm getting back on track with my grades and practicing every day to get my body back in condition to the point where I can compete in athletics again. And I'm working to regain the trust of my parents and teachers. So like I said, I'm getting back on track—even when I'm at the beach! But the even bigger "back on track" is that I'm not drinking or using again, ever. I have too much going, and I've made the choice not to lose any more time.

Wyatt Atkins, 16

Do the Math!
Real Reasons "a Little Bit" Can Hurt

As Wyatt Atkins' story shows, a little bit can hurt. One of the most persuasive arguments not to use "even a little," or to just "try it," is that experimenting is how people get started in the first place. Experts in the field of substance abuse confirm that experimenting "opens the gate" to harmful drugs, and cigarette smoking and drinking are the most common "gateway drugs." Smoking cigarettes, for example, is considered the most "predictable" gateway drug to marijuana use, which is considered a predictable "gateway" to experimenting with other drugs.

The statistics below speak for themselves. Take a thoughtful look at these eye-opening statistics and ask yourself, "If I experiment with or try alcohol or drugs, will I become one of these statistics?"

- Nearly 65 percent of teens "try" cigarettes before reaching seventeen. Of these, nearly 52 percent will become "regular" smokers, smoking from two to ten cigarettes on a daily basis.
- Of the teens who smoke cigarettes, 65 percent will try marijuana; of those, 49 percent will smoke marijuana on a regular basis.
- Of the teens who smoke marijuana, 65 percent will experiment with other drugs, from inhalants, to crystal, even heroin.
- Of the 65 percent who experiment with other drugs, 47 percent will become "addicted."
- Of the teens who smoke marijuana, 71 percent will use alcohol.
- Of the 58 percent of teens who drink alcohol, 82 percent will develop a serious drinking problem.
- Teens who "try" or "experiment" with "gateway drugs" are 266 times more apt to use hard drugs.

Are There Any Parts of Your Life You'd Be Willing to Forfeit?

"I really get it how hard drugs can totally devastate your life," fourteen-year-old Cassandra Lyton said at a recent workshop. "I have a cousin whose whole life was ruined because of cocaine. So I'm clear on saying no when it comes to hard drugs. I have absolutely no problem with that—crystal, ecstasy, coke, heroin are out for me—no ifs, ands or buts about it. And I know that it's a proven fact that cigarettes cause cancer, so I'd never smoke. But I don't feel as 'scared' about taking a puff of a joint or sipping a beer. I mean, can just a little bit really hurt?"

It's a fair question. And of course, you see your friends (and adults, maybe even your own parents) using a "little bit" at parties—and they still get up the next day and fix meals, go to school or work, and so on.

So, can just a little bit hurt? Here are facts to help you decide, as well as some questions to ask yourself.

- As a minor, it's illegal to use or be under the influence of alcohol or drugs. Other than prescription drugs, it's illegal to use drugs even as an adult, and it's illegal to drive while impaired by alcohol. If, as a teen, you are caught using or with alcohol or drugs in your possession, you will have legal problems on your hands. Ask yourself:
  - ✓ How will I feel to be handcuffed and put in a police car, then taken to juvenile hall or jail, or *mandated* to do community service as a result of my using?
  - ✓ How will I feel about myself if I'm arrested, and how will I feel about others knowing I put myself in this situation?
  - ✓ How will I feel when I fill out applications (for employers, college boards and other licenses) that ask if I've ever been arrested?

- Thinking and decision-making abilities are impaired by alcohol and drug use. Just watch as others who use even "just a little" say (or do) some really embarrassing, mean or stupid things. And consider this: Nearly 60 percent of teens who become pregnant say that "being under the influence" led to unplanned, and unprotected, sex. Speaking of unprotected sex, one out of every four new cases of HIV is reported to be a teen. The implications of this possibility are worth your serious consideration. Ask yourself:
  - ✓ How would I feel knowing I had put myself at risk in some way, such as driving while under the influence (or getting in the car with someone who is)?
  - ✓ How would I feel if I found out that I (or my girl-friend) was pregnant or caught a venereal disease—or had possibly exposed myself to AIDS?

✓ How would I feel about myself knowing I had made a fool of myself at a social gathering with everyone watching embarrassed for me?

- Motor skills and coordination are impaired by alcohol and drug use. It's outright dangerous to be behind the wheel of a car after using "even just a little bit" (or to be a passenger in that car). Of the eight thousand teenagers who die behind the wheel of a car each year, more than half test positive for alcohol or chemicals. Ask yourself:

  ✓ Do I want to take the chance of being in a car (or driving) with someone who is not able to be fully aware of everything going on around him or her?

  ✓ How would I feel if I woke up in the hospital after driving while under the influence of even "just a little bit" of alcohol or drugs?

  ✓ How would I feel if someone was seriously injured or even killed because of me or my friends?

- Cigarettes, alcohol and drugs are addictive substances. "A little bit" of use can lead to "a lot" of use. A national survey on drug abuse reveals that there are 2.3 million teens who are chemically dependent: addicts. The definition of an addict is someone "whose thinking is controlled by the desire to use" a particular substance or chemical. As the statistic you read in the previous section confirms, teens who "try" or "experiment" with gateway drugs are 266 times more apt to use hard drugs. In short, addiction begins with a "first-time use." Of course, not *every* user becomes addicted. Ask yourself:

  ✓ Am I willing to risk that my mind and body won't become addicted?

  ✓ Do I want to chance becoming addicted?

  ✓ Am I willing to give up being in control of the choices I make and instead, become a prisoner to my mind and body's dependency on a chemical?

- Drugs and alcohol are toxic and poisonous to the human body. If you think that "just a little bit" means staying away from "hard drugs," remember that it's well-documented that tobacco (or smoking) causes cancer and drinking causes body breakdowns from liver damage to dementia. Whether from related diseases or accidents, tobacco and alcohol are responsible for one-third of all deaths. Each month, more people die from tobacco and alcohol use than do in a full year from using all the other "hard drugs" put together. What's more, even "just a little bit" of any substance is still "a little bit" of poison to your body and can tax your system. Ask yourself:

  ✓ Do I want to poison my body—even "just a little bit"?
  ✓ Am I willing to feel bad—sick, headachy, depressed—because I've used?
  ✓ Am I willing to subject my mental and physical health and well-being to the potential for health impairments, breakdowns, serious illnesses, even put my life at risk?

- Under the influence of alcohol and chemical use, you "aren't you." You give up your full-on integrity. When you use, even that little bit for the first time, the secrets and lies begin. It's doubtful that you'll be able to tell your parents, grand-parents (or other relatives) that you are using, nor will you want your "non-using" friends to find out, so you'll keep it a secret and hope they won't find out. If they do, you'll prob-ably lie about it. You're left feeling less-than-honest—and this begins to hammer on your self-esteem. Ask yourself:

  ✓ How would I feel to know that I'm living a lie, or that *I am the sort of person who lies?*
  ✓ Do I really want to become that sort of person?
  ✓ Am I willing to give up my freedom to be open and authentic?

You're a Smart Teen: Make a Smart Choice

As you can see, there are real prices to pay for using even just a little. Make the decision not to use, not even "just a little." Don't risk your health or put yourself in jeopardy with the law, or ruin your reputation with your friends, or your relationship with your parents. Don't kid yourself about the potent effects of drugs.

Saying no to "just try it" or using "just a little" makes it easier to say no to hard drugs, as well as to say "yes" to your life and all its rewards—which include being the real you and having a real life.

Questions to Think About

♥ When do you feel most tempted to "try just a little" and how can you avoid those feelings or situations?

♥ What are your top-five personal reasons for saying no to "just try it" or to using "just a little"?

♥ Do you know anyone who tried "just a little bit" and changed afterwards? Who and how did the person change?

♥ What are the five qualities you like most about yourself that could be placed at risk if you try even "just a little bit"?

Source of Research on Statistics: Indiana Prevention Resource Center; University of Michigan's Institute for Social Research; The Center on Addiction and Substance Abuse at Columbia (CASA)

Unit II

If You (or a Friend or Family Member) Are Using, Here's What You Should Know

If anything is sacred, the human body is sacred.
—Walt Whitman

*Addicts don't have relationships —
they take hostages.*
—Source Unknown

*It doesn't do to leave a dragon out of your
calculations, if you live near him.*
—J. R. R. Tolkien

READER/CUSTOMER CARE SURVEY

We care about your opinions. Please take a moment to fill out this Reader Survey card and mail it back to us.
As a special **"thank you"** we'll send you exciting news about interesting books and a valuable **Gift Certificate.**

Please PRINT using ALL CAPS

First Name |_____| MI. |__| Last Name |_____|

Address |_____|

City |_____| ST |__| Zip |____|-|____|

Phone # (|___|) |___|-|____| Fax # (|___|) |___|-|____|

Email |_____|

(1) Gender:
_____ Female _____ Male

(2) Age:
_____ 8 or younger _____ 17-20
_____ 9-12 _____ 21-30
_____ 13-16 _____ 31+

(3) What attracts you most to a book?
(Please rank 1-4 in order of preference.)

	1	2	3	4
3) Title	O	O	O	O
4) Cover Design	O	O	O	O
5) Author	O	O	O	O
6) Content	O	O	O	O

(7) Other than school books, how many books do you read a month?
_____ 1 _____ 3
_____ 2 _____ 4

(8) How did you find out about this book?
Please fill in ONE.
1) _____ Friend
2) _____ School (Teacher, Library, etc.)
3) _____ Parent
4) _____ Store Display
5) _____ Teen Magazine
6) _____ Interview/Review (TV, Radio, Print)

(9) Where do you usually buy books?
Please fill in your top TWO choices.
1) _____ Bookstore
2) _____ Religious Bookstore
3) _____ Online
4) _____ Book Club/Mail Order
5) _____ Price Club (Costco, Sam's Club, etc.)
6) _____ Retail Store (Target, Wal-Mart, etc.)

(11) Did you receive this book as a gift?
_____ Yes _____ No

(12) What do you like to read? *(Please check all that apply)*

Magazines:
12) _____ Teen People
13) _____ Seventeen
14) _____ YM
15) _____ Cosmo Girl
16) _____ Rolling Stone
17) _____ Teen Ink
18) _____ Christian Magazines

Books:
19) _____ Fiction
20) _____ SelfHelp Books
21) _____ Reality Stories/Memoirs
22) _____ Sports
23) _____ Series Books (Chicken Soup, Fearless, etc.)

TAPE IN MIDDLE; DO NOT STAPLE

BUSINESS REPLY MAIL
FIRST-CLASS MAIL PERMIT NO 45 DEERFIELD BEACH, FL

POSTAGE WILL BE PAID BY ADDRESSEE

TASTE BERRIES™ FOR TEENS
3201 SW 15TH STREET
DEERFIELD BEACH FL 33442-9875

FOLD HERE

(24) Do you prefer to read books written by:

1)_____ Teen Authors?

2)_____ Adult Authors?

3)_____ No Preference

Comments:

4

Plain Facts About Drugs and Their Effects

When I Come Knocking . . . Knocking . . . Knocking . . .

I am more powerful than the combined armies of the world.

I have destroyed more men and women than the wars of all the nations.

I have caused millions of accidents and have wrecked more homes than all floods, tornadoes and hurricanes put together in your lifetime.

I am the world's slickest thief—I steal trillions of dollars each year.

I find my victims among the rich and the poor alike, the young and the old, the strong and the weak.

I loom like a huge, ominous cloud, casting a dark shadow as far as the eye can see.

I am your highest high—and your lowest low.

I give no added value for having known me, in fact,

I will leave you empty, lonely—and will devastate your self-esteem.

I am relentless, insidious and unpredictable—I am everywhere,
Making my home in your house, on the street, in the factory, in
    the office,
I bring sickness, poverty, insanity. Even death.

I am your worst enemy.
I am drugs.
When I come knocking, knocking, knocking
Will you have the willpower to turn me away—or lock me out?
Are you sure?

Leeah Jenn, 17

Leeah Jenn's poem is a stark warning about the powerful effects of drugs. In this chapter of "plain facts" on drugs and their effects, you'll discover Leeah's warnings have merit. Each entry in the following information is a sobering reality of the price for using on physical, mental and emotional health, so we've offered little to no commentary. Any smart teen should be able to read the following "profiles" on "commonly" used drugs and make the choice to stay drug-free; or if you "use just a little," to stop before you become chemically addicted. If you already are chemically dependent, this information is persuasive evidence to get the help you need to overcome your addiction.

Here then are the "scientific" facts about drugs and their effects on the human body.

Drugs and Their Effects
"DESIGNER DRUGS" AND/OR "CLUB DRUGS"

Drug	Common or Street Name	Effects Sought	Physical Signs & Symptoms of Use	Possible Risks & Long-Term Effects	Withdrawal Effects
Hallucinogenic amphetamine-based compounds MDA MDMA	Disco biscuits Ecstasy Essence Hug drug Love drug Lover's speed Scooby snacks X XTC	Enhanced emotions Euphoria Hallucinations Heightened attention Increased stamina Insight	Accelerated heart rate Blurred vision Chills Clenching teeth involuntarily Distorted sense of reality Faintness "False memories" Hallucinations (seeing and hearing things that aren't there) Increased blood pressure Insomnia (unable to sleep) Nausea Sense of floating or lightness Shakes and tremors (trembling or shaking) Sweating Tense muscles Vomiting	Anxiety Brain damage Convulsions Death Depression (sadness) Fatal dehydration Inability to control body movements Irrational and/or violent outbursts Kidney and cardiovascular system fail (caused by "hyperthermia"; see below) Lack of inhibitions "Malignant hyperthermia" (sharp increase in body temperature) Muscle breakdown (caused by hyperthermia) Panic Paranoia Psychosis	Discomfort Insomnia (unable to sleep) Irritability

Drugs and Their Effects
"DESIGNER DRUGS" AND/OR "CLUB DRUGS"

Drug	Common or Street Name	Effects Sought	Physical Signs & Symptoms of Use	Possible Risks & Long-Term Effects	Withdrawal Effects
GHB (gamma hydroxy buterate)	Cherry meth Easy lay Everclear Fantasy Georgia home boy Goop Grievous bodily harm Jib Liquid ecstasy Soap	Bodybuilding (anabolic effects) Euphoria Intoxication Relaxation Sociability (to feel more comfortable with others)	Drowsiness Impaired coordination (clumsiness) Impaired hearing Impaired judgment (trouble making good decisions) Lack of motor control Lowered heart rate Reduced inhibitions Slowed breathing	Coma Date rape Death Dependence/addiction Difficulty breathing (when used with alcohol) Headaches Loss of reflexes Nausea (when used with alcohol) Overdose Seizure Vomiting	Anxiety Insomnia (unable to sleep) Sweating Tremors (trembling or shaking)
Ketamine	Black hole Cat valium K Kit kat Special K Super C Vitamin K	Altered state of consciousness Dreaminess (dreamlike states) Hallucinations Intoxication	Delusions (believing things that aren't real or true) Disassociation (belief the mind has separated from body) Incoherent speech (babbling and talking jibberish) Increased blood pressure Terrible taste in mouth and throat	Amnesia Death Delirium (extreme mental confusion) Depression (sadness) High blood pressure Impaired motor function (lack of coordination) Respiratory problems (loss of ability to breathe)	Unknown

Drugs and Their Effects
"DESIGNER DRUGS" AND/OR "CLUB DRUGS"

Drug	Common or Street Name	Effects Sought	Physical Signs & Symptoms of Use	Possible Risks & Long-Term Effects	Withdrawal Effects
Rohypnol	"Date rape drug" Roach Roofies Rope Rophies	Calmness Induced sleep Intoxication Relief from tension	Detachment Disorientation (confusion) Impaired motor control (clumsiness) Sleepiness Slowed or slurred speech	"Anterograde amnesia" (blackouts/inability to remember events while under the influence) Confusion Date rape Death (especially when mixed with alcohol and/or other depressants) Dependence/addiction Double vision Loss of consciousness Loss of motor control	Agitation Cramps Nausea Nervousness Tremors (trembling or shaking)
Fetenyl (synthetic narcotic)	Synthetic heroin	Euphoria Pain relief	Constricted pupils (pinpoint pupils) Decreased heart rate Drowsiness Dry mouth Inability to think clearly Nodding head (inability to stay alert) Slowed respiration (slowed breathing)	Constipation Death High risk of dependence/addiction Parkinson's disease Unconsciousness	Anxiety Chills Cravings Diarrhea Excessive sweating Stomach cramps Tremors (trembling or shaking)

Drugs and Their Effects
STIMULANTS

Drug	Common or Street Name	Effects Sought	Physical Signs & Symptoms of Use	Possible Risks & Long-Term Effects	Withdrawal Effects
Amphetamines Methamphetamines	Bennies Crank Crystal Dexies Go fast Meth Pep pills (Diet pills) Speed Tweek Uppers	Alertness Euphoria Physical energy Stimulation Weight loss	Agitation Dilated pupils Elevated blood pressure Elevated body temperature Grinding teeth Impulsiveness Increased respiration (breathing faster) Insomnia (unable to sleep) Involuntarily clenching jaw Irritability Loss of appetite Obsessive, repetitive activity Overactivity Rapid heart rate Sweating Talkativeness	Cardiovascular problems Confusion Convulsions Delusions (believing things that aren't real or true) Depression (sadness) Elevated body temperature Headaches High risk of addiction/dependence Inflammation of the heart lining Involuntary facial movements (twitches, clenching) Irrational paranoia Moodiness Outbursts of unprovoked violence Severe anorexia Strokes (due to irreversible damage to the brain's blood vessels)* Suicidal thoughts and feelings Toxic psychosis	Anxiety Convulsions Delirium (extreme mental confusion) Depression (sadness) Extreme sleepiness Irritability Suicidal thoughts and feelings

*This damage and strokes can also occur with overdose.

Drugs and Their Effects
STIMULANTS

Drug	Common or Street Name	Effects Sought	Physical Signs & Symptoms of Use	Possible Risks & Long-Term Effects	Withdrawal Effects
Caffeine (from kola nuts, cocoa beans, coffee beans, tea leaves)	Chocolate Coffee Cola No-Doz Tea	Alertness Arousal Increased energy Sociability (to feel more comfortable with others) Stimulation	Increased heart rate Mild muscle tremor Perspiration	Anxiety Gastric pains Insomnia (unable to sleep) Jittery nerves Restlessness	Fatigue Headaches Irritability Nervousness
Nicotine	Cigarettes Cigars Cigs Coffin nails Grit Pipe tobacco Smokes Snuff	Calmness Sociability (to feel more comfortable with others) Stimulation	Coughing Increased blood pressure Increased heart rate Reduced appetite	Cancer (linked to cancer of the lungs, mouth, larynx, pharynx, esophagus, lungs, pancreas, cervix, uterus and bladder) Chest pain Chronic bronchitis Decreased sense of smell and taste Dependence/addiction Early wrinkles Emphysema Heart disease Respiratory infections "Smoker's cough" Stroke Wheezing	Aggressive feelings and behavior Cravings Headaches Inability to concentrate Irritability Overeating Social discomfort (uncomfortable around others)

Drugs and Their Effects
STIMULANTS

Drug	Common or Street Name	Effects Sought	Physical Signs & Symptoms of Use	Possible Risks & Long-Term Effects	Withdrawal Effects
Cocaine Crack (chemically altered cocaine that is smoked)	Blanca Blow Coke Nose candy Snow Toot Zip	Euphoria Freedom from pain Stimulation	Accelerated breathing Clenching teeth Constricted blood vessels Dilated pupils Dry mouth Elevated body temperature Increased blood pressure Increased heart rate Loss of appetite Obsessive, repetitive activities Overactivity Talkativeness Stuffy nose	Anxiety Brain seizures "Cocaine psychosis" (out of touch with reality) Confusion Depression (sadness) Eroded nasal septum Failure to resist infection Feeling like bugs are crawling over the skin Gastric problems Headaches Heart attacks and disease High risk of addiction/dependence Insomnia (unable to sleep) Irrational violent outbursts Little or no interest in other people or activities Loss of interest in eating Paranoia Seizures Severe birth defects Strokes	Anxiety Cravings Delusions (believing things that aren't real or true) Depression (sadness) Extreme fatigue Pain Sleepiness Tremors (trembling or shaking)

Drugs and Their Effects
STIMULANTS

Drug	Common or Street Name	Effects Sought	Physical Signs & Symptoms of Use	Possible Risks & Long-Term Effects	Withdrawal Effects
Ritalin (methylphenidate)*	Unknown	Energy Euphoria Increase in focus/attentiveness Weight loss	Agitation Elevated blood pressure Increased heart rate Increased respiration (breathing faster) Insomnia (unable to sleep) Irritability Loss of appetite Perspiration Talkativeness Wakefulness	Anxiety Dependence Insomnia (unable to sleep) Jittery nerves Restlessness	Fatigue Headaches Irritability

*Ritalin is primarily prescribed to treat ADHD; however, recently, it has been increasingly abused. The above information reflects the effects of Ritalin on those who have no legitimate medical need to take it and are not taking it as prescribed.

Drugs and Their Effects
DEPRESSANTS

Drug	Common or Street Name	Effects Sought	Physical Signs & Symptoms of Use	Possible Risks & Long-Term Effects	Withdrawal Effects
Alcohol	Beer (brew)	Euphoria	Aggressiveness	Blackouts	Aches and pains
	Booze	Freedom from inhibitions	Blurred vision	Cancer (liver, mouth, esophageal)	Delirium tremens ("D.T.'s"—include hallucinations, uncontrolled shaking and elevated blood pressure that can lead to stroke and death)
	Hard liquor	Intoxication	Distorted sense of reality	Central nervous system damage	
	Juice	Relaxation	Exaggerated or erratic emotions	Damage to the liver (possible cirrhosis)	
	Sauce	Relief from pain and anxiety	Impaired coordination (clumsiness)	Death	
	Spirits	Sociability (to feel more comfortable with others)	Impaired hearing	Dependence/addiction	Depression
	Wine		Impaired judgment (more apt to make poor decisions)	Endocrine disorders	Elevated blood pressure
			Lack of motor control	Heart damage	Extreme thirst
			Reduced inhibitions	Memory loss	Fear, panic
			Slurred or incoherent speech	Pancreatitis	Hallucinations
				Poor appetite	Restlessness
				Sexual impotence	Seizures
				Stomach problems (such as ulcers)	Sweating
				Susceptibility to disease	Tremors (uncontrolled shaking)
				Vitamin deficiencies	Upset stomach

Drugs and Their Effects
DEPRESSANTS

Drug	Common or Street Name	Effects Sought	Physical Signs & Symptoms of Use	Possible Risks & Long-Term Effects	Withdrawal Effects
Barbituates Nembutal Phenobarbitol Pentobarbitol Secobarbitol	Barbs Blockbusters Downers Goofballs Reds Stumblers Yellow jackets	Intoxication Reduced pain and anxiety Sedation (relieve tension)	Argumentativeness Bloodshot eyes Confusion Dizziness Drunken behavior Impatience Irritability Memory problems Sleepiness	Brain damage Breathing problems Coma Death High risk of dependence/addiction Fetal defects (birth defects) Liver damage (jaundice) Loss of coordination Lowered immune system Skin rash Tremors (trembling or shaking) Unresponsiveness	Convulsions Cramps Delirium (extreme mental confusion) Nausea Toxic psychosis Trembling Vomiting
Tranquilizers Ativan Benzodiazepines Klonopin Librium Valium Xanax	Big V Downers Sleeping pills Tranks	Calmness Induced sleep Pain relief Relaxation Relief from tension	Detachment Disorientation (confusion) Sleepiness Slowed or slurred speech	Abnormal heart rhythm Anxiety Confusion Dependence/addiction Double vision Drowsiness Headaches Muscle contraction Weakness	Agitation Cramps Nausea Nervousness Tremors (trembling or shaking)

Drugs and Their Effects
CANNABINOIDS

Drug	Common or Street Name	Effects Sought	Physical Signs & Symptoms of Use	Possible Risks & Long-Term Effects	Withdrawal Effects
Marijuana	Bud Chronic Doobie Ganja Grass Herb Home grown Joint Kind Magic dragon Mary Jane Pot Puff Rasta Reefer Roach	Calm Escape Intoxication Relaxation Sensory distortion Sociability (to feel more comfortable with others)	Craving for sweets (increase in appetite; "munchies") Distorted sense of time Dry mouth Fast pulse Forgetfulness Increased heart rate Less inhibited Red eyes Self-consciousness Sensitivity to light Uncontrolled laughter	Denial of effects Dependence Disruption of central nervous system Increased cancer risk Irritability Lethargy (lack of energy) Liver and lung damage Memory loss Moodiness Paranoia Psychological dependence Psychosis Reproductive problems Weakened immune system	Anxiety Decreased appetite Fatigue Feelings of despair Insomnia (unable to sleep) Jittery
Hashish Hashish oil	Hash	Escape Euphoria Hallucination Relaxation Sensory distortion	Bloodshot eyes Distorted senses Dry mouth Forgetfulness Immobility Inability to think clearly Increased heart rate Lack of inhibitions Talkativeness	Dependence/addiction Impotence Inability to reason soundly Lack of motivation Lung disease Mental deterioration Psychosis Weakened immune system	Anorexia Anxiety Hiccups Insomnia (unable to sleep) Lowered appetite Restlessness Sweating

Drugs and Their Effects
CANNABINOIDS

Drug	Common or Street Name	Effects Sought	Physical Signs & Symptoms of Use	Possible Risks & Long-Term Effects	Withdrawal Effects
LSD (lysergic acid diethylamide)	Acid Blotter Cid Doses L Microdots Tabs Trips Window pane	Altered state of consciousness Hallucinations Insight Sensory distortions	Accelerated heart rate Dilated pupils Distorted sense of direction and distance Feeling out of control Hallucinations (seeing and hearing things that aren't there) Increased blood pressure Insomnia (unable to sleep) Loss of appetite Loss of sense of time Mild nausea Paranoia Rise in body temperature Sense of disconnection from the world Sensory distortion Sweating Swings in emotions and moods Tremors (trembling or shaking) Violent outbursts	Anxiety Bad trips Becoming catatonic Behaving in ways that resemble schizophrenic psychosis Coma Confusion Convulsions Depression (sadness) Heart failure Heightened risk of self-inflicted injury (due to reduced sense of pain and touch) Flashbacks (spontaneous recurrence of being under the influence without taking the drug again) Incoherent speech Irrational behavior Loss of coordination Lung failure Permanent distortion of reality Suspicion	Flashbacks Insomnia (unable to sleep)

Drugs and Their Effects

HALLUCINOGENS (as a group hallucinogens are known as "psychedelics")

Drug	Common or Street Name	Effects Sought	Physical Signs & Symptoms of Use	Possible Risks & Long-Term Effects	Withdrawal Effects
Mescaline	Buttons Cactus Mescal Peyote	Altered state of consciousness Hallucinations Insight Sensory distortions	Delusions (believing things that aren't real or true) Distorted sense of reality Feeling out of control Hallucinations (seeing and hearing things that aren't there) Insomnia (unable to sleep) Intoxication Loss of appetite Loss of sense of time Nausea Panic Paranoia Vomiting	Bad trips Confusion Irrational thoughts and behavior	Unknown
PCP (phencyclidine)	Angel dust Dust Rocket fuel Sherm Whack	Altered state of consciousness Feelings of omnipotence (being all-powerful) Hallucinations Intoxication Sensory distortions	Delusions (believing things that aren't real or true) Distorted view of reality Insensitivity to pain Numb extremities Self-destructive behavior Unnatural stare Violent behavior	Anxiety Death Dependence Distorted sense of reality Flashbacks Inability to think clearly Isolation (withdrawing from others) Paranoia Poor concentration Slurred speech	Aches and pains Cravings Depression (sadness) Headaches Insomnia (unable to sleep) Loss of appetite Memory loss Nausea Tremors (trembling or shaking)

Drugs and Their Effects

HALLUCINOGENS (as a group hallucinogens are known as "psychedelics")

Drug	Common or Street Name	Effects Sought	Physical Signs & Symptoms of Use	Possible Risks & Long-Term Effects	Withdrawal Effects
Psyllocybin (mushrooms)	Magic mushrooms Mushrooms 'Shrooms	Altered state of consciousness Euphoria Hallucinations Insight Sensory distortions	Delusions (believing things that aren't real or true) Distorted sense of reality Feeling out of control Hallucinations (seeing and hearing things that aren't there) Insomnia (unable to sleep) Intoxication Panic	Unknown	Unknown

Drugs and Their Effects
NARCOTICS

Drug	Common or Street Name	Effects Sought	Physical Signs & Symptoms of Use	Possible Risks & Long-Term Effects	Withdrawal Effects
Heroin	H Brown China white Chiva Dope Horse Junk Smack Tar	Euphoria Pain relief Warm, flushed sensation	Apathy Constricted pupils (pinpoint pupils) Decreased heart rate Drowsiness Dry mouth Inability to think clearly Itchy skin Needle marks (if used intravenously) Nodding head (inability to stay alert) Slowed respiration Stupor Vomiting	Collapsed veins (if used intravenously) Coma Constipation Death Hepatitis High instance of arthritis or other rheumatologic problems High instance of liver and kidney disease High risk of dependence/addiction (whether smoked, inhaled or used intravenously) Impotence Increased risk of pneumonia Muscle weakness Loss of appetite Overdose Restlessness Severe withdrawal	Anxiety Body aches and pains Chills Cravings Crying Diarrhea Excessive sweating Extreme agitation Feelings of despair and hopelessness Goose bumps Kicking movements Muscle cramps and spasms Nausea Panic Restlessness Runny nose Stomach cramps Tremors (trembling or shaking) Vomiting Watery eyes Yawning

Drugs and Their Effects
NARCOTICS

Drug	Common or Street Name	Effects Sought	Physical Signs & Symptoms of Use	Possible Risks & Long-Term Effects	Withdrawal Effects
Codeine/Vicodin	Pain pills	Euphoria Pain relief	Apathy Constricted pupils (pinpoint pupils) Decreased heart rate Drowsiness Dry mouth Inability to think clearly Slowed respiration	Constipation Dependence/addiction Dizziness Lightheadedness Nausea	Anxiety Chills Cramps Cravings Loss of appetite Nausea Restlessness Seizures Tremors (trembling or shaking) Vomiting
Opium	Bird's eye Button Hop O Op Poppy	Detachment Dreaminess Euphoria Pain relief	Constricted pupils (pinpoint pupils) Decreased heart rate Drowsiness Impaired coordination (clumsiness) Lethargy Nodding head (inability to stay alert) Slowed respiration	Chronic feelings of hopelessness Constipation High risk of dependence/addiction Impotence Loss of appetite	Anxiety Body aches and pains Chills Cramps Cravings Crying Diarrhea Excessive sweating Nausea Restlessness Twitching Vomiting

Drugs and Their Effects
NARCOTICS

Drug	Common or Street Name	Effects Sought	Physical Signs & Symptoms of Use	Possible Risks & Long-Term Effects	Withdrawal Effects
Morphine	Dreamer M Morf White stuff	Euphoria Pain relief Sensation of floating	Constricted pupils (pinpoint pupils) Decreased heart rate Drowsiness Dry mouth Inability to think clearly Nodding head (inability to stay alert) Slowed respiration	Constipation High risk of dependence/addiction Mental deterioration Muscle weakness Loss of appetite Reproductive problems	Chills Cravings Diarrhea Excessive sweating Goose bumps Insomnia (unable to sleep) Kicking movements Loss of appetite Muscle spasms Nausea Runny nose Stomach cramps Tremors (trembling or shaking) Watery eyes

Other opiates are Dilaudid, Percodan, Oxycodone and Demoral. Methadone, Darvon and Talwin are synthetic opiates.

Drugs and Their Effects
INHALANTS

Drug	Common or Street Name	Effects Sought	Physical Signs & Symptoms of Use	Possible Risks & Long-Term Effects	Withdrawal Effects
Consumer aerosols Fluorocarbons	Cooking sprays Correction fluid Deodorant Freon Hair spray	Mental excitement	Drowsiness Irrational behavior Nausea Reduced sense of smell Runny nose Slurred speech Watery eyes	Brain damage Coma Death Freezing of larynx Headaches Hearing loss Liver and kidney damage Suffocation	Confusion Discomfort Headaches
Depressive inhalants Amyl nitrite Butyl nitrite	Amyl Poppers Rush Snappers Whippets	Surge of euphoria	Distorted view of reality Flushed face, neck and shoulders Rapid heat rate	Blood vessel damage Death Feeling of suffocation (trouble breathing) Headaches Heart attack Limb spasms Liver and kidney damage Loss of oxygen to the blood	Unknown

Drugs and Their Effects
INHALANTS

Drug	Common or Street Name	Effects Sought	Physical Signs & Symptoms of Use	Possible Risks & Long-Term Effects	Withdrawal Effects
Gaseous and vaporous anesthetics Chloroform Ether Nitrous oxide	Blue bottle Ethyl Gas Laughing gas	Euphoria Intoxication Pain relief	Confusion Distorted view of reality Drunken behavior Giggling Hallucinations Impaired judgment Irrational thoughts and behavior Loss of motor coordination (clumsiness) Nausea Vomiting	Brain damage Death Heart failure Limb spasms Liver damage Loss of muscle control Reduced sense of smell Stupor	Confusion Discomfort Feelings of hopelessness and despair Loss of motor coordination

Drugs and Their Effects
INHALANTS

Drug	Common or Street Name	Effects Sought	Physical Signs & Symptoms of Use	Possible Risks & Long-Term Effects	Withdrawal Effects
Organic industrial solvents (etc.)	Adhesive spray Airplane glue Cleaning fluid Gasoline Nail polish Nail polish remover Paint remover Paint thinner	Mental excitement	Delusions (believing things that aren't real or true) of grandeur (exaggerated opinion of own abilities) Dilated pupils Distorted view of reality Dramatic mood swings Drunken behavior Impaired judgment Irrational thoughts and behavior Lightheadedness Loss of motor coordination (clumsiness) Nausea Vomiting Wild eyes	Asphyxiation Blurred vision Bone marrow damage (gasoline) Brain damage Coma Damage to central nervous system Death Delirium (extreme mental confusion) Dizziness Headaches Hearing loss Heart attack Limb spasms Liver, kidney, lung damage Loss of bladder or bowel control Muscle weakness Nosebleeds Numbness and tingling in hands and feet Psychosis Reduced sense of smell Stomach pain Suffocation Violent or erratic behavior	Confusion Discomfort Drowsiness Headaches

Drugs and Their Effects
OTHER DRUGS

Drug	Common or Street Name	Effects Sought	Physical Signs & Symptoms of Use	Possible Risks & Long-Term Effects	Withdrawal Effects
Nonprescription stimulants (used in combination) caffeine + ephedrine + phenylpropanolamine	Coke-alike Legal speed Pea-shooters	Mental clarity and awareness	Accelerated blood pressure Dependence Grandiosity (exaggerated opinion of abilities) Hyperactivity Shakiness and tremors (trembling or shaking)	Discomfort Headaches Insomnia (unable to sleep) Irritability Nervousness (jittery)	Anxiety Depression (sadness) Lethargy (extreme tiredness)
Clove cigarettes	Cloves	Excitation	Numbing of mouth, lips and tongue	Bleeding in mouth or throat Cancer of mouth Dependence/addiction Lung diseases	Irritability

These "plain facts" speak for themselves. Chemical use poses grave risks to your emotional and physical well-being. Be aware that the risks of using don't end with the effects of the substances themselves; they include dangers caused by the way the substances are taken—such as the risk of contracting HIV, the virus that causes AIDS, to those who inject drugs by sharing needles. Those users who inject drugs by sharing needles are also at risk for getting the liver disease hepatitis (including hepatitis C), tuberculosis, bacterial infections and other infectious diseases, and are also putting themselves at risk for infection of the heart lining and valves, and having their veins collapse and/or scar and develop abscesses.

There are other risks as well, such as:

- Even first-time users of any drug are at risk of overdose.
- Any mind- or mood-altering drug carries the risk of leading to addiction.
- Any drug that impairs your judgment can lead to your taking dangerous risks—whether sexually, to your health or to your mental well-being.

Where to Learn More About Drugs—
And How to Break Free of Them

If you'd like to know more about drugs and their effects, the following are resources to provide such information, as well as to direct you on how you can get help and support in overcoming chemical dependency. Also be sure to check out the Suggested Readings in the back of this book.

CDC National AIDS Hotline
800-342-AIDS
800-344-SIDA (Spanish)
800-AIDS-TTY (TDD)

Center for Substance Abuse Treatment
National Drug and Alcohol Treatment Referral Service
800-662-HELP (twenty-four-hour, toll-free service)
800-487-4889 (TDD)
877-767-8432 (Spanish)
www.findtreatment.samhsa.gov

800-ALCOHOL
800-COCAINE
800-448-3000, Boystown

National Clearinghouse for Alcohol and Drug Information (NCADI)
P.O. Box 2345
Rockville, MD 20847-2345
301-468-2600
800-729-6686
800-487-4889 (TDD)

National Council on Alcoholism and Drug Dependence (NCADD)
20 Exchange Place, Ste. 2902
New York, NY 10005
212-269-7797
800-NCA-CALL
www.ncadd.org

Questions to Think About

♥ Do you think doing drugs is worth the risk they pose? Explain.

♥ What "facts" about the effects of drugs did you learn that you had never before known? How will they influence you to make a choice to live drug-free?

♥ Do you think most of the teens who "try" drugs are aware of the risks? Would it make a difference if they knew them? Why or why not?

♥ What do you feel is the most dangerous of all the drugs you've learned about? (Or is there a difference?)

♥ Looking over the "facts," what do you think are the three greatest risks or dangers of using?

5

Do You (or Someone You Know) Have a "Problem"?

Alien Abduction

A couple of my friends and I decided to go to a Saturday matinee. We agreed to all meet at Chloe Batina's house. I was the first one to get there. When I arrived, I was a little surprised to find Chloe holding a really pretty, decorative wine glass. I thought it was strange to drink water from what was obviously a fancy (and maybe expensive) wine glass, but I dismissed it as just the glass she'd wanted to use. Within minutes one of our other friends, Melania, arrived and Chloe sort of gulped the remainder of what was left in her glass. Then, she quickly went to the sink, washed out the glass, dried it off and set it up in the cabinet.

Within another couple of minutes, our other friend, Elizabeth—we call her Lizzy—arrived, and we friends went off to the movies. We had a really good time, just like we usually do when the four of us get together. And we decided that we'd reserve next Saturday for a "repeat performance."

The next Saturday, we did just that. Then we went back to Chloe's after the movies, took out frozen pizzas and began our "party." As promised, I'd brought a six-pack of Pepsi, Lizzy brought a six-pack of Coke, and Chloe and Melania furnished the pizza. But Chloe didn't drink soda; instead, she poured vodka into a small water glass. She asked us if we wanted some, and then told us that she couldn't serve us "a lot" because her parents "would notice." No one took her up on this—not one of us friends had ever had alcohol before, and drinking vodka sounded especially terrible, and with pizza it sounded positively gross. Still, while none of us had ever known Chloe to drink before, it wasn't like it was earth-shattering. But we were surprised when she poured yet another small amount of vodka for herself after she'd drunk the first "helping." Seeing Chloe drink hard liquor was kind of unsettling. At least I, for one, was troubled by it. By the time we were ready to leave, Chloe had done this a total of three times!

At that point, I no longer thought that it *wasn't* a big deal: She became really argumentative with Melania over a simple comment Melania had made about the value of not taking trig during the regular school year and waiting to take it in summer school. Her argument was pointless and senseless, too, because she wasn't taking an advanced math track like Melania. And she got really loud and started telling some really dirty "boy" jokes, as well as filling us in on the latest gossip on some of our more "colorful" classmates. Her gossip seemed really farfetched, so I chalked it up to exaggerations.

Because it was finals time at school, the next three weeks passed really quickly. During this time, we friends didn't get together for our regular "matinee date," but we did meet one Saturday morning to cram for a civics final. Chloe didn't join us for that.

The weekend following the finals, Terrance Connelly had a "FINALS ARE OVER!!!!" party, and so we four friends made plans to go together. I was more than ready to be with my friends to dance and have some fun.

It was a good party, and everyone had so much fun—especially Chloe, who not only could be heard across the room but was also the center of attention as she danced on top of the coffee table—which, as you can imagine, made Terrance nervous.

And when he called to her, "Scratch that, and I'll be grounded for life," she came back with a really rude comment, one that I could never put in writing. It was clear to everyone she'd had "way too many" as someone said. Well, she really made a spectacle of herself, and I think it's fair to say that like me, most all of her friends were embarrassed for her. Her behavior was that bad—though I'm pretty sure she had no idea what a fool she made of herself.

The next Monday at school, as you can guess, everyone who had gone to Terrance's party teased her about her behavior there. But you know what? Chloe didn't remember any of the worst of the way she acted. Feeling sure that she would want to know that she had been really wild, even weird—basically, drunk—Lizzy and I "filled her in" about how she had acted. We were hopeful that by telling her, she wouldn't let it happen again.

We were wrong. She did nearly a repeat performance the very next weekend at Tanya Williamson's party (a birthday party for Jordanne Guy); as well as two weeks later at Brian White's long-planned "end-of-soccer-season" barbecue. Watching Chloe do this to herself over and over again throughout the following semester was really confusing to me; she acted so "slutty" when she drank, but it was just one phase of her now fairly predictable chain of events. She'd drink, then get loud and then louder and then obnoxious and then start swearing louder yet. Then, she'd get really argumentative no matter what subject or topic was being discussed (sometimes we even had to pull her off someone she was trying to fight). Then she'd become quiet and withdrawn, and go off in a corner and fall asleep.

All of this got her nicknames around school, everything from "Party-Hearty" to "Party-Central" as well as an assortment of other not-so-good names, all having to do with the way she acted "while under the influence." It wasn't only embarrassing that my once-good friend had become such a "freak show," it was also sad, especially because while her "popularity" grew in notoriety—if that's what you can call it—so did her reputation as someone typically out of control. Chloe had become the hub of the party, as well as the "butt" of jokes.

My embarrassment had grown to being concerned for her, and I felt I should do something—but what?

My first decision was to part ways with her, or at least hang out with her less. I invited her to my house next to never, and never asked her to join me for studying. Though we didn't see each other as much, I always heard about what she was up to. Everyone always talked about her or was reporting on her. The drama and rumors at school were always about some of the "more stupid" things she'd done, or about Chloe being "true to form." "Alien abduction, alien abduction, alien abduction" was the phrase (the "password") that classmates repeated and passed along as they hurried to their classes when they knew that Chloe had been drinking and was "in space" because of it. Like I said, it was sad. I kept wondering, "How could Chloe go from being such a nice and normal person, to someone who, as Chad Brenner described, was a 'real drunk'?"

Our classmates all talked about Chloe; even trashed her, and yet we all liked her—and covered for her. I guess maybe we were all minding our own business—and completely ignored the danger she was putting herself in. I mean, it was obvious that she wasn't just drinking at parties, but also at school. Practically everyone knew when "Chloe's loaded." Thinking we were doing her (and ourselves) a favor, we covered for her, like the time in history lab when the teacher called on Chloe. Karen Torres, knowing Chloe was "really gone," spoke right up and answered the question for Chloe. I'm sure she did this because she knew that if Chloe answered for herself, she'd make it obvious that she was "out of her mind" and then she'd get in trouble—like being expelled from school. So in a way, we all protected her "secret."

Unfortunately, Chloe spiraled down to a place that was, as she later called it, "really dark."

Then one day, Lizzy called to tell me that Chloe had attempted suicide. Lizzy said that Chloe had been out drinking with some guy from another school and had been date raped. The feelings of shame, along with her despair over not being able to control her drinking, had caused Chloe to feel so helpless that she'd actually wanted to take her own life. Luckily, she didn't die. And luckily, she was placed in a hospital for "observation" and treated for depression—and her alcoholism. Our friend Chloe was an alcoholic.

Her suicide attempt scared me. It's made me think about the responsibility we have for looking out for each other. I mean, what if I had told my parents about Chloe's drinking early on—and they had called her parents (which is exactly why I hadn't told my parents)—and they had gotten her help for her drinking? So what if she hated me for it—would that have been as bad as her ending up in a position where she was easy prey for date rape? Would it be as bad as her becoming willing to take her own life? And what if us friends at the parties with her didn't egg her on by showing her all the attention we did when she was drinking? Why hadn't we tried to stop her from drinking as much as she did and take her home when it was obvious she was on her way to passing out in the corner? Often she even drove: Why on Earth did we allow her to get behind the wheel of the car in her condition—her "stupor" as we called it? Certainly when we saw her stumble out the door, or even if we didn't see her leave because we left before she did, we always wondered how she managed to make it home in her condition. Sometimes we would ask, and when we did, she'd say, "My car knows the way!" We're all smart enough to understand the nervousness we felt behind our chuckles.

And what if we allowed the teacher to see that Chloe couldn't answer the question because she was barely conscious? The teacher would have gotten a counselor involved immediately, and then maybe Chloe's condition wouldn't have gotten as bad as it did. I mean, I'm sure that none of the friends at school wanted to admit out loud, "Our friend Chloe has a problem," but we all knew it. I just wish that early on I'd confronted Chloe myself—not just about her behavior while drinking, but about the fact that she was drinking in the first place. Instead, mostly I'd smile that smile that says, "Glad it's you making a fool of yourself and not me!" Why hadn't I spoken to her directly and tried my best to convince her that not only did she have a "real problem," but she needed help? I wish I had.

Doing nothing doesn't do justice to our friends. My advice for anyone and everyone is: Don't run from your friends' drug or alcohol problems, but do all you can to help them get the help they need. Speaking the truth is often the ransom you need to pay when your friend is "abducted" by drugs and alcohol, like Chloe was. You just might be able to intervene before they've crossed the line from "using" to losing control of themselves and being chemically addicted—like my friend, Chloe.

Delia Anne MacNaughton, 17

Crossing the Line: What's the Difference Between "Using" and "Addiction"?

There are a lot of good reasons to live a drug- and alcohol-free life. The risk of becoming chemically dependent (addicted) is just one of those reasons. Reading about Chloe's progression from beginning to drink to eventually attempting suicide makes it clear where that risk can lead. But maybe you're a little more cynical, a little less sure that using means you're going to want to end your life, or even that it'll impair your ability to study for your next test.

Sure you know that, yes, as a minor, alcohol and drug use is illegal, but you don't intend to drink and drive, nor use and drive— nor be with anyone who is driving while under the influence. You're smart enough to know that many teens do "experiment" with alcohol and drugs, and many simply say, "It's not for me" and never use again. And you know that some will use from time to time without becoming chemically dependent (addicted). Maybe you (or your friends) use "every now and then"—you have a "sip of beer" or take "just a little hit." You know that while you've earned the right to say, "I used," it doesn't mean you're necessarily going to become chemically dependent.

So you also know that while using can lead to dependency, you also know that not everyone who uses will become "dependent." So the question is, if you "try it," how do you know whether you will or won't become like Chloe—who is now "chemically dependent," an "alcoholic"—an "addict"? And if you use, how will you know if and when you may have crossed that line?

The difference between "using" and "chemical dependency" is this: "free will." But it's not as simple—or as easy—as it sounds, because the mind and body of someone who has become chemically dependent demands "yet another dose" regardless of the consequences. Even in spite of wanting to stop, the demand of the craving is there. The chemically dependent person will do whatever it takes to get some more of the alcohol or drug he or she is addicted to (craving).

Here is another way to understand the difference between someone who is an addict and someone who uses but is not an addict: One may embarrass himself at a social gathering, get a low grade in school, or get in trouble with his parents or teachers—and see these as consequences for having "used." These experiences are enough for this person to know that alcohol and drugs impair him and that's "not good," and it's all it takes for him to stop using altogether.

Not so for the person who is (or is well on his way to being) chemically dependent, who doesn't "process" these or similar experiences in the same manner. The chemically dependent person will use in spite of the problems it causes—including harming relationships with people she loves and cares about deeply. She will skip school, steal, lie, cheat, drop out of school— do whatever it takes to use. Why? Because her brain and body are being controlled by chemicals and screaming for more. This person—now an addict—has to use regardless of how much chaos and destruction she brings upon herself. She will even use against her own desire not to use.

Who is an "addict"? Many times the word *addict* conjures up visions of tattooed criminals, vampire-like "junkies" or a disheveled street person. But as you can see from Delia Anne's story about her friend Chloe, there is no stereotype: Chloe has all of the signs of being an addict. *An "addict" is any person who has become (physically or emotionally) chemically dependent.*

While the telltale signs of Chloe's drinking problem grew more and more apparent to those around her, perhaps her classmates didn't associate Chloe's problem with full-blown alcoholism. After all, Chloe went to the same school, and liked the same movies and music as most of her peers. She looked and dressed and even acted much like many other high-school teens. Yet Chloe was chemically dependent—an alcoholic. (Alcohol is a drug.)

What does it mean to be an "addict"? The word "addiction" can bring to mind some false impressions. Often, it brings up spooky images of dark street corners in seedy neighborhoods, barren-looking jail cells, horrific crimes, the mention of dirty needles and senseless violence. But addiction doesn't always include these things. Although it can lead to all of them, addiction can also exist in "nice" homes and neighborhoods and in the "nice" people who live there, just like it existed for Chloe. *An addict is any person who has become dependent—hooked—on chemicals.* So what, exactly, is addiction?

Addiction means someone is dependent on drugs or alcohol. It is linked with the words *obsession, compulsion* and *tolerance* because once the chemical begins to wear off, the mind and body demand more—or else a painful process of "withdrawal" sets in.

The mind and body want "gratification"—the chemical—and they want it right now! The price may be serious and painful consequences, but the chemically dependent person is willing to pay it in order to get that instant satisfaction.

The pain and shame the user feels at being so out of control can make him or her feel like a "terrible person." So this person will use again in order to escape the problems and emotions as a means of coping. Of course, this only makes for more problems. Eventually the chemically dependent person ends up using to escape the pain created by using or drinking! If this sounds insane, it is—as anyone who has escaped from his or her "abduction" by drugs will tell you.

The Vicious Cycle of Chemical Dependency: Why It's Tough to Stop— Even When You Want To

Those who become chemically dependent don't start out by saying, "I use because I want to be chemically dependent!" In the beginning, they "try" drinking or using drugs for any number of reasons, whether to feel like "one of the crowd" to fit in, or because they believe that using will make them feel a certain way—such as happy, relaxed, energized or confident. The person who becomes chemically dependent will continue to use for other reasons, the first of which is that her mind and/or body are dependent on the drug and demand it the quiet the cravings for the chemical. And she will use because she is under the illusion that she needs the chemical in order to feel "happy, relaxed, energized or confident"—even though using makes it unlikely she will feel any of these! And then, when she doesn't have the chemicals, she'll get physically sick and go through "withdrawal"—bouts of anxiety along with painful physical symptoms—all of which indicate that the body is running out of "chemicals" and making demands for some more. If you don't provide the body with a "fix" of chemicals, then it begins a process of adjusting to being without them.

So chemical dependency begins by using, and as the user's tolerance for the drug grows, she needs more and higher doses of the chemical to reach the same effect. Let's look at the cycle the chemically dependent person lives as a result:

- The user can't stop thinking about using. (This is called an *obsession*.)
- The chemically dependent person constantly craves the drug, even though she knows there are painful consequences to pay for using it.
- The user begins to do and say whatever it takes to guard her use: She denies that there is a problem with drugs; she blames her frustrations and mounting problems (such as her showing up late, or not showing up at all for school or work) and all the ways her life is beginning to get chaotic, on other people or things; and builds a wall of lies that even she believes to protect her using or drinking.
- She develops a greater and greater tolerance for drugs or alcohol, needing more and more of the substance in order to get the same physical and emotional sensation ("high"). If it once took five dollars' worth of the substance, over time it could take fifty dollars (or more) to even come close to feeling the same satisfaction the five dollars' worth once gave her.
- An addict's days become centered around having and using the drug—she thinks about it, plans for it and looks forward to it. She wakes up knowing she needs to have the drug and goes to any and all lengths to make sure she gets it. All her other daily activities take a backseat to it—using is her priority.
- Once she's used, she begins this thinking and planning all

over again. The desire to use is never-ending. Once satisfied it goes right on to crave the next "high"—there is never either "too much" or "enough."

- She can't control her use because she is ruled by the obsession. Totally overwhelmed by the stress of these thoughts and feelings—as well as knowing her life is total chaos and not wanting to confront it—she is once again driven toward her chemical use as a way to escape her pain, shame and feelings of guilt.
- As the chemically dependent person continues to use, her health begins to suffer (for example, she experiences weight loss, tooth decay, vitamin deficiencies, damage to internal organs—lungs, liver, heart).
- Driven by the need to have the drug, the addict's conscience begins to shut down. A chemically dependent person will go against her own morals in order to get the chemical "fix" she craves. Of course, the addict feels terrible because of this—guilty, ashamed, lonely, frustrated, even angry—so she wants more drugs to ease the pain.
- Numbing the pain through drug use strips the addict of the ability to feel how much her drug use is hurting her and others, keeping the vicious cycle of addiction spinning.

And so the addiction continues. The chemically dependent person cannot stop using through willpower—though at some point she is sure to try. Chloe no doubt made prior attempts to control or stop her drinking. But unless Chloe (or any person who becomes chemically dependent) gets help to break the cycle of addition, she either won't be able to stop at all, or she will return to drinking or using at some point. This is why an addict needs to do more than just not use drugs; otherwise she won't stay clean and sober.

Why Is Addiction Called a "Disease"?

Why is addiction considered a disease? Addiction has specific symptoms, which can be identified in order to be diagnosed and treated. Medical professionals consider addiction a disease because it meets certain criteria. It is:

- **Chronic.** While it is treatable, it is incurable: Once an addict, you are always going to be an addict (although you can live drug-free and be in recovery).
- **Progressive.** Without treatment, the disease will progress in severity.
- **Predictable.** Without appropriate treatment you can predict where the symptoms and progression will lead.
- **Terminal.** You can die from it unless you get the help and treatment that you need to "arrest" it.

Understanding that chemical dependency starts a "disease" cycle is the basis for "respecting" the reality of putting chemicals in your body. Again, you're a smart teen: Read all you can about this. It is sure to be your most convincing argument to not use (or if you do, to stop using, and if you cannot do that on your own—and most cannot—then seek help in breaking free of your chemical dependency).

So someone whose alcohol or drug use has progressed to the point of addiction can no more just stop even if he or she wants to stop. Just like cancer or diabetes, addiction is a chronic illness that causes long-term damage to the body. It can also cause long-term damage to the mind, emotions and personal relationships. In short: Addiction is a "primary physical disease" that affects every area of the addict's or alcoholic's life.

Addiction usually begins gradually and grows progressively worse and worse. Eventually, it reaches what is known as the "chronic" stage. During this stage, the ability to reason clearly and make sound judgments is ruined not only by "addictive thinking" (such as the obsession) but also by the mental and physical effects of the drugs or alcohol on the brain.

Another way to gauge the progression of addiction is to see it divided into three stages:

Stage 1: Using. During this phase you may be "just using a little bit." Still, problems caused by using start to appear: You're having difficulty concentrating, your studies take a backseat to your using, and you're sometimes in trouble with your parents, with school, with friends, maybe even with the law. What you do in response to these problems—either quit using and drinking, or continue—will determine whether or not addiction (chemical dependency) sets in.

Stage 2: Chemically Dependent. Your using creates even bigger problems in every area of your life. Most things take a backseat to your using. You're beginning to hang around those who use and losing interest in your life as you once knew it. You are at a crossroads: You can determine that your problems are caused by using or drinking, or you can place the blame for those problems on something or someone else.

Stage 3: Chronic Addiction (commonly referred to as "hitting rock bottom"). Your life is usually in total chaos, and your mental and physical health have paid a toll (you're feeling and looking sickly, and not thinking rationally). You may have "cleaned up" any number of times, going to various treatment programs, only to relapse again and again. There's no way to escape the fact that your problem is severe and your problem is addiction—even you know it.

Do you recognize yourself or someone you care about in these stages? Has this "disease" got a hold on you or a friend or family member? It can be frightening, but it is better to be frightened than to be in denial of the problem. Some fears are very healthy—it's the fear of the oncoming train that motivates you to leap off the railroad tracks! Just like that fearful instance requires taking action, so does the fearful recognition that you or someone you care about is—or is becoming—chemically dependent.

How to Get Help

It can sound overwhelming, but don't feel there's no hope. Addiction is treatable—you can overcome it. Recovery is possible. But it requires rigorous honesty and taking positive action. So first things first, if you're still using drugs and alcohol:

- Stop using. This is the first step in healing the symptoms—and certainly the most critical one.
- Talk to your parents. Even if you think they will be upset, even if you feel you have let them down, tell them anyway. Yes, at first they will be upset, but your well-being is their number-one concern, so brave their reaction and enlist their support in getting you the help you need.
- If you feel you simply cannot tell your parents, ask a trusted adult, such as your family doctor, a clergyperson, or school nurse or counselor what you should do and where they suggest you turn for help and treatment.
- You need help: Get treatment. (Read chapter 12 in this book to learn more about all the different types of treatment available.)
- Join a support group. Don't try to go it alone. A support group can help you stay on the path of living drug-free. Look in the yellow pages for the hotline numbers of the various agencies that assist teens and call them to see what help they have to offer you. There are also hotlines for Alcoholics Anonymous or Narcotics Anonymous that you can call to find out when and where they have meetings near you. (See chapter 12, "Referrals and Resources to Find Help Near You.")

Questions to Think About

♥ Are you or a friend or family member beginning to have a problem with using?

♥ Have you ever missed school because of drug or alcohol use?

♥ Has your use of drugs or alcohol caused problems between you and your parents?

♥ Have you done things under the influence of drugs or alcohol (or in order to get them) that you never would have done otherwise?

♥ Do you use drugs or drink so you don't have to feel worried or depressed—to escape painful feelings?

♥ Have you lied or felt defensive when asked about how much or how often you use drugs or alcohol?

Ties That Bind: How "Using" Makes Each Member of Your Family "Sick"

Jekyll and Hyde—And the Rest of Us

The first time I had any idea that my family was less than an "ideal" family was when my brother, Robert, began to "make waves" when he was fourteen. I was really bummed because I considered myself a happy kid with a cool family. Unlike so many of my friends whose parents had divorced, my parents were still together and really loved each other. I was sure they really liked being parents to me and my two brothers and my sister. One of the many things I liked about my family was the sense of security I felt. I knew I was loved; I was sure all us kids in my family knew that. Other than the typical "wrestling" over who got to watch what on the TV or use the computer when, we all got along.

But suddenly, my brother became really rebellious. Almost eleven at the time, I didn't exactly understand it all, but I was smart enough to know that things had changed. It seemed that there was always an argument going on, and Robert was always the reason for it. In the first few months when he began to "take on" my parents, it didn't bug me as much as impress me that he was trying to lobby for more time with his friends, to have dinner in his room, get a later curfew—things like that. I wasn't surprised that it came with a few arguments—but I did think he went about it all the wrong way. I mean, he yelled, stormed off, and sometimes would even swear at my parents—which I thought was way out of line. Oh, and he slammed his door to his room a lot, which wasn't too cool. But then, over the next few months, he got even worse. He just got more and more bold in the things he said and did. His rebellious nature kept growing and growing and growing. I didn't like this at all—he was my older brother, and I'd always looked up to him. He could do no wrong in my eyes. But that was changing—fast. I mean, many times when he talked back—actually it was more like "yelled" back—I thought he was wrong, and my parents were right. So that really bothered me, because I didn't understand why he was acting like such a jerk.

Just when I thought things couldn't get any worse, they did. Coming home from school one day, I saw broken flowerpots and glass scattered everywhere. Some of the furniture was tipped over—things were strewn everywhere. The family room was a disaster! I was very confused about what had happened—until I noticed a "note" in Robert's handwriting laying on the counter. It was an angry note, mostly just words aimed at hurting my parents' feelings. I was baffled—and really worried. "Why would he do this?" I wondered. My parents weren't home, so I went to my older sister, Karlie. She tried to make me feel better. "Don't worry about it, Marcus. I'll clean it up—and well, Robert—he's just being a complete and total idiot again."

But my mother got home before my sister and I had managed to put things back in place. The moment my mother looked around, she sat down and explained to my sister and me the truth behind Robert's actions: He was using drugs. Apparently, the chemicals drove him to be violent, because he was one angry person when he used. The reason he was totally hostile and unreasonable was because of his using. My idea of our perfect family was shattered. I was shocked, mad—and scared, too.

After that, the whole family had a big talk about Robert's use. I learned that he'd been using for a while. My parents had actually known about it for some time, but I guess they were hoping they could convince him to stop using, and that he could quit on his own, or whatever. I found out they'd been covering up for him quite a lot. But with all the damage he'd done to our house on his latest "binge," my parents decided they wouldn't cover up for him anymore.

Things got even worse. The effects of his using brought our family to its knees, so to speak. And the drama was never-ending—one incident after another. This unspeakable thing wasn't supposed to be happening to our family. We were "normal"—"cool." Cool families don't do drugs. Now, one family member did.

My brother continued to use for some time. And it's just amazing how his using changed our family and everyone in it. It was like his drugs "ruled" the family; certainly they seemed to have a strange control over all of us. We stopped functioning the way we used to: We stopped being happy—you could see it in our eyes, and in our smiles, which came less often and were sometimes forced. Each of us stopped acting the way we once did. I tried to make it up to my parents that my brother was so hard on them. I tried to bring home perfect report cards and do everything I could think of to make sure they didn't feel so bad about having a son who used drugs—and treated them as badly as he did. My older sister, Karlie, tried to make sure everyone was happy—especially when we were upset over something Robert did—like not coming home for nights on end. She was forever trying to smooth things over after my brother had one of his outbursts. Then as time went on, she spent more and more hours in her room. If there was some really huge drama she couldn't smooth over, she headed straight for her room and stayed there.

I guess you could say that everyone changed. My little brother, Josh, started being the family clown. He was always coming up with a joke—knock-knock jokes of all things! It was really pathetic because the moment things got tense when my brother was around, he'd break out his jokes—even if it meant telling the same ones over and over. Or he'd act silly or goofy should some big drama be happening because of something my big brother had just done. It was like he thought he was in charge of tension-control. And there was a lot of tension: When Robert came into the room, the conversation stopped—and when it started again it was sort of phony, everybody saying "pleasant" things—sort of like each of us were letting the other know that at least all of us hadn't turned angry and mean. If my brother was having a temper tantrum, we looked at each other to see if we should speak up or stay silent so as not to rile him up any more than he was. And if he was being rude or inconsiderate—which he was a lot—we had to gauge if it was safe to speak up and say what was on our minds, or if it was better if we just left "well enough alone." When Robert was in one of his "really dark moods," we had to be careful what we said or even did for fear we'd tip him over the edge. More often than not, he'd yell accusations, knock things around, run to his room, or worse yet, run out the door and who knew if he'd return that night—or the next day for that matter.

My parents tried twenty million ways to deal with our "drug-using family member." They pleaded; they reasoned; they counseled; they sometimes got angry; they spoke gently and persuasively; they put him on restriction; they begged him to change; they tried silently ignoring the behaviors. Nothing worked. It was like Robert was someone we didn't recognize any longer. It was like he was two people: Dr. Jekyll and Mr. Hyde. He had changed that much.

My once-thoughtful, cool big brother now acted as if he didn't have a conscience. He didn't care who he hurt, and all he thought about was himself. None of his old friends ever came around anymore, and none of his old dreams for the future seemed to mean a thing to him. His grades fell, and he was nearly flunking out of school. He didn't even look like himself anymore—he was skinny and pale. His eyes were sunken and looked empty, and he was always sullen—either that or mad.

Things got even worse, and eventually, Robert's drug use got him arrested, which was both good and bad. It was good in that, as embarrassing as it was, it freed our family—finally someone else would deal with him. Robert's arrest was a turning point for him because that's when the courts mandated that he get into a treatment program to get help to recover from his drug use. After he finished being in a treatment program, he continued to get help—so did our whole family. So I guess you could say that in some ways, our family is closer than before. While in the beginning we all pulled together and vowed to "get through it," the counseling we all went through was good for us individually and as a family.

I didn't ever think I'd tell this story, because it is both sad and hurtful. But I've discovered that many, many teens have problems with using. I've learned it doesn't take much to get hooked. And it's sad but true that once you've used, your life starts to fall apart in a lot of ways. And all because drugs are more addictive than anyone wants to believe.

So that's my story, and why I now have a new definition of what is "normal" for a family. Luckily, we are a strong and close family, and we love each other. The good news is that we now have our brother back. We don't love Robert any less and know that he is not a "bad" guy. He is just someone who used drugs and paid the price. Still, there is a sadness and a painful loss of innocence because of it all—to him, and to each of the rest of us. I can tell you that the price of using drugs is more than you'll ever want to pay or put your family through.

Marcus LaMont, 15

Addiction: A Family Disease

We often hear about how devastating drugs are to the user, but as you can see from Marcus's story, when someone uses drugs, it takes a toll on everyone around that person. Alcoholism and addiction are said to be "family diseases." This isn't because they necessarily run in the family (although medical professionals have said there can be a "family tendency" toward alcoholism or addiction). The reason addiction and alcoholism are called a "family disease" is because the addiction of one family member can affect the entire family. Certainly this was true for Marcus and his family in the previous story.

Perhaps no relationship is as basic as our family, and there are many ways that having a chemically dependent member impacts the family. When addiction sets in, the relationship with the drug becomes the chemically dependent person's primary relationship in life . . . a relationship that becomes more important than all others. This is bound to stand in the way of creating healthy family ties.

All of us need and want our parents' approval—no matter how old we are. As a teen, while you seek to create a "space" of your own and want to grow into your "own person," you still need and want love and acceptance from your parents—even if you don't always get it. What's more, almost no one wants to hurt their parents—but that's exactly what using does. Since using is harmful (and can even be life-threatening), parents will take a stand against it. As a teen you have probably gone through times when you felt you were "on the outs" with your parents. Using can make "the outs" an ongoing state because it creates a secret that stands between the user and his or her parents. What once may have been a trusting relationship may now become shrouded in secrecy, dishonesty, guilt, fear and suspicion. This can take on a life of its own, distancing the teen more and more from his or her parents.

If you have any brothers and sisters, you know there are often spats and arguments—this is normal and to be expected. But when a family has a member who is chemically dependent, these spats and arguments aren't as harmless because they are driven by a need to survive the "family disease" and feel like one has a place in the family. This can stand in the way of brothers and sisters being able to have caring, positive ties with each other.

Family members are connected and their lives impact each other—for good or for bad. So, of course, addiction takes its toll on the entire family.

Is Someone in Your Family "Changing"?

Once dependency sets in, the addict's life can't help but unravel. The family probably knows something is wrong before anyone else does. And no wonder: As the family member uses, his or her behavior changes. He or she no longer goes along with "normal family life"—such as talking and listening to each other in respectful and loving ways, or honoring the rules (such as timelines and curfew and other activities) that keep a family functioning in an orderly way. As these changes take place, confusion sets in. When stress, pressure and tempers rise, yelling and arguing seem to become the daily norm. Family members look into the chemically dependent person's face and wonder what has happened. It seems this person has become an unrecognizable stranger, and in many cases, he has. And yet, as painful and frustrating as this dilemma is, it can be expected. Addiction renders the user sick and unable to behave in ways that are rational or responsible. To expect a person who is chemically dependent who is not in recovery to be trustworthy, responsible and rational is like expecting someone with emphysema or pneumonia to run a twenty-mile marathon.

The longer the normal pattern of family life is disrupted, the more likely it is that family members experience emotions rang-ing from confusion, to concern, fear and anger. As you would expect, the "dynamics" of the family change.

Sometimes each family member begins a new pattern of doing and saying things with an intent to keep the family "feeling okay." Yet covering for the "user" is not good because it prevents this person from being responsible for the consequences of his actions. When Marcus and his sister picked up the mess of papers, glass and strewn furniture from Robert's "tantrum," their covering for him lessened the appearance of the chaos he caused. They made it appear less dramatic and less harmful than it really was. When a family member is using, it's easy for others to become what professionals in the field of chemical depen-dency call a "codependent."

What Does It Mean to Be a *Codependent*?

It's only natural that when someone in the family has become chemically dependent, it's going to affect each person in the family. As each family member tries to "cope" with the person who is using, they adapt their behavior to that person. In the process, they are at risk of becoming a "codependent." Melody Beattie, considered a leading expert in the field of chemical codependency, defines a codependent as, *"Anyone who has let another person's behavior affect him or her, and who is obsessed with controlling that person's behavior."** For example, the other family members may become obsessed with the chemi-cally dependent family member's using or drinking, making the user the center of their waking thoughts—and *always* the topic of their conversations, and thus normal family life suffers.

When this happens, just as an individual can hurt emotionally

---

*Melody Beattie, Codependent No More, *Center City, Minn.: Hazelden Information Education,* 1996.

(even to the point of becoming physically ill), the family as a "unit" can become "sick." Because it's normal for family members to care and look out for one another, each person may lose sleep as they worry about the trouble their family member is going to get into, or try to cover the bases of the user, trying to guard him or keep him out of harm's way (or to shield the fact of his drug use from one or more of the other family members—as Marcus's parents did in the beginning of Robert's drug use). They may even blame themselves for their family member's addiction, or turn on their chemically dependent family member in anger. They want "the problem" to go away, and while coping themselves, they end up changing the way they react to the member using, as well as the way they relate to each other.

In fact, professionals in the field of chemical dependency identify specific "roles" family members take on in response to another family member using. Just a few of these roles include:

- The "Rescuer," who is always trying to rescue the chemically dependent person—and prevents the "addict" from suffering the full impact of the consequences of his using.
- The "Hero," who is a high achiever, who seeks the approval of others and works very hard to be as close to perfect as possible in order to compensate for the chemically dependent family member.
- The "Scapegoat," who draws the attention away from the chemically dependent person by acting out in self-destructive ways.
- The "Mascot," who is usually the family clown and gets a lot of attention by providing comic relief. His need to create laughs is to cover up pain—both his own and the family's.
- The "Lost Child," who does whatever it takes to adjust to any and all circumstances. Her easygoing nature gives some relief to the family—and she has the payoff of escaping notice altogether.

Do you see Marcus and his family members in any of these roles? What about you and your family members? This is just a brief description of different roles that play out in the dynamics of a family with a chemically dependent member. There are a number of others; and usually family members take on variations and combinations of the traits represented. This allows you a glimpse of how each individual is affected by the addiction of one of its family members.

The real problem with "assuming a role"—as opposed to being yourself and expressing your true feelings—is that it chips away at your integrity, your reputation with yourself. It also stops the user from the consequences of his addiction. As such, it actually keeps him in his cycle of using, thus preventing him from reaching a "bottom" so that he can see for himself that he does not want to continue using.

How to Talk to Your Family So They'll "Hear" What You'd Like to Tell Them

Communication is such an important part of healthy relationships. Often there are problems in relationships because family members don't know how to communicate. They are not able to express themselves openly and honestly. What each person in the family expects of each other is not clear. Other times, assumptions prevent effective communication. You can assume you know something about your family member, or assume he (or she) knows how or what you think or feel. Then you end up basing the way you act on something that might not even be true—the other person may not know what you think or feel at all. You may feel like you don't have to say positive things about your family members because they already know how you feel; besides, you reason, surely they already know all these positive things about themselves. But this simply isn't true—especially in relationships involving drugs or alcohol.

Unexpressed expectations and assumptions aren't the only possible problems in relationships where drugs and alcohol are involved. Since the communications in these relationships are bound to become tense, many subjects are avoided altogether. "Secrets" may be kept for any number of reasons but they have the power to be very destructive to relationships. If you were to take a few minutes to think of some subjects that you avoid discussing or feelings that are uncomfortable for you to talk about, you would no doubt come up with at least a couple of them. To get started on improving communication in your family, share the following information with your family member(s). If you like, you can write down what you'd like to say and then share your answers; or you can simply find the right time and words to talk about them.

Clarify your expectations of your family member(s) and yourself.

- Talk about those times when you feel close to your family member, and how you want to experience more of those times. <u>Try starting with these words:</u> *I feel we are so close when:*
- Share what it is that you like and want most in your relationship. <u>Try starting with these words:</u> *What I like most about our relationship is:*
- Commit to taking specific actions in order to make your relationship more healthy and positive—and share those actions you're willing to commit to with your family member(s). <u>Try starting with these words:</u> *In order to make our relationship more healthy and positive, I am willing to:*

Clear up any assumptions—learn and communicate the truth.

- Take the time to think about and then openly share those things that you assume your family member(s) knows, just in case he or she (or they) doesn't know those things. <u>Try</u>

starting with these words: *These are the things I've just assumed you knew, but just in case you don't, I'd like to tell you:*

- As often as possible, sincerely share the qualities you value most in your family member(s). Try starting with these words: *I want you to know I value these things:*
- Ask your family member(s) to share those qualities they value most in you; start by showing that you know what you value in yourself. Try starting with these words: *The qualities I value most in myself are:*

Get the secrets out in the open.

- Talk about how your family member's drug use (or your own) has had an effect on your relationship. Try starting with these words: *I feel my (or your) drug or alcohol use has had these effects on our relationship:*
- Share openly and fearlessly about some subjects you put off bringing up because you are uncomfortable with how your family member might respond. Try starting with these words: *Here are some subjects I put off bringing up because I'm uncomfortable with how you might respond:*
- Admit to those feelings that you have a difficult time sharing with your family member. Try starting with these words: *I have a hard time sharing these particular feelings with you:*
- Talk about those times when you feel very far away from your family member. Try starting with these words: *I feel far away from you when:*

Questions to Think About

♥ How have you been affected by your family member's use—for example, do you have trouble concentrating, getting your homework done, or have your grades dropped? Do you seem to enjoy life less—your time with friends, your pet, life in general?

♥ If you are the one who uses in your family, how has your using affected your family?

♥ When did you begin to either "walk on eggshells" or act out on your feelings with the chemically dependent family member?

♥ Have you tried to control your family member's use of alcohol/drugs by doing things such as getting rid of his or her supply?

♥ When did you start to make excuses for the behavior of the chemically dependent family member? For example, do you blame others, rather than expect that person to behave responsibly?

7

If a Friend or Family Member Is Using, What Can You Do?

Catch Me—If You Can!

I started using drugs mostly because many of my friends were drinking and using. I'm sixteen, and most of my friends are older than I am. When I started using, mostly I hung out with friends who were using. Since many of these friends didn't go to school, I didn't want to either. A lot of them didn't even have jobs. They just "hung out" all day. That looked cool to me! As time went on, everyone in this group—including me—began doing more drugs—and harder drugs. It wasn't long before I got seriously hooked.

Using drugs messed up my life in a lot of ways. Having dropped out of school, I felt like a failure. Then I'd use so as not to think about it. Of course, then I felt even more like a failure, because not only had I dropped out of school, but I was using, as well. So then I'd use some more so I could drown out feeling "even more like a failure"! It was a never-ending battle. Then I began to stay away from home, sometimes for a day or two—or three—at a time. It was like I was playing "catch me if you can"—because I was going to do what I wanted to do—and I wanted to use drugs. That led to Mom and me fighting all the time. It got to the point where she told me that if I was going to be a "druggy," I had to leave, which was fine with me. Every kid using drugs wants to get "permission" to leave the house and crash at a friend's place. It's very easy to find a place to stay if you're a good-looking girl.

Mom had tried everything she knew to help me get straight. Even though my mother had resigned herself to the fact that I needed to "reach bottom"—to make a decision that I wasn't going to do drugs any longer—she wanted me to stop using drugs and get healthy, not just leave home because she had a rule of no drugs—or else.

My choice was to do drugs. So then my life was spending time at one friend's place and then on to the next. It wasn't as "glamorous" as I had thought. We were always out of food, and when rent came due, someone always had their hand out for money—and, of course, I didn't have any. I found out that even your "druggy" friends only want you around as long as there's something in it for them—and just hanging around doesn't account for too much. One day, I got sick of it all, and I called my mom. She asked if I was done with drugs, and when I said no, she tried to reason with me about getting help.

Well, I guess she decided that I was pretty bad off, because even though I hadn't told her where I was staying, she found out, and the next Thursday at two o'clock in the morning, she drove there. Even though she was scared and didn't know what she was walking into, she came into the rented house where I was hanging out at the time. I was there with five of my "friends," all of us really wasted from doing drugs.

My mother knew from looking at me that I needed medical help. Good thing, too, because I was really messed up. Though she looked calm on the outside, Mom has told me since then that from the way I looked, she was really afraid of how much damage I'd done to myself. I can only imagine how difficult it must have been for my mother to see me in the condition I was in. I mean, here I was, her daughter, once an okay student and athlete, now looking lifeless, stoned out of her mind. I've seen pictures that were taken of me when I was using. They are pretty scary looking. When I look at those pictures now, it still scares me. So it must have been an especially terrible thing for her.

What courage she had! I mean, it's not like I was happy to see her when she showed up. It's not like I wanted to be taken from my friends and from my addiction. Because I was in no condition to walk, let alone be reasoned with, my mother didn't even try to force me to leave. Instead, she calmly announced that she was staying until I decided to come home with her! The standoff between the two of us lasted almost the rest of the night—what was left of it. As the drugs began to wear off, and when I got so tired I would have done anything to get some sleep, I finally gave in and we left together. I'm sure I didn't sing and skip to her car—though I don't remember too much other than waking up in the hospital.

Over the next few days, my mother set in motion a million plans—all designed to get me some help. She got a drug "intervention" to take place. This is where the people dearest to you come together and, along with a drug counselor, try to convince you that they're fearful that you may kill yourself—or hurt someone else (like in a car accident)—if you continue doing drugs. As Mom had hoped, it worked. I agreed to go for help at a drug rehab center. Even when I was released, Mom continued to help me get my life back together. And that's what I'm up to now, living in a healthy way, day-by-day, one day at a time—rather than failing day-by-day like I had been.

Mom says it was the "most harrowing experience" of her life. I am so lucky she loves me and believed that with help I would break free of drugs and get my life together. It took a lot of courage for my mother to do what she did. Still, whenever life seems tough, and I wish I didn't have to feel what I was feeling, I think about getting high. But only for a moment. What keeps me from relapsing, from using again, is thinking of how horrible that time was for me and of the misery I felt. I got so sick, and I'm sure I came close to overdosing any number of times.

I do thank my mother for her courage. I'm very grateful for her love and loyalty. I think one of the greatest examples of courage I've ever seen is what my mother did for me. I credit her with saving my life. But next to her, I am the most courageous person I know. Every day of my life I play "catch me if you can" with my own thinking and behavior—to make certain my addiction stays in check. It can be a struggle. So if you aren't using drugs, don't. If you are, go to your parents. Even if they yell at you—which they probably will—go to them anyway. When they're done being mad that you're slowly killing yourself because of doing drugs, they'll help you get well.

Gianne Warren, 16 (Adapted from Taste Berries for Teens)

If Someone You Care About Is Using, Consider This Before You Say, or Do, Anything

Gianne Warren's mother was relentless in trying to see that her daughter got the help she so badly needed. Helping a friend or family member understand that by using they are on a path that only leads to self-destruction is a noble act.

It doesn't always work. Sometimes the person chooses his drug over the thought of living without it. As you've learned, the greater the addiction, the more the user—the "addict"—will refuse help. Sometimes he or she has to do what is known as "hitting bottom" (more on this in chapter 9) before he or she is willing to get help. To someone who doesn't use, needing to "hit bottom" can seem simply crazy. Keep in mind that when someone uses to the point of becoming addicted, the chemical is in control and not the person using. The addict may no longer be able to "choose" to be without the drug.

Is someone you care about chemically dependent? It can really hurt to watch someone you love self-destruct. If your friend or family member is using, you can help that person get a hold of her life before she damages her health or maybe even dies. Here are some things to keep in mind about "getting help" for your friend or family member:

1. You can't force anyone to get help, but you can suggest it, and you can offer your support in their seeking treatment.
2. No matter how "bad" the person you care about has been acting, he is not "bad" but rather "sick." Addiction—whether to alcohol or drugs—is a disease that can lead to all sorts of destructive behavior, including doing things that hurt the people the addict cares about most. Remember, the chemical is now in control of your friend or family member—and not the other way around. However, it is crucial for you to know that if this person is abusive, you have the right to get help for yourself immediately—and should do just that. Always protect your own health and well-being, and don't allow yourself to be placed at risk.
3. Before you do or say anything to your friend or family member, talk to one or more adults—whether your mom or dad, a counselor, family doctor, teacher or clergyman. Tell them about the problem and ask what they think is the best thing for you to do. It's important to get support and direction to make certain your plans are as safe and effective as possible.
4. Getting help for your friend or family member isn't "betraying" that person, nor is it being a snitch, a tattletale or stirring up trouble. It is an act of bravery and courage—and compassion—one that might even save a life. It's also the moment when your friend or family member gets a chance to stop the self-destruction, work to restore her health and begin to put her life back together.

5. Don't underestimate the value of saying something: Health experts tell us that seven out of every ten people who attend treatment programs for chemical abuse are there because a friend or family member spoke up about their using and urged them to get help.
6. If you believe that your friend or family member's drug or alcohol abuse is endangering his or her life, a professional in the field of chemical dependency may be the most effective way to get this person to seek the help he or she needs.

Once you've taken into account these considerations, you may then want to go ahead with a "intervention."

What Is an "Intervention"—
And How Does It Work?

An "intervention" is a way to take action in helping someone who has a problem with drugs and alcohol. It is an attempt to try to get a friend or family member to stop using drugs or alcohol and seek help. Of course, you can always encourage your friend or family member to get help and share your concerns with them. You can even have a planned conversation between just you and your friend or family member to do this, but it's best to do an intervention with other people who also care. This not only protects you from trying to present your concerns alone, it also shows your friend or family member that several people are concerned—making the concerns seem more valid. There can be strength in numbers.

Following are some ways for you and those helping you to make your discussion as effective as possible:

• Plan to talk to your friend or family member when they are most likely and able to listen, as opposed to when that person is tired or under the influence.

- Share your care and concern without making accusations. Don't say, "You are a drug addict (or alcoholic)." Instead say, "I'm concerned for you because you are using drugs. . . ." You want to keep your friend or family member open to listening to what you have to say, so avoid anything that sounds like blame. Speak with compassion, not with pity. Speak exactly as you'd want someone to speak to you if the roles were reversed.

- Share how you feel. Feelings you might include are: scared, worried, terrified, sad, frustrated, hurt. You might say, "I'm so scared that you are going to black out and hurt yourself." Or, "I miss the way we used to have heart-to-heart talks."

- Share the things you've seen your friend or family member do while under the influence, the changes you've witnessed, the consequences you've seen her pay. Start your sentences with "I" and be specific: You might say, "I was worried about you when you fell down at the game and knocked into someone," rather than saying, "You're dangerous when you drink."

- Know ahead of time where your friend or family member can go for help. If he agrees help is needed, you need to be able to suggest where this person can turn for assistance. (See chapter 12 for more direction and information on treatment options and resources.)

- Make it clear that you want to help—even offering to go with your friend or family member. This can show that you truly care and want to do all you can to be there for her. If it's a friend you might say, "Will you talk to the school counselor about this? She knows where you can turn for help. I'd be glad to come along and be there for you." If it's a parent you're concerned about, you might say, "There is an AA meeting at the Community Center twice a day every day of the week. Will you go this evening? It's an open meeting, and I'd like to come with you."

- You may not meet with success. Don't be surprised if your friend or family member responds with complete denial or tells you in no uncertain terms that he does not have a problem. That person might even suggest that you're the one with the problem for accusing him of such a thing.
- If you've talked to your friend or family member alone, and that person refuses to get help, let him know that you're going to have to tell someone who can help. If you hold his secret, you're helping protect his disease, which will allow it to grow more and more destructive.

Doing an Intervention with a Professional Counselor

Sometimes an informal intervention is not enough. If this is the case, a formal intervention may be what's needed. In fact, whenever possible, it's best to solicit the help of a professional in the field of chemical dependency. This person, often called a facilitator, is trained to do formal interventions. This chemical dependency professional will organize, guide and direct the meeting. She will ask you about the person who is chemically dependent, and which four or five people that person loves and/or respects the most (such as best friends, brothers or sisters, a grandparent, mom and dad, maybe even a coach or teacher). These will be the people who will be asked to participate in the intervention.

Different professionals handle interventions in different ways. Fourteen-year-old Kelly Calhoun told us about her experience with an intervention: "When my family decided on an intervention for my older brother, we called a local family therapist in our community who gave us the name of someone she thought would be good, and we met with that person. He told us that we should hold the intervention at our home, and to plan it at a time when we were sure my brother would be at home. Then, we were told to each write a letter to my brother that we would read to him during the time we were all going to meet. I think this made it easier, because we could think about what we were saying and rewrite it so that we were honest with him without blaming him."

Sometimes the professional "facilitating" the intervention has the friends and family members in attendance simply tell the chemically dependent person—face to face—about their concerns and the things they're worried about, giving examples of specific behaviors.

The facilitator is there to make certain the meeting unfolds in a way that best gets the message across to your friend or family member that help in the form of treatment is needed. Another advantage to having a chemical dependency professional facilitate a formal intervention is that he or she will usually know the best treatment referrals and be prepared to assist with getting your friend or family member there immediately. To find this professional, you might start by asking your school counselor who to call. Or you can look in the yellow pages under some of the following possible sections or listings:

- Drug and Alcohol Treatment/Substance Abuse Treatment/ Chemical Dependency
- Community Drug Hotlines
- City/Local Health Departments
- Local Community Treatment Services

"Tough Love": Three Important Reasons to Be "Tough" with Someone Who Is Using

What do you do if your friend or family member still refuses to get help? It's easy to fall into the habit of making excuses for the chemically dependent person. It's natural to try and protect someone you love or care about. But when "enough is enough" it may be time to get "tough"—and practice what is called "tough love." This means letting your friend or family member suffer the consequences of his or her drug use. Here are three good reasons to be "tough" with a friend or family member who is using:

1. **Hitting bottom may be necessary.** When you protect your friend or family member from the consequences of using, you cushion the "bottom" he needs to "hit" in order to admit there is a problem and get help (you'll find more about "hitting bottom" in chapter 9). As sixteen-year-old Rachel Lund explained, "My sister, Rena, who is twenty, just wouldn't stop using drugs. To help her come to a place where she would admit there is a problem and get help, all of us had to stop covering up for her. We don't say she's sick when her work calls, like we used to. My parents don't lend her money to make her car payments anymore. Basically, Rena is on her own until she admits she has a problem and gets help. The rest of us have finally reached that point where we understand that we can no longer 'enable' her—which means we used to make it easy for her to keep using. We are all in agreement that we each do our part not to make it easy for her to use. It can be really hard, because when she comes to me and begs to 'borrow' a few dollars, I have a really hard time telling my own sister no. But now I do, and I feel okay knowing that it wasn't because of me that she just put more drugs into her body."

2. **Your friend or family member has to acknowledge that using is a problem.** When using drugs or alcohol, there are consequences. When a person doesn't show up on time (or skips out) or isn't where he's supposed to be, or doing the things he's supposed to be doing, he gets in trouble with teachers, or gets suspended or expelled from school. If he steals to support his habit, it is likely he will get into

trouble with the person he stole from, maybe even be "charged" with a crime. If he spends money on alcohol or drugs rather than spending it wisely on the things he needs, then he should go without them. If you prevent these consequences from playing out in the life of your friend or family member, you are denying that person the reality of his decisions and actions. In short, you take away the chemically dependent person's need or motivation to stop using.

3. **Taking care of yourself requires that you distance yourself from the chaos.** Holding and harboring your friend or family member's secret—or trying to make things right in spite of the drug use—is very stressful. It also creates a lot of confusion and chaos and can even become an obsession of its own. As you sacrifice your integrity to cover up for your friend or family member, your self-esteem suffers—and you can find yourself not being helpful to either your friend or family member, or to yourself, as you fail to do what's best and right for you.

It is difficult to sit back and watch another person spin out of control, especially when that person is also hurting emotionally, maybe getting sick physically, and when he doesn't have the things he needs—such as lunch money. And, not "helping" can run counter to what you believe about friendship: Being a friend means helping each other out. So, if your friend is using, your first instinct is probably to keep him out of trouble—cover for him. This can include anything from harboring his secret, helping him lie to his parents, letting him copy your homework because he can't ever seem to get his done anymore to letting him hide drugs in your locker. The plain truth is you are not helping him by allowing him to avoid the consequences of his actions.

The best thing you can do right from the start, from the first time you see someone using, is take a stand. If the person you are trying to help is a friend who refuses to get help on his own, you may want to talk to his parents. It's worth remembering that people end up in jail, in mental institutions and can die because of drug and alcohol abuse. If you feel your friend is having serious mental and/or physical health problems or is endangering the lives of others, say something to his parents, or to a school nurse or counselor. It may be what saves that person's life.

When It's Time to "Detach and Let Go"

In the end, the decision to stop using drugs and alcohol and to begin working a program of recovery always lies with the chemically dependent person. As sixteen-year-old Rachel Lund, who told us about her sister Rena earlier, explained, "I can't make Rena do anything—neither can my parents. No one can control another person and make the decision to get clean for them. At some point, Rena has to want to clean up and live a life of recovery."

If you've done all you can to be there when your friend or family member needed your love and support most, it may be time to walk away, "detach" or "let go." She and her family having come to that point, Rachel said, "Knowing that we've done our very best helps give us some comfort. We're still there if Rena decides she wants help."

Are You Feeling Overwhelmed and Drained by Your Friend or Family Member's Use? Where to Turn for Help and Support —For Yourself

Your friend or family member's chemical dependency can take its toll on you, too. Knowing what to do with all the feelings it brings up—fear, anger, loneliness, worry, frustration, confusion, sadness—can be hard. It's important to talk to someone about how you are feeling and how you are coping. Perhaps your counselor at school can help you or refer you to someone who can. Following is a list of support groups and organizations that provide information for friends and family members of chemically dependent people. It's always good to get help to understand what you're facing, and then to get the help and support you need in order to cope in healthy ways.

Al-Anon/Alateen Family Group Headquarters
P.O. Box 862, Midtown Station
New York, NY 10018-0862
212-302-7240
800-356-9996 (Literature)
800-344-2666 (Meeting Referral)

Children of Alcoholics
555 Madison Ave., 4th Floor
New York, NY 10022
212-754-0656 or 800-359-COAF

Nar-Anon Family Group Headquarters
P.O. Box 2562
Palos Verdes Peninsula, CA 90274
310-547-5800

National Clearinghouse for Alcohol and Drug Information (NCADI)
P.O. Box 2345
Rockville, MD 20847-2345
301-468-2600
800-729-6686
800-487-4889 (TDD)

National Council on Alcoholism and Drug Dependence (NCADD)
20 Exchange Place, Suite 2902
New York, NY 10005
212-269-7797
800-NCA-CALL
www.ncadd.org

National Organization of Student Assistance Programs and Partners
4760 Walnut St., #106
Boulder, CO 80301
800-972-4636

Questions to Think About

♥ If you were worried about someone and wanted to write that person a letter, what would you say in the letter? How would you tell that person you were worried without placing blame or sounding like you were accusing her of being "bad"?

♥ How can you use "I feel" messages in your life (even if not in a situation like an intervention)?

♥ Is someone you know doing something harmful? What do you think you can do about it? What can you do if she doesn't stop the harmful behavior?

♥ Have you made excuses for someone else that may have harmed the person or kept the person from consequences he should have experienced?

Unit III

You Want to STOP Using: What to Do and How to Do It

*If you always do what you've always done,
then you'll always get what you've always got.*

—Source Unknown

Experience is the truth that finally overtakes you.

—Katherine Anne Porter

*When you want to believe in something,
you also have to believe in everything
that's necessary for believing in it.*

—Ugo Betti

*Minds are like parachutes:
They don't work unless they're open.*

—Source Unknown

8

Denial: Are You Kidding Yourself About "I Can Stop Anytime I Want"?

"If Her Mouth Is Moving, She's Lying"

I started drinking and smoking pot when I was thirteen. At first it was just on weekends with a couple of my friends—and maybe just a little toke now and then at school. I still got okay grades and while I was sometimes late for soccer practice, I managed to stay on the team. So at least for the first year, if smoking pot "affected" me in any way, I didn't consider it a big deal. It wasn't like my being a little more laid-back than usual was any glaring red flag or anything.

By the time I was fourteen, I was smoking more, like after school nearly every day with my friends, and a couple of times a week over the noon hour. At this point I was having trouble concentrating in class, and my grades were falling—but probably I figured it was because I never did my homework—and teachers were always on my back. I constantly promised myself I was going to do better and start getting my homework done. But then every evening after dinner, I'd go outside, saying I was going to "shoot a few hoops," and smoke a joint. Then I'd go to my room, close the door, put on some music and, well, I'd fall asleep and before you know it, morning had arrived.

It wasn't long before my parents began to be on me all the time about my grades or yelling at me about getting in too late. It was always something. I'm sure they suspected something because before I left the house every morning, they'd inspect everything from my backpack to my purse! They even accused me of smoking pot outright, but of course I told them they were paranoid and crazy. I saw my parents as way too nosy and way too strict. When they asked what was wrong with me, I told them I hated the school I attended. When my mom asked me why, I told her, "I don't fit in there—all the kids are preppy, and they're just all so happy. They make me sick."

That summer I met a cool guy, Jason. I fit in with him and his friends. They all went to another school, but he had a car, so that was cool. He'd come and pick me up, and we'd drive around or hang out with his friends. Jason smoked pot, too. He also used "crystal"—and as I found out, a lot of his friends did, too. Probably because he'd become my boyfriend, I started using crystal with him. I'll never forget his words on the day he gave me my first "line" of crystal methamphetamine: "You'll be able to stop whenever you want—you're just not going to want to stop." He was my boyfriend so I didn't even question his logic. It wasn't the first drug I'd ever taken, but it would affect my life like no other.

What Jason failed to tell me with his line were two very important facts: One was that the not wanting to stop could signal a much bigger problem than wanting to; and two, there can be a huge part of you that does want to stop, even though it's overtaken by the stronger part of you who doesn't! After using crystal for even a couple of weeks, I'm sure I had become addicted to it because I was using all the time, and really anxious and "crazed" when I didn't have any. I always wanted some—and my favorite amount was "more."

For the first four months of using, I managed to function—at least on some level: I still went to school, and I got a part-time job at a music shop. My parents even bought me a car. But after that, "functioning" took on a different tone: My life centered on using each day—and everything about the day was focused on getting and using. I lost the part-time job, and my grades hit rock bottom—not just because I wasn't doing homework, but because now I wasn't even going to school. It's hard to function in the "real world" when you have to make time for getting "high" first, because you sure won't get to school or work when you're "coming down," since you'll be too tired and irritable to function, let alone to think.

Still, I was certain drugs weren't my problem: Teachers and parents were my problem. I was sure that anyone would use if they had teachers and parents like mine, who were always on their back. Besides, I had plenty of friends who thought I was just fine—not that they didn't use, too. Still, none of them thought anything was wrong with me. I also liked to tell myself that I couldn't be that bad because my using was nothing compared to Jason's. But it must have been bad, because things kept getting worse, especially when I started to stay out all night and practically never go home. It started with just one night, then it was two, then a week or more—and soon I was actually a "runaway," hanging out with Jason and his friends, or wherever.

At one point, my parents found me and brought me home. When they tried to talk to me about it, I accused them of being at fault for making me go to that stupid school. Then, when they took the keys to my car, I realized that if I wanted them off my back, I'd better just tell them what they wanted to hear. So I promised them I wouldn't use drugs anymore. Of course, they were only too happy to believe me. Two days later, I took off again—stealing back the car and money for getting high. A couple of weeks later, having gotten what I believed was the cause of my "stress" out of my life (my parents and school), it was getting harder to understand exactly what my problem was. Even I had to admit there was something wrong. I went to the library and researched all sorts of mental illnesses. Carefully looking up and copying down different disorders and symptoms, I tried to diagnosis my problem. I wrote all my "findings" in a letter and sent it to my mother, as if trying to prove to someone my problem had nothing to do with my drug use—or else trying to justify my drug use. I still had Jason to help prove that drugs weren't my problem, because he was someone with a drug problem—not me.

I ended up staying in this shack behind Jason's house. Jason lived with his family, so I couldn't live with him, but we fixed up the shack like a room for me. But it was cold and cramped and not as clean or comfortable as my room at home. Now I became convinced that Jason's family was my problem. I was miserable, and I simply had to use crystal every day. Somewhere about this time, I also came to the conclusion that my problem was just bad luck—and that I had really bad luck. That being the case, I shouldn't have been surprised when I got really sick. What started out as a cold and a cough grew so bad I could hardly breathe, and I was almost delirious with a fever. Jason told his mother, and she called my mom. My mom came and got me. She said she was taking me to the hospital. I was so sick, I didn't argue. Well, she took me to the locked adolescent unit of a psychiatric hospital.

Once I felt a little better, I was so mad! I was in the unit with kids who were so depressed they said they had wanted to die. I certainly didn't belong with them! I didn't want to die; I just wanted to do what I wanted, to have a little fun. I wasn't sick like they were. When the doctor and counselor told me I needed help for my drug addiction—and then kept calling me an "addict"— I told them they were the ones who needed help, not me. Drugs were not my problem, and I was *not an addict*. Then the doctor quizzed me about a couple of "big" issues going on in the world, and I have to confess, I didn't even know who'd won the presidential election. That's when I decided that what I needed was to start reading the newspaper so I could know what was going on in the world. My problem was that I'd just lost touch with current events. But once I knew what was going on in the world, I could get a job and go back to school and rent my own place. I'd be fine. Just fine.

Fortunately, no one was going along with my plan this time.

During a "family session" at the hospital, my parents told me that Jason's mother wasn't going to let me stay in the shack any-more and that Jason was going into treatment for his addiction. Just hearing them use the word "addiction" so matter-of-factly gave me a sick feeling in my stomach. Still, I held to the fact that I had never had that big of a "problem" with drugs—although I believed that Jason did. But I couldn't escape this terrible feel-ing of despair: I was a high-school dropout who didn't have a job or anywhere to go. And now I didn't have Jason to turn to, nor to fight with—which is one of the reasons I gave myself for needing to use. Jason had gone into a treatment center some-where, and I didn't know where. And I was in some psychiatric hospital recovering from pneumonia and being told I was an addict. It all looked like a crisis to me. I was really panicked.

There were these twelve-step meetings at the hospital every week. Young people who weren't in the hospital came to them to share how they had stopped using drugs. I hated those meetings. I went because they made me go—but that was the only reason I went. One day, one of the guys at the meeting shared how in the beginning all he had to do was "be willing to be willing." Somehow this stuck with me: "willing to be willing." With my life such a mess and looking so hopeless, I still wasn't "willing" to admit my problem was with drugs, I wasn't really "willing" to quit using drugs—but I was "willing to be willing." After all, it would make it so much easier if I could be willing; if I was willing then there were all these things I could learn to do in order to stay clean. So I decided I would start with being "will-ing to be willing."

After that things slowly started to change. I continued to work with the doctor and my counselor, and I kept going to those meetings. Eventually, I started to really listen to what people were saying. Finally, I heard another girl my age share about "denial" and how she used to "rationalize" and "justify" the most gnarly behavior with some of the craziest lines of reason, just so she didn't have to admit she had a problem and needed help. Even while I was laughing at some of the stories she came up with, I suddenly knew that I was exactly like her. I had been in denial, too. It wasn't until later that I fully realized how outrageous and dangerous some of my own denial had been. Once my parents had asked one of the counselors for some advice on when they should believe that what I was saying was really the truth. "She's just like any other addict. When she's using, if her mouth is moving, she's lying!" he replied. I remember how mad I was at that man. Now, I can see he was right. But you know what? My mouth didn't have to be moving. I was being told lie after lie right in my own head—and believing all of them!

I now have nearly a year "clean and sober." I was released from the hospital after thirty days and went on with counseling and an outpatient treatment program where I went for six months. Now I'm back in school and doing okay. I have new friends, and I have some peace of mind. Life's just not as complicated as it used to be. I don't see Jason anymore; last I heard he was doing okay after completing a six-month residential treatment program in another state.

I still go to those twelve-step meetings I used to hate. Now, I really look forward to them. I'm doing everything that's suggested when it comes to working on my recovery. When I remember all the bizarre things my denial had me believing, I know I have to stay totally "on it" when it comes to my recovery. Today, I'm not just "willing to be willing." I am completely and totally willing to do what it takes to remain drug-free— which includes giving up denying, lying and rationalizing my actions—first of all to myself, and then to everyone else.

Kylie Mienke, 17

Denial:
"Don't Even 'No' I Am Lying"

We're glad that Kylie is getting the help she needs to continue to "bust" the deceit of her denial—which included lies about not only the extent of her use, but all the ways drugs had taken a toll on her life. As was true for Kylie, using once can lead to using twice—to using more and more. Using more leads to a greater tolerance for the drug, and so you use more and "need" more to achieve the same high. Once dependency sets in, you begin to live your life around getting and using the drug (or alcohol). You'll say—and do—most anything to find and use drugs, including becoming "a professional liar"—spinning a web of lies and deceit about your using. Once you've developed an emotional or physical dependency on a chemical, your addiction is now in command—and it commands that you do and say anything that will lead to satisfying its craving for the chemicals you're in the habit of using.

The difference between denial and lying is this: *Lying* means you know you're not telling the truth. *Denial* means you don't even know you're lying: You actually believe the lies. Does all this deception and denial make the user a "bad" person? No. If you were to ask almost anyone, "Would you like to use to the point where neither you or others can count on what you tell them?," undoubtedly anyone's answer would be, "Of course not!" But in fact (as experts in the field of chemical dependency confirm), denial is a symptom of the disease and a predictable stage of chemical dependency. When you use denial as your defense mechanism long enough, it becomes second nature. All those lies of denial serve a purpose: When you lie about your ability to control your use—to take it or leave it—you don't have to face the truth about your addiction, which is that *the chemical is now in control of your life!*

Below are three ways "denial" filters in the lies for the user—
so that you will continue to delude yourself about your using.
Let's look at each of these self-deceptions:

1. **Justifying: Do you make excuses—justify—your using?**
   Do you justify your behavior as okay? Do you make something right that's really wrong? For example, do you (or a
   friend) "use" because "the day was stressful and I need to
   mellow out," or take speed because you need to "rev into
   high gear to study, party or play sports"? Kylie justified her
   using by saying that "everyone used" and that anyone
   would use if they had parents like hers.

2. **Rationalizing: Do you make "inexcusable" behavior logical
   —at least in your mind?** Do you come up with good reasons
   for using, for getting alcohol or drugs, even when it's wrong,
   even illegal? Do you ever find a "good reason" for doing
   things that aren't right? For example: Do you steal things in
   order to afford your using, telling yourself it's logical since,
   after all, your body was facing the agony of withdrawal?
   Kylie reasoned that the drugs weren't the reason for her
   problems and behaviors—they were the fault of other
   people, maybe even a "mental disorder."

3. **Minimizing: Do you downplay the effects of your using?**
   Do you tell yourself that what you're doing isn't really so
   bad? Minimizing means claiming that what you've done is
   not all that bad, or at least "less wrong" than it actually is.
   For example: Do you say you "only" smoked pot at the
   party—at least you didn't take Ecstasy? Kylie minimized
   her drug addiction by saying her boyfriend used way more
   than she did—implying that since she didn't use that much,
   she didn't have a problem.

Was the Lead Singer Really Singing Right to You? How (and Why) We Lie to Ourselves

It's easy to see that Kylie was lying to herself and everyone else. What about you? Even if you've never used, have you ever convinced yourself that something was all right when deep inside you knew that it really wasn't? It can be something that seems harmless. For example, is it possible that the lead singer at the rock concert wasn't really singing right to you? It's important not to lie to yourself; even seemingly "small" lies begin to erode our sense of trust in ourselves. And, of course, if you're not honest with yourself, you can't be honest with other people. Being honest with yourself is a quality—and value—that enriches your relationships with others, allows you to learn and grow from your mistakes, and builds your self-esteem. It's great to "own" this kind of honesty. You know all this, of course, yet when you use, you'll not care about truth. It's a huge loss.

If you use but your life still looks and seems normal, you may be tempted to conclude that you don't have a problem. Depending on how much and how often you are using, it's easy to think everything's okay. Early on in addiction, the user can sometimes keep things together—though she really has to work at it. With continued use, it will be fairly impossible to hide the effects of alcohol and drugs—most especially when *dependency* sets in.

Kylie had a classic case of denial. Let's look at the way denial and its deception played out in Kylie's addiction:

1. **"I can stop anytime I want. . . ."** In the beginning, Kylie was still able to convince herself that she was in control of her life—and her drug use. The changes weren't yet radical: Being late to practice didn't mean the world was coming to an end. She passed her classes, and was still a member of

her soccer team, so it was easy for her denial to set in, or as she said in the early days of her using, "Using isn't a problem for me." There were no physical problems, and Kylie hadn't changed the activities of her everyday life—yet. Other than a few friends who knew Kylie was using, no one else even suspected that she was. But once you've used to the point of addiction setting in, you can't quit "any time you want." You'll need treatment to stop the powerful cycle of addiction.

2. **"I don't have 'a problem.'"** With her continued use, more and more changes and problems started to show up—even Kylie spotted them. Now she had to make a decision: If she admits to herself that the changes—bad grades, teachers and parents "on her back"—are caused by her drug use, she either has to stop using or admit that using is bringing down her life around her. But since she's chemically dependent, the choice is no longer hers and hers alone. When her body screamed, "I need" (the chemicals), she knew stopping was out of the question. So, Kylie blamed her problems on other people and other things. To admit to being addicted, or to acknowledge the destruction using caused, meant she would have to stop using. So Kylie said anything to get what she needed: the freedom to use more drugs—including promising her parents she wouldn't use drugs anymore.

3. **"I'm fine—even my friends think so."** Kylie's denial, like that of most addicts, is shared by others around her. When Kylie's using friends (and boyfriend) tell Kylie she is fine, Kylie's denial is deepened. These are just the kind of friends she and her disease were looking for—friends who will continue to allow her to use. Using friends weren't about to let Kylie think doing drugs was a problem. After

all, if doing drugs could be a problem, they'd have to consider how it caused havoc in their own lives as well. And that she continued to hang out with them was proof that they, too, were "okay."

4. **"I promise not to drink or use anymore."** People often don't understand how easy it is to go from "using" to "dependent." When her parents first knew that Kylie used drugs (no doubt wanting to believe that she wasn't at the point of being chemically dependent), they thought they could persuade her not to use, and that it was as easy as that. So Kylie promised her parents she wouldn't use drugs anymore, and her parents believed her. But Kylie was already chemically dependent, and turning away from drugs would not only be difficult for her to do, but without professional help, impossible. If they knew that Kylie's use had progressed to the point of being a "disease" or an illness, they would know that they couldn't accept her promises. If someone had cancer and promised not to have it anymore, but didn't go get the necessary treatment, you wouldn't believe them. What's more, you wouldn't think that having cancer was something they were doing on purpose and could therefore just stop having on their own.

5. **"My life is crazy—but not because of drugs."** Finally, because her using had gone on for some time, and because the body needs more and more of the chemical to get "high," her addiction had grown even more advanced. There was no way to deny she had a problem, but she still refused to see it was caused by her drug use. She thought a mental disorder caused the insanity in her life, not the drugs she was using. As her addiction advanced, it became impossible for her to reason clearly and make sound judgments, not only because of her "addictive thinking" but also

because using had impaired her ability to think rationally. She even thought it was a sane choice to live in a shack where she could use drugs, rather than to live at home where she had a nice room and was loved, fed and clothed, but couldn't use drugs the way she wanted.

Are You "Willing to Be Willing"? Getting Help and Support

We can see how Kylie denied she had a problem with drugs because if she didn't have a problem with drugs then she didn't need help—and Kylie didn't want help, or at least wasn't yet "willing to be willing." But it is also very clear that Kylie did have a problem, and Kylie did need help to stop "needing" the chemicals. Getting professional help to stop using the chemical is a necessary, and often a lifesaving, move.

Being aware of the lies you've told yourself, which lead you to be dishonest with others, is a first step in stopping those lies and living with the honesty and integrity that are so vital to a drug-free life. What can you do to stop the denial that would keep you from the honesty that is so important for staying clean and sober? Here are three suggestions:

- **Stop using drugs or alcohol.** If you're using drugs or alcohol, this is the first step in stopping the denial—and certainly the most critical one. Turn to your parents. If you feel you cannot, make an appointment with your school counselor to talk over what's going on with you. With or without your parents' help or support, if you are dependent on a chemical, and regardless of whatever you see as the "reasons" for your use—get help. Depending on what you're using and how long you've been using, you may need the medical attention of a "detox" facility, as well as a drug treatment program. (You'll find more information on treatment programs in chapter 12 of this book. This book will also give you guidance and direction on how to continue to live your life free of alcohol and drugs.)

- **Ask your family and friends to "call you on it" when you start to make excuses and lie.** Often others are able to see what we are not able to see in ourselves. If you are ready to take a look at these things, ask people you care about and trust to be respectful, to help you see where you are being less than honest with yourself. Ask them to point out when you rationalize, justify or minimize. A professional counselor can help you break through your habits and patterns of lies and deceptions. Such a professional is also able to help you understand how and why you use those deceptions, and how you can get back to communicating in an open, honest and straightforward manner.

- **Work on developing a level of honesty that helps you stay drug-free (whether you've never used, are now in recovery or have just relapsed).** One way to do this is to work with a professional counselor, as well as to journal on how, when and why you are being less than honest with yourself or others. Unit VI in this book is a guided journal that will help you work through your thoughts and feelings about being honest.

Questions to Think About

- ♥ Do you (or anyone you know) lie about using drugs or alcohol? Do you (or anyone you know) refuse to believe or admit you have a problem with using?

- ♥ When have you lied but convinced yourself it wasn't really a lie? Did you know "deep inside" that you were really lying?

- ♥ When was the last time you were not being honest with yourself? What was the situation and what were you telling yourself? What was the truth about the situation and how could you have handled it more honestly?

♥ When was the last time you told a lie to someone else? What was the lie? Did you know at the time that you were telling a lie? Why did you feel like you had to lie?

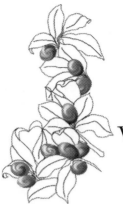

9

"Hitting Bottom": What Will It Take for You to Stop Using?

"Bottoms Up!"

I lay there quietly as I tried to clear my head. My eyes felt like they were glued shut, my head kept pounding, and I could feel the heaviness of my breathing as it swelled forcefully against my chest. I felt as if I was driving through a heavy, dense fog where I could not even find my hand in front of my face. My stomach felt like it had been wrenched completely out of me, and fear began to wash over my body as I tried to move my head. I couldn't move. It was as if I was frozen in time, yet I could faintly hear noise in the background. There was buzzing and beeping from some kind of machinery, and I heard voices of people yelling and crying and footsteps running all around. "Oh God, what is happening to me?" I wanted to shout—except that I couldn't utter a word out loud.

I tried to stop all the throbbing in my head as I leaned over to vomit into a bucket that had somehow appeared on my chest. It was then that I felt my mother's hand brush over my forehead as she whispered it was going to be okay. I just lay there and wept. It was then that I heard another voice in the room, and as I peeled my eyes open I could faintly make out a man in blue scrubs standing at the foot of my bed.

"Michelle, can you hear me?" he shouted.

I winced at his volume and managed to whisper a crackly, "Yes."

"Good, good, then we are making progress. I'm going to leave you on this IV for another few hours, and then I'll be back to see you again." It was then that I began to realize that I was in an emergency room in a hospital.

It had been as normal a Friday night as any other that brisk December night, and my two best friends and I were getting ready to go support our football team at a championship game. At fifteen, Friday nights had become a focal point for finding my independence and defining my character, or so I thought. I'm not exactly sure who initiated the conversation, but one of us thought it would be cool to empty our water bottles and put in some vodka. We thought we were so clever; since vodka is clear no one would ever know the difference, right?

We arrived at the game just as it started and found a spot on the bleachers toward the end. "Bottoms up!" my friend Leeza said, and we began drinking. After a while, we didn't feel cold anymore; the alcohol was "warming" us up. So we drank a little more, then more. My boyfriend and a couple of guy friends arrived, and once they saw our condition they wanted nothing to do with us. By this time our bodies were numb, including our throats, and we couldn't tell how much we'd "guzzled." We finished off what was in our bottles and tossed them.

It wasn't long before I started to feel very strange. Time passed, and I grew more and more intoxicated. I began to feel really sick, dizzy and nauseous, and just wanted it all to stop! But I'd gone too far, and the effects of the alcohol in my body were doing—well, what alcohol does to the body! So I just tried to sit still and keep my friends quiet, and we would wait it out. But things kept getting worse. I tried to focus my eyes on the game, but I could barely make out the field. Everything was blurry, so I closed one of my eyes and tried to focus, but nothing helped. Now things were getting scary; I couldn't feel anything in my body at all and I could barely see. What had I done to myself? I just wanted everything to stop, but it wouldn't.

The next thing I knew someone was shaking me and yelling, "Michelle, Michelle. What is your telephone number? Do you know your telephone number?"

"Umm, yeah I think so," I slurred. They dialed the number, walking away from me as I was left on the cold, hard, unwelcoming chair all alone. I felt as if I was not inside of my body; everything was completely numb. Somehow, they managed to find my sister in the crowd at the game, and I remember saying to her, "I just want this feeling to go away," as she wiped away my tears and gave me a hug. "Nicole, what's wrong with me? What's happening?" She just stood there looking at me in disbelief as tears rolled down her young, innocent face.

"Why, Michelle, why?" was all she could say, then she hesitantly walked away, now crying uncontrollably. What had I done? Everything went black again as I faded away, trying to forget. Someone yelled that my mother was on her way. I tried to grasp what was happening around me; everything just kept fading in and out. It was then that I noticed my friend, Leeza, a few feet away from me. "Let go of me. You're not calling my mom. I'm fine, let go of me." The lady next to me asked if I knew Leeza's number as I heard Leeza yell, "No, Michelle, you better not tell her."

The number just came out.

"I hate you, Michelle. I don't ever want to talk to you again," she screamed.

"I'm sorry, I'm sorry," is all I could whisper.

As they strapped me onto the gurney and slid me into the back of the ambulance, I saw my friend Leeza again. I could barely make out where she was because I couldn't keep my focus. "Leeza! Leeza, look at me. Keep looking at me. You can't go to sleep. Stay awake. Stay with us, stay with us, Leeza," I heard the paramedic scream to her. I moved my head slowly to the side, trying not to cause an eruption from my stomach again. I saw Leeza laying on a gurney next to me. I heard her crying, but I couldn't seem to get any words out of my mouth to tell her that I was there for her (like I could be in the condition I was in!). I looked over at her and saw her body shake. I blinked, trying to clear my vision and stop my head from spinning at the same time. "What was happening to her?" I tried to ask, but again no words came. "Hold that side of her. She is convulsing," the paramedic screamed, and then everything went dark.

As I slowly began to regain consciousness, I looked around. Nothing looked familiar. Everything was spinning uncontrollably, and my eyes began to feel like lead weights were tied to them. I didn't know where I was. Then I heard a familiar voice beside me telling me to relax and that we were going to get through this. I began to drift and my eyes slowly rolled back into their sockets. Suddenly, a man lightly grabbed my arm and told me that I had to stay awake, but I couldn't. I ached all over and began to feel what appeared to be an enormous needle attached to a tube going into my arm. I tried to follow the tube with my eyes. It led to a large pole with a bag of liquid hanging on it. Next to the IV stand were two empty bags, and before I could figure out what they were for, I was keeled over into my bucket. I tried to shake away the feeling and come back to reality, but it just wasn't happening.

I don't remember what happened after that. I was suddenly being prodded awake again, as I heard them say, "You can't go to sleep. Wake up, Michelle. You have to stay with me, okay?" I couldn't seem to control my body as I tried to open my eyes. Everything began to spin again, and it was not long before I was bent over the side vomiting again. It was then that I noticed my mother standing next to me, leaning over to wipe my mouth. My lips were raw, and it felt like she was rubbing sandpaper across them. Finally I managed to say, "Mom, I just want to go home. Please make this all stop and take me home."

"In a little while, honey, just lay back," she said.

Suddenly, nurses were all around me, literally tearing off my clothes and poking needles into my arm, yelling at me to stay awake, pulling back my eyelids, constantly telling me that I had to stay awake.

My mother never left my side that night. And she had no harsh words, no admonitions. I will always love her for that unconditional love at that defining moment. I can't say the day after or the weeks that followed were as forgiving—but hey, if my child had done this, I don't even know how I'd respond!

A few days after the incident, I was given a hearing before the disciplinary board at my high school. There was zero tolerance for this type of behavior in my school, and I was instantly asked to either remove myself from school or I would be subjected to expulsion. I sat there before my teachers, my principal and the parents of students I had known and felt that I had let everyone down, mostly myself. It was then that my mother removed me from a school that I had attended for most of my life, with friends who had been my entire existence. I had no idea what was going to happen to me, but I knew that whatever punishment was given it would never be enough to take away all the pain and guilt that I was feeling at that moment. I knew all the kids at school were talking about me, and the parents and teachers would look at me in disgust when I walked by. I was now labeled, but it didn't matter because regardless of what anyone was saying, I was thinking and feeling even worse things about myself. I wasn't certain about anything in life anymore except that my mother still believed in me even at my worst moment. She helped me enroll in another school, and as I was happy to be alive, there was no complaining from me.

I don't need to tell you that my experience—my ordeal—with drinking was a lesson I learned the hard way.

I attended the new school with a new attitude and outlook on life. It wasn't easy to walk into an environment halfway through my junior year when people knew what had happened. Yet, I wasn't about to let that affect another day of my life. I had stood before my friends, peers and teachers and apologized. Now it was my turn to forgive myself. I began a new chapter in my life in a new environment with new friends and peers, and it worked out. I did well in school the remainder of that year, but more importantly I began to really like who I was, and believed enough in myself not to let others sway me into making bad decisions. I realized through this pain that in the darkest of times, there are people out there who want to help you. It is through persever-ance and faith that you find your way back from difficult deci-sions in life; how you choose to deal with those decisions defines your character. I am a much stronger person now, and I am con-fident that my future holds great things for me.

I returned to my old high school for my senior year and was received with open arms by everyone there.

I wish that everyone's encounter with alcohol could end as quickly as mine did. After that awful night, I absolutely knew that the consequences of drinking hurt a lot more than any fun it could give me, and I wasn't about to risk the pain of those consequences again. But that just isn't the case for many people; they have to go through a lot more before they get it. Still, I altered my life drastically by making a mistake that could have taken my life. Sitting on the cold, concrete bleachers that night, I would never have imagined this would have happened. But it did, and I am just thankful that I "hit bottom" so quickly—and my bottom was hit for sure in that experience. I'll never drink again. The other good news is that I am alive to warn other teens who are naïve to drugs and their lethal effects just as I once was. It was a lesson I learned the hard way—but at least I learned it. Still, I wouldn't want anyone to go through what I went through on that brisk December night!

Michelle Langowski, 18

When "Enough!" Is Absolutely, Completely and Totally Enough!

There comes a time when it simply hurts more to keep on using or drinking than it hurts to stop. This, as Michelle in the previous story mentions, is called "hitting bottom." Michelle's near-fatal alcohol overdose was a very dangerous experience. Even though it was her first experience using alcohol, Michelle definitely "hit bottom." Unfortunately, many chemically dependent people have to suffer terrible consequences for a very long time before they hit bottom.

Even when the user finally realize it hurts more to keep on using than to stop, it still doesn't mean there's no pain in quitting or in staying drug-free—especially in early recovery. Not only is there the very real experience of physical (and emotional) withdrawal, but the user must confront painful emotions he or she may have been escaping. What's more, it's never pleasant for any of us to look at all the mistakes we've made and feel the guilt and shame that can come from it. With no drugs or alcohol to mask those feelings, the days, weeks and months following "abstinence" (not using) can be a rough time.

Michelle's "hitting bottom" was a physical crisis. But sometimes the user finally reaches an emotional crisis: The pain of not feeling good much of the time, the disappointment of losing friends and always being on the outs with your family, the pain of losing self-respect, of getting poor grades, of waking up knowing you have to find a way to get your next high, of living with the threat of being "busted" and ending up in jail—all these are finally seen as more painful than the pain of not using.

Hitting bottom can be different for each of us. In Michelle's case, drinking once was enough. For one thing, she almost died from it. And there were other consequences: having to change schools and leave all her friends, being treated differently by others, and suffering a loss of self-esteem with her own guilt and shame. These were enough for Michelle to never want to use again. When you decide you've had enough, you get to draw that line and claim, "This is it; this is my bottom." This is the beginning of "recovery."

So recovery begins with a shift in the way you look at things: What was once seen as more painful is finally seen as less painful than its alternative. It is at this point that you'll be willing to commit to abstinence. This is why you hear people talk about addicts and alcoholics needing to "hit bottom"—it's a big opportunity for change. When you hit bottom, it's finally obvious—to you (because those who don't use have probably wondered why you have put up with the pain and chaos in your life for as long as you have)— that the pain of using is greater than the pain of quitting.

If you are using, what will it take (or did it take) for you to hit bottom? Will your "bottoms" include:

- Ending up in an emergency room because of an overdose or an accident?
- Having your parents take your car away from you?
- Totally embarrassing yourself in front of your friends because of doing something stupid while under the influence?
- Losing friendships, or a boyfriend or girlfriend, because of using?
- Being arrested and ending up in juvenile hall or in another locked correctional facility?
- Being suspended or expelled from school?
- Feeling sick and unhealthy—and looking it?
- Committing crimes to get high, and realizing you have to keep on doing them over and over again to stay high?
- Doing something totally against your morals to get high that makes you loathe yourself?
- Losing a friend who drinks or uses to a related accident or overdose?
- Being asked by your family to leave the home?

Of course, there are other possible consequences. For some, the consequences it takes to hit bottom are horrendous; for others they can be less drastic. For some, they can include daily consequences for years on end; for others, like Michelle, they can occur as the result of a single event.

You don't have to suffer one of those horrendous "bottoms." You can decide at any time that you are done using and choose to get the help you need to stop.

Four Ways to "Hit Bottom"

Those in recovery talk about hitting four different kinds of bottoms:

Emotional Bottoms: When a person hits an emotional bottom, his consequences are shown in the way he feels emotionally. An emotional bottom means the person feels miserable because of his drug or alcohol use, and he is depressed, angry, hopeless or frustrated. The pain of those feelings is greater than any escape from them that using can offer.

Physical Bottoms: When a person hits a physical bottom, his consequences are paid for in his health and physical circumstances. A person may hit a physical bottom when he continues to get sick over and over again because using has weakened his immune system. His physical bottom may be seeing himself in the mirror and realizing he is ten to twenty pounds underweight, gaunt and pale. His physical bottom may be waking up with tremors and terrible hangovers, or even soreness in his liver. His physical bottom may be waking up in the emergency room because of an overdose or an accident caused by his drug or alcohol use. Another person's physical bottom may be what is called "being sick and tired of being sick and tired."

Then again, his physical bottom may have more to do with the physical circumstances his using has caused. He may hit a physical bottom when he is told that he cannot come home any longer because of the things he has done while using, such as stealing from his family or being violent in the home. He may hit a physical bottom when he finds himself sleeping in bushes and panhandling to eat. He may hit a physical bottom when he ends up incarcerated and loses his physical freedom.

Financial Bottoms: When a person hits a financial bottom, her consequences are paid for in the loss of money, physical comforts and material things. A teen may hit a financial bottom when she has no money for meals outside the home or gas for her car (because she's spent her lunch and gas money on alcohol or drugs), or for any other "extras" because of using drugs or alcohol. Because you're still at home, your financial bottom probably won't include going without shelter or any food at all—unless you're told that if you don't stop using, you can't live at home. A financial bottom can mean losing your source of income as a result of your drug or alcohol use—such as losing your job, losing your allowance or losing your parents' financial support.

Social Bottoms: When a person hits a social bottom, the consequences of her drug or alcohol use can include loss of friendships, family and other important relationships. Those consequences can also include loss of social status—such as being cut from a sports team or being sent to court-ordered program because of using or related behavior. A social bottom can be anything from having one friend decide not to hang around with you, to being on bad terms with your parents, losing all your friends, living in nearly total isolation, or being kicked out of school and ending up in juvenile hall, even jail.

So a chemically dependent person's bottoms can include any

of the above consequences or any of a combination of them. Many times they are related to one another. For example, when your friends don't want to hang around with you, you feel the pain both emotionally and socially. There could be severe consequences or less painful ones—the defining point is that they motivate the person to stop using.

Why You Shouldn't (Necessarily) Interfere with Someone's "Hitting Bottom"

So for some people the consequences it takes to hit bottom are far more extreme than for others. There is a great deal of difference between "getting it" when your grades slide from Cs to Fs versus "getting it" with a jail sentence. Even so, the experts say you shouldn't necessarily interfere with someone's hitting bottom.

Of course, if someone is about to kill himself, we should do what we can to make sure that doesn't happen—calling in whatever law enforcement or medical professionals it takes to save the person's life. Being aware of this, it's also important to recognize that "hitting bottom" helps the addicted person see the truth of his chemical dependency, so you should not soften the consequences that result from his drug or alcohol abuse. Why? Because doing this can keep him from hitting bottom—which means it stops him from having that painful experience that he needs to realize how destructive his chemical dependency has become.

In chapter 7, you learned about assisting someone who is chemically dependent to seek help or treatment for his or her addiction. Sometimes that isn't convincing enough to help the addict understand that help is available for him and to get him to want to stop using (because those who love him would like him to get the help he needs). So when that fails, about the only thing you can do is wait for the chemically dependent person to "hit bottom"—his own bottom—consequences that for him are evidence enough to make him willing to get the help he needs to overcome his addiction.

So when you (or others) cover up for him, make excuses for him or his behavior, "bail him out" of trouble or lend him money, you are taking away an opportunity to see that change is needed. Sure, he may still be suffering other consequences, but as you soften the force of the blows that his actions have caused, you ease the user's pain. While his pain is difficult for you to watch, and no doubt for him to suffer, it may be that exact amount of pain that is needed to motivate the change that will result in getting help to break free of his addiction.

Of course, your intentions can be completely pure—you don't want to see someone you care about suffer. But ultimately you are only prolonging the suffering—and as you do this, the "disease" progresses, the tolerance increases, the obsession gets stronger and the physical toll grows worse. This means that it could end up taking even harsher consequences than those you are trying to ease in order for your friend or family member to see the truth about his chemical dependency. If you recall Chloe from chapter 5, you'll remember how her classmates covered for her, and how ultimately this didn't help her at all. While she didn't "get caught" in the classroom, her alcoholism progressed to the point where she felt taking her life was preferable to living. If her classmates hadn't stepped in to cover for her, it is possible she may have gotten "in trouble" that proved to be the "bottom" that helped her recognize how badly she needed to get help.

In chapter 7, you learned about "interventions" to help your friend or family member get the treatment she needs. You should also know that just because she doesn't yet see or admit she has hit bottom, it doesn't mean she cannot be helped. Treatment and the period of clean time that it can provide for the mind to clear may lead to a person's seeing the need for change, even though she doesn't initially see that need. Still, in the end, the decision to stop using drugs and alcohol and to continue to get the help needed to stay drug-free always lies with the chemically dependent person. Being able to admit there is a problem—and the problem is using drugs or alcohol—marks the first step toward change.

Once you or someone you care about has hit bottom, you'll need to find help for staying drug-free. A substance-abuse counselor should be able to direct you to the best treatment option and support group to meet your needs. The yellow pages in your phone book should have listings under "Drug and Alcohol Abuse" or "Drug and Alcohol Treatment" that you can call to find a counselor to help you. You can also find out when and where AA and NA meetings are held in your area by calling the local branches listed in your phone book. Additionally, chapter 12 will tell you much more about the different kinds of help that are available.

Questions to Think About

♥ Have you (or a friend) ever hit bottom? If so, what consequences made you reach bottom? If not, what consequences would make you "hit bottom"?

♥ What consequences would you consider "bottom" but still didn't stop you (or a friend) from continuing to drink or use? Why do you think that was so?

♥ Has someone ever "interfered" or stopped you from hitting bottom? If so, who was that person? Did he know he was being "codependent"?

♥ How have you interfered with someone else's hitting bottom? What consequences have you "softened" for them? Is that person still using? What would you do differently now?

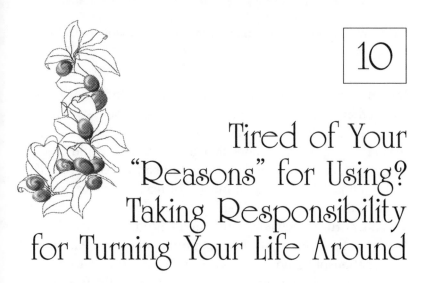

10

Tired of Your "Reasons" for Using? Taking Responsibility for Turning Your Life Around

Flipped Off—For the Last Time

Flipping through the chapters of the past, I've concluded that what I'm about to share is definitely the worst page of my life. I say this because drugs had an extremely tight grip on me: I sometimes used three to four times a day. Any form of mind-altering possibility, I used. I don't say this flippantly. Being on this side of having been through what I would now call a "harrowing" experience, I know there's a lot of utter stupidity in having ever used in the first place.

Still, the insanity of using doesn't mean you can just quit—at least that was the way for me. "Just say no"—yeah, right! That approach may work before you start, but it has no basis in reality once you've been down the road of using. It's just not that easy, and I should know. I was absolutely positive I could walk away—"take 'em or leave 'em."

I started out using cigarettes, and not just because I wanted to inhale some cancer-causing agents, but because, well, I wanted to look cool. Funny how you think that. Somehow, in my little mind, lighting a cigarette would show I was no kid. I was a man! A man cool enough to smoke! And oh, did I mention that if I was cool enough to smoke cigarettes, you should see how cool I thought I was lighting up a joint with my friends. I'm sorry to report that I didn't stop at using marijuana, either.

I'm sure I thought I was cool long after others thought I wasn't. I'm quite sure now that everyone else could see that drugs were beginning to have a pretty bad effect on me. They could tell just by looking at me. (I got really thin, was nervous most of the time, and my skin got pasty-looking.) Even worse was how drugs screwed up my mind—I couldn't think for crap! But what I noticed most—but not until I got clean—was how all my relationships, how can we say, "Went to hell in a hand-basket." The obvious ones were with my straight friends, and then my girlfriend, and my parents and teachers. Of course, I always thought the other person was to blame. I think it's fair to say that with using, you don't really have a relationship with anyone other than drugs. I'm a really bright guy (well, I'm sure that you're questioning that since I've admitted I've used a lot of drugs), and I got great grades until drugs took over.

It was like I'd made a "deal with the devil": The unstoppable cravings were so firmly planted in my body and in my brain, I couldn't escape even when I wanted to. Using pervaded my every thought, even when I tried to will them away. Then of course, I felt like a loser for not being able to do what I wanted— quit. My whole life completely revolved around defeat. It was "past time to quit."

The first time I tried to quit, I went for the legendary "cold turkey"—quitting without any kind of treatment for the with-drawals. I figured that I'd just "tough it out"—simple enough, right? Ha! No! The first day passed—it wasn't easy—but I made it through without much problem. The second day, still no defeats. Immediately following the third day, the indescribable craving overcame the little faith I had in willpower. Quickly, I veered uncontrollably back to my repetitive and destructive old habits, but this time I was using in even larger quantities. The consequences grew worse and worse, and my drug use went totally out of control. Constantly wallowing in my failure, I drifted into deeper and deeper feelings of worthlessness. Despair is a dark and ugly feeling. I'd finally descended to the bottom of the pit.

I tried to commit suicide two years into my use. Trying to kill myself stripped away what little dignity I had left. Though I was ecstatic that I woke up the next morning, I couldn't welcome the joy and relief that finding myself still alive had brought.

Desperate, scared and more sober than I ever trusted myself to be, I sat down and wrote out what I thought was going on with me, and how I might quit—yet again. I sat there for nearly three hours. I made the most life-changing conclusion that I'd ever made. I didn't have any reasons to use. All the reasons, including to be cool, were just nuts. As I tried to point to who was to blame for my having used in the first place, and then who or what was to blame for why I continued to use, I came to a startling realization. There was no one to blame—except me! Trying to point my finger at someone to blame only produced the stark image of four fingers all pointing back at me.

I remember actually laughing, because those fingers I pointed were flipping me off. No one else was to blame: My teachers weren't holding grudges against me. My parents weren't destroying the most productive years of my life. There was no undiscovered force making my decisions. I'd run out of fingers to point, because the only one still remaining was pointed directly at me. I was devastated. All this time, the people who were deliberately destroying my happiness never existed.

As a senior in high school, I'm happy to say that I got help for my drug use and as a result, I've survived the destructive disease that has taken over many brilliant minds and killed many people. I have to work at staying drug-free—every day—but I feel victorious over drugs. Day by day, I'm getting more confident that I'll stay drug-free. I'm getting more comfortable with the idea that while remaining drug-free is a lot of work for someone who used as much as I did, I can do it: I've come face to face with bigger problems and have succeeded. When I'd really rather run than stay and confront something, I remember that it was by taking responsibility that I got through getting clean. If I'm ever trying to avoid something that will mean working on me, I remember how owning my part, finally stepping up and admitting it was me who had to change, resulted in the most incredible change—from the misery of addiction to a full and happy drug-free life.

So, while I won't forget those past chapters, I don't dwell on them so much anymore. Since taking responsibility for my life, I spend more time focusing on the present and the future, rather than the past. It's been a long haul, but finally, I'm beginning to look to planning for a future again—a future I intend to live without being chemically dependent.

Christopher Brackett, 17

Taking Stock:
Is the Finger Pointing at You?

There was a time when Christopher, like most "users," placed blame on others for all his circumstances. His "reasons" for using were all someone else's fault. Luckily, in the process of "taking stock," Christopher finally saw himself as the problem—and the solution: He needed to take responsibility for giving up drugs so that he could get on with his life. He began attending NA meetings and working a twelve-step program (discussed in chapter 13) so he could change what he called "thinking like an addict." His "change" didn't happen overnight. As Christopher explains, "I was trying to get the recovery thing straight—going to twelve-step meetings and to counseling—but I didn't change anything else. I still hung around with my same friends, still skipped school when they did, still lied about where I was going—and I still couldn't figure out why I seemed to get in so much trouble and had such a hard time staying clean. I was talking to this guy in the waiting room at my counselor's office. I'd seen him at a few twelve-step meetings, and he seemed pretty cool. I was telling him about some of the trouble I was in—again. And he said, real matter-of-fact, not preachy, 'You know what they say, "If you always do what you've always done, then you'll always get what you've always got."' That's all he said—but I got it. At that point, I realized I was doing the same things and expecting different results. But when I decided to change my actions, I finally turned my life around."

Nine Things You Can Do to Turn Your Life Around

Admitting that *you* are the person who is ultimately responsible for making your life better is an important first step in turning your life around. In short, taking control of your life and recovery rests with you. This doesn't mean that others can't and won't help you break the self-destructive cycle of using. But it does mean that the only person who can make the change is *you*. No one but you can make the decision to diligently work for your ongoing recovery.

When you give up blaming others and acknowledge that the fingers all point back at you, here are some ways to take action and responsibility. (The first three are standards. You've read them in previous chapters, but they merit starting again.)

1. **Stop using drugs or alcohol, totally, no matter what.** It's a well-known fact that by using, you have altered your brain's chemistry so that it now not only desires the drug but demands it. It's not easy to get the brain to let go and "un-learn" this craving. Freeing yourself of the desire to use is a long process and one that you have to commit to.

2. **Ask for help and get into a treatment program.** Get into treatment—you need to break the cycle of addiction. (Chapter 12 will give you an overview of types of programs available.)

3. **Join a support group.** Look in the yellow pages for the hotline numbers of the various organizations that are there to help you—such as Alcoholics Anonymous or Narcotics Anonymous—and find out when and where there are meetings near you. Start going to meetings—going every day for the first ninety days is strongly suggested. If you're still in school, check to see if your school provides "Peer Counseling," a program where teens in schools are trained to support teens going through tough times. You are also well advised to find a twelve-step sponsor and start to work on the twelve steps as your sponsor directs (again more on how to do this in chapter 12).

4. **Learn all you can about the disease of addiction.** As you learned in chapter 5, addiction has specific symptoms that can be identified in order to be diagnosed and treated. Your chemical addiction can only get worse until you get help to stop its destruction on your mind and body, and stop it from wreaking havoc on your life. If you have access to a computer, go online and read about its symptoms and stages. Buy, borrow or go to the library and check out the *Basic Text of Narcotics Anonymous* and/or *The Big Book of Alcoholics Anonymous* and start to read them. Understanding is power—it helps you know what you're up against and helps you prepare your defense and run interference on potential problems and setbacks.

5. **Admit that your chemical dependency is "stronger" than your ability to fight it, and that you are "powerless" over it.**

Experts in the field of chemical dependency confirm that a person who has become chemically dependent cannot stay drug- and alcohol-free through willpower alone. However, this does not mean that a chemically dependent person is not responsible for his own life and recovery, nor that he is powerless to make healthy decisions for his life. Commit to undertaking a rigorous program—recovery for life is your desired goal (more on this in chapters 12 and 13).

6. **Practice self-discipline.** Taking responsibility doesn't end with the decision to stay drug-free. It is an ongoing practice in life and in recovery. Just as addiction represents a vicious, negative cycle, self-discipline can represent an inspiring, positive cycle, leading to new and more positive coping skills. This, in turn, contributes to self-esteem and a positive self-image, all-important to living a healthy drug-free life.

7. **Keep a journal.** Journaling is a powerful tool to help you clarify your feelings, as well as see your progress and setbacks in breaking free of your chemical dependency. Journaling about what you think and feel can help give you a clearer perspective of your problems and their solutions. (Unit VI in this book is designed for this purpose.)

8. **Make a new plan—today—for "tomorrow."** While you're using your journal, write about what you want out of life, set new goals and begin a course of action. Get back to doing those things that help you discover your talents, aptitudes and hobbies. Ask your parents, teachers or counselors for help and support with things such as tutoring if you have fallen behind in certain skills or classes, or if you dropped out of school as a consequence of your using. Do all you can to get back on track.

9. **Be hopeful and optimistic.** Cut yourself some slack when you're feeling down and vow to stay in your program of sobriety no matter what. Using the "Emergency Support List" found in chapter 18—and also at the back of this book—keep a list of phone contacts handy of those people who will support and encourage you in getting and staying chemical-free.

You are responsible for your behaviors—good or bad. You are in charge of the thoughts you choose to dwell on, the actions that you take, and the way you live your life. If, like Christopher Brackett, you take responsibility for the consequences of your actions, you are in a truly powerful position. Yes, it can be humbling to see where the destruction of using has led you, but when you take responsibility for those past mistakes, as well as for your present and future recovery, you are able to begin the "freeing" process of change. Admitting that you are the one who is responsible for it is the first step.

Questions to Think About

♥ How do you "take responsibility" for your own life?
♥ How do you think taking responsibility means practicing self-discipline?
♥ When did you decide it was time to stop blaming others and simply change your own life? How did you do that?
♥ When have you had to "'fess up" because you "messed up"? What were the circumstances? What was the outcome? How did you feel after "'fessing up"?
♥ What changes have you seen in your life because you took responsibility to "make change"?

Why "White-Knuckling It" Isn't Enough: Abstinence Versus Recovery

Dear Crystal . . .

Dear Crystal,

It's over. And I'm done with you. I'm ending my "love affair" with you—once and for all!

I'm done believing all your lies, especially those about how good you'd make me feel. As it turned out, nothing could have been a further stretch of the truth. For starters, being with you left me feeling guilty and ashamed of myself. But no more! Oh, the headaches and heartaches you caused me.

The truth is, you're a liar and a cheat. You not only lied about who you really are, but what you wanted from me, and what you were offering me in return. And I was so gullible. I know it's my fault for believing in you as I did, and for staying in the relationship for as long as I did—even when I realized you weren't good for me.

The thing is, I turned to you to help me feel better about myself—yet being with you made me feel anything but that. In fact, being with you made me feel just terrible about myself. I thought you'd help me accomplish anything I wanted, including "flying without a parachute." I thought you were the solution to my feeling more confident, "with it," cool, likeable and fun. Oh, you worked your magic for a while. But when all was said and done, I felt tired, exhausted, emotionally whipped, shamed, stupid—basically, like the lowest form of life in the world.

But it's over now. I'm out of your life and intend to find my way back to my own life. I know you doubt that I can live without you; I heard talk from my friends that you thought I'd be back by your side in no time. I know you think I'm dying to be with you, but the truth is, I'm lucky I didn't die *because* I was with you. And that is why I'm writing this letter to you: I want you to know that it's my choice to go on without you.

I now realize how cunning you were to have made me believe so many lies about you—and about myself. You know, I actually feel better without you! And, hey, it's going to be okay. You know, I've discovered that I can be myself and people still like me. I've found out that I haven't forgotten that life can be fun—even "extreme"—without you. I'm happy to report that I have not forgotten how to have fun and to feel happiness without you, and that it's really not so bad to be sad and lonely once in a while. Best of all, I've learned that I can do for myself what I thought you did for me: I can feel good about myself without you—the only difference is, I have only myself to credit.

My dear friend, Pot, I thought you could make me happy but honestly, I have to say good-bye to you also. The idea that your tar will linger in the fat cells of my body and brain totally grosses me out. I had no idea you, too, were as destructive as Crystal. You made me lazy and caused me to forget that I can survive stress and anxiety on my own. And when I need to "mellow out," well, music will work just fine, thank you! You made me lose my ambition and drive. Thanks to you, I became moody and lived in a fog. All this cost me countless lost and unproductive days, needless fights with my parents, as well as teachers who nearly gave up on me. Because of my friendship with you, I've lost some really dear friends and gained a strange assortment of weird, lost and sometimes "shady" losers. You have not added to my life in positive ways, and in fact, have kept me from the life I should have, could have, and now intend to reclaim for myself.

Crystal and Pot, it's like this: Essentially, you both prevented me from being the person I was before I met you. It's a sad fact, and I'm upset about it. And so I'm moving on.

I've apologized to me, and I am reclaiming myself!

Beginning today, I will always remember that I am a girl learning how to live life without drugs. I intend to deal with the shame and guilt I have because you were in my life. But I will. Do not think I'll be running to you and your false comfort when things get tough. I know such times are ahead, but they can never be as difficult and destructive as the times I spent with you. So count me out of your circle of obsessed and spaced-out friends. As of today, I intend to stay clean and sober.

Paige Olds, 19
(Adapted from Taste Berries for Teens #3)

Which Is Better, a "Drunken Horse Thief" or a "Sober Horse Thief"?

As Paige's heartfelt "letter" to her "former friends" illustrates, breaking free of drugs and getting on with your life means that you must say good-bye to all using. You must commit to never using again, a day at a time. It's admirable that Paige has bid her "former friends—Crystal and Pot" good-bye. It's absolutely a first step in getting and staying drug-free. But it's only a first step.

Doing completely without drugs (called "abstinence") means you're not using. And what a milestone that is! But when a chemically dependent person decides he is done using, he can't afford to think that stopping his use means he's broken the spell of his addiction. Experts in the field of chemical dependency confirm that more than just abstinence is needed if a person is to break his physical and psychological dependency on alcohol and drugs and continue to live drug-free. Toughing it out, saying "no" to using, but not "cleaning house" of all the habits and patterns that go along with using (often called "*white-knuckling* it") are rarely enough to *stay* clean and sober. Certainly you need abstinence, but you need it as the first step in working on your "recovery" (which means doing specific and prescribed things that are known to help you stay drug-free and not relapse).

Paige explains how she came to understand the difference between *abstinence* and *recovery*: "I wasn't one of those teens who could just take one hit off a joint. I had to have several. And I couldn't just smoke now and then, like at a party with a friend. I had to find a way to do it nearly every day. It was the same way with the other drugs I was using. So then I'd tell myself that I'd be okay if only I didn't use so much and so often. But that didn't work either. So I knew I needed to quit altogether—then I'd be fine; things would be back to normal. I tried quitting and managed not to use for a while.

"But even when I wasn't using, things didn't change. It's not like I was just excited to jump out of bed in the morning and get off to school where I merrily went to class on time. After school I didn't just head for the library to eagerly get my research papers done, nor did I get on my homework once I was home. Not only did my poor study habits plague me, but so did a bad attitude. I mean, it's fair to say that I was miserable! What's more, I still found myself lying about where I was and what I was doing (and for no reason at all), and just being angry and mean most of the time. So then I'd use again.

"Finally, I got desperate enough to try doing something different, and I started to go to counseling and twelve-step meetings. At one of those meetings I heard someone say, 'If you just take the booze away from a drunken horse thief, you'll just have a sober horse thief.' I finally 'got it': Unless I changed the way I thought—my reasons and excuses for using—nothing would really change when I quit using. I had to work on recovery—which means doing those things that keep you on a path of not using, as well as not *wanting* to use. My quitting alone didn't make my life return to 'normal.' Abstinence wasn't enough. I had to work at recovery—at doing those things that made it possible to continue to stay clean."

Seven Goals for Moving Forward in Your Recovery

In order to stay drug-free—and not have bouts of cravings and constantly wanting to use—you'll need to change some things. Here are some of the things you'll need to do in order to get and stay on the path of "recovery":

1. **"Re-learn" how to think clearly.** Using distorts the way you see life and your ability to handle things, and as a result, you'll need to "recover" a clear way of thinking and coping. You'll need to "re-learn" how to be yourself, or as Paige says, to "reclaim" the former you. (In some instances, it may even mean developing effective coping skills for the first time if, for example, you always had low self-worth.) A counselor can help you to learn effective skills to cope with your life in a realistic and healthy way.

2. **Change "old" behaviors.** When you used, no doubt you not only thought like someone who used, but you almost surely behaved like someone who used: You did whatever you had to in order to use. Maybe you stole things in order to support your use. Maybe you violated rules (even laws), such as your curfew, as well as other rules set in place to look out for and protect the family. If you've violated such rules, now you'll need to stop behaving in old ways and abide by the rules. If you were in the habit of lying or manipulating others

to get what you wanted, that has to stop—even when what you want now isn't drugs or alcohol. If you were irresponsible, now you must be responsible. These are the kinds of "old behaviors" that need to change in order to stay clean and sober.

3. **Rebuild your reputation.** Having violated rules, been less than honest and acted irresponsibly, chances are you've broken the trust with everyone from family to friends, from teachers to peers. It will take some time and doing on your part to get others to trust you and to see that you mean what you say and say only what you mean. But in time, as others observe that you're regaining integrity, they'll begin to trust you once again. Recovery means you can begin the work or repairing the wreckage of the past. Be patient as you begin the process of relationship-building. Lean on your parents for love and comfort, and honor the house rules once again. As you feel the satisfaction of being trusted once more, your self-esteem—the reputation you have with you—will improve, as well.

4. **Be vigilant in finding and staying close to a twelve-step sponsor** (explained in chapter 12). This is very important as you work toward resisting all temptations to use—whether it be "old" friends trying to rope you back into using; coping with your body's physical and psychological dependence; as well as coping with the often painful pangs of even later stages of withdrawal (PAWS—more on this in chapter 14). The time-honored experience of a twelve-step sponsor and a professional counselor trained to help those overcoming chemical dependency are the best ways to help you develop effective strategies to deal successfully with life, as well as support you as you go about learning to readjust your actions and reactions to the ups and downs of life.

5. **Let go of false illusions.** Chances are, in order to protect your using, you've become good at lying—even to yourself.

Maybe you've fooled yourself into thinking that you're a "better you" when you use, and that you *need* to use in order to cope with your life. Addiction is a cunning disease. As such, you'll need to free yourself of some of its common illusions, such as:

- I can't have fun unless I use.
- I can use just this once.
- I can use this alcohol (and not the other drugs).
- Using makes me "feel better."
- I'll only use to lose weight.
- Using makes me more creative.
- Using makes me forget my problems.
- Using gives me confidence.
- Using helps me fit in.

Again, a counselor can help you to break through these distortions and to cope with your life in a more realistic and healthy way.

6. **Don't ever forget how it hurts to use.** To feel free of pain is a normal human desire. Just because you're no longer using, that doesn't make you an exception. If reality seems painful, and the pain is eased by drug use, it's difficult to muster up the desire to stop using drugs. But if you've "hit bottom" you know that this is a lie, so you must remember that the pain that using drugs creates for you is far greater than the pain that using drugs could take away. Remember where using leads you by taking yourself beyond that first "high" or drink and to the pain of your last bottom.

7. **Learn how to take care of yourself.** When you were using, you were doing more than bringing chaos into your life. You were hurting yourself physically and emotionally. Recovery is about genuinely loving yourself and willingly taking responsibility to care for yourself—to the extent that

you'll not put yourself at risk to suffer the physical or emotional toll of using. Caring for yourself in recovery includes:

- Developing healthy and supportive friendships with those who support you in living drug-free.
- Learning healthy new ways to process feelings and emotions.
- Learning to care for your body. (Learning healthy ways to eat, exercise and relax are all part of recovery.)
- Learning to live according to your real values—as well as claiming and developing those values.
- Putting yourself in drug-free environments where you can have fun.

As you're learning, being drug-free is an ongoing process. But you can do it. Just as using took a lot of work—and yes, a lot of energy, determination and resourcefulness—recovery will take some work as well. "Honest self-examination" is easy enough to say, but it takes time and dedication to actually perform, as do changing old habits and putting in place new ones to support you in your recovery from chemical dependency. The rewards are real—and you're worth it!

Questions to Think About

- ♥ How many times have you tried to quit using drugs and alcohol? What happened with each past attempt? How long were you successful?
- ♥ What illusions have you "let go" of for the sake of your recovery?
- ♥ What does "honest self-examination" mean to you?
- ♥ What actions are you taking to create changes in the way you think and behave?

♥ What three areas do you need to work on changing most? (For example, do you need to work on being more assertive? Or do you need to work on not feeling sorry for yourself? Do you need to work on being honest? Or do you need to work on dealing with anger?) What are some healthy ways that you can think of to work on these changes?

12

Getting Help: Types of Programs to Help You Get and Stay Clean

"24-7"

I'm writing this from a residential drug-treatment program, where I've been "24-7" for the past seventy days. As I listen to the people around me, I can tell that everyone who ends up in one of these places has his or her own story. All those stories, just like mine, come down to the same thing: I had a serious problem with drugs, and I needed help. Luckily, my family saw that—because I was sure busy trying not to see it.

The end of my using "24-7" and ending up here "24-7" happened when I came home one afternoon, and my parents, my sister, my little brother, my grandmother, two friends and a man I didn't know were all sitting there, waiting for me. "Come in and sit down, Trey," my dad said. He sounded so serious that my heart dropped to my stomach. Of course, I was wondering, *Why is my dad home at this time of day and what's happening—has someone in our family died?* Well, it turns out everyone was there to convince me to stop using drugs!

I'd started out smoking cigs at the ripe old age of eleven, was using pot by age twelve, and even before I turned thirteen, I was smoking it all the time. By fourteen, I'd used a couple of other things—and well, my need for drugs became a monster I

155

couldn't control—but boy could it control me. So now, at fifteen, I was addicted in a pretty bad way. Even I'd admit that my behavior was so up and down that sometimes I'd have to look in the mirror to see "which way the wind (me) was blowing."

As it turned out, my mom had called all sorts of substance abuse treatment programs and learned about interventions and drug and alcohol treatment programs—and decided I was in for both.

I walked over to the couch, sat down and just looked at everyone, not knowing what to expect. So everyone was sitting there, looking pretty grim. The man was a substance-abuse counselor. He just said, "Trey, you're a lucky guy to have family and friends who love you and want what is best for you. They're gathered here today because they have some things they'd like to say. I think we'll start with your little brother." So then he turns to my little brother, who is just a little squirt of nine, and says, "Jamey, what would you like to say to your big brother?" Well, my little brother looks at me with his big brown eyes, squirms in his chair, fiddles with his fingers and then totally breaks down and cries. Through sobs he says, "I want you to stop! I don't want you to die, and I'm scared you're going to die and then I won't have a big brother." Well, I didn't know what to say, but I realized my using had really scared my poor little brother. I felt just awful for the little guy.

So then my thirteen-year-old sister, who was sitting next to Jamey, put her arm around him to comfort him and looking at me, her eyes really defiant, blurted out, "Please stop using drugs. It hurts me that you don't talk with me and Jamey like you used to, and you don't shoot basketball hoops or cook macaroni for us when Mom works late anymore. I feel like you're never here, and when you are, you don't want to do anything with us. I miss you, and I don't like it that you love drugs more than being my friend." Then she dropped her head and just glared at me.

I knew what she said was right: We'd been so close, and my

using had changed her feelings about me. So I sat there sort of stunned, because frankly, I never considered how much my using hurt them, and how they just wanted to trade in this big brother for the one they *used* to know. It was almost the exact words my mother had said, "I am so worried for you. Please come back to us, Trey . . ." My dad, who hardly ever says anything, said, "I'm worried, too. Please get help, son. You can lick this thing, and I want you to know I'll stand by you."

One by one, everyone had their say, while I listened to each person in the room tell me how they'd seen me change and how they cared about me and wanted me to get well.

I didn't know if I could be helped, but having heard my family say what they had, I knew I couldn't continue to hurt them. So then the counselor turned to me and said, "You're a lucky guy to have people love and care about you in the way they do. Obviously you deserve their love and support. They've said some really important things, like what a terrific son, brother and friend you are—when you're not using. Are you willing to get the help you need?"

"Yes" was all I could manage to get out.

Then the counselor said, "Good. There's a local treatment center with a place for you, and they are holding a four o'clock appointment open to see you."

I looked at my watch. It was 2:21!

So literally, I went to my room and packed—my mother and dad helping . . . probably to make sure I didn't leap out of my bedroom window. Believe me, I thought about it—except that I kept remembering my little brother's sobs and my sister's angry and hurt glare. I'd hurt them, and my parents, so much. It was time. It was time to stop my own madness.

To be honest, as I was packing, I felt better, freer than I'd felt in a long while. So, in the end, I went into treatment.

When I packed up my stuff to come here, I had no idea what I was getting into. All I had were questions: Was I going to be locked up? Could I talk on the phone? What would I be doing all day? Could I have visitors? How long were they going to make me stay? It turns out I was going to a ninety-day residential treatment program. I'm not locked in, but my days are all structured. We're up by seven, to breakfast by seven-thirty, to meetings at nine. Every day we have group counseling and educational groups to learn about addiction and recovery. Then anyone like me who is still in high school spends time with the tutor five times a week, keeping up (and most of the time catching up) on their classes. And there are assigned chores that are rotated every week and inspected every day. There are also groups on things like family dynamics, self-esteem, stuff like that. Twice a week, I meet with my counselor one-on-one. We have a twelve-step meeting at night. There's also time set aside for us to work on writing assignments and "step work." As you can probably tell, there's not a lot of free time, but there's some. For the most part, what we're going to do is all mapped out for us 24-7—and it's all about recovering from drug or alcohol addiction and learning how to deal with life, beginning with getting back to normal patterns of sleeping, eating and doing things all day. There are family visits once a week and family group once a week, too.

Some of the kids in the program were "repeating" it. They explained how they'd made the mistake of going into treatment thinking of it and "all they were leaving behind" as something they were unwilling or just didn't want to do. They say having that attitude will make it tough—and you'll spend a lot of time "playing games" and you won't "work your program" as seriously as you need to in order to stay clean. So this time around, they said they were here voluntarily, happy to be in a program that took them away from the temptation to use, and happy to have a chance to learn how to put their lives back together.

My parents came for family group. We had to do a communication exercise together. I have to tell you, my dad looked more uncomfortable than I felt. The chairs were arranged so that family members sat across from each other and had to look at each other when they spoke. We were each given a page of questions and were told to answer each one to each other. My dad went first, reading the question, "What I value most about you is . . ." Looking down he read it the second time, and then looking at me, he said, "Son, what I value most is that you are a kind, thoughtful and ambitious young man"—all the things I most definitely wasn't when I was using. I didn't know whether to cry or get angry; maybe he was making fun of me, maybe he was being sarcastic. I told him kind of defiantly, "I'm none of those things!" My dad looked at me, his expression somewhere between surprised and hurt, and said, "You're all of them when you're you." The counselor asked my dad to tell me more about what he meant, and my dad explained, "Who you are when you're not using drugs is all of these things—and I value and admire them. This is the real you, the you I know and hold to and believe in no matter what. This is the you we're fighting to get back—this is who you really are."

Somehow something in me shifted when my dad said that. (My mom always says those kind of mom-like things to me.) Knowing my dad really believed in me hit me pretty hard. I think it's something I always wanted—for my dad to see my good side and believe in me. And here I had it all that time and didn't know it—and all because using had blinded me to it. After that, something changed. That's when my mind opened, and I finally believed this treatment thing just might be what I needed.

When it came time for my parents and I to leave group and go visit with the whole family outside on the lawn, I got to spend time with my little brother and my sister. Well, Jamey was happy and all smiles—like a million tons had been lifted from his little shoulders. All he could do was smile and sit as close as he could squeeze to me. "I'm taking good care of your room," he promised, "and I hope you don't mind that I've renamed your pet lizard, Freddie, but you can still call him Slash and Burn when you get home." When we ate the lunch my family brought with them, I told my mom her famous ham sandwiches were still "the bomb." My sister, smiling and obviously happy, remarked, "But they're not as good as your macaroni and cheese—no one can make it like you." Funny how much I missed my family now that I was away from home—and now that I was clean and sober and could feel my love for them.

I only have twenty days left here in treatment, but I know that whenever I'm awake I'll be working a program 24-7 for the rest of my life, and I'll sure be glad to be home with my family again busy working that program.

Trey Oberg, 16

Three Important Reasons
to Attend a Treatment Program

Admitting that you need help is a crucial first step toward getting a hold of your life and starting down the road to living drug-free. Good for you for reaching that point! Whether you've made that decision alone, whether a friend, family member or even the courts have ordered you to get some help to stop using, you're at this point and that's what counts. It doesn't matter whether you walked here, drove here, a friend or family member brought you here, or a police car or ambulance delivered you here. What matters now is that you accept this as a point where change can begin.

And that is what treatment is all about. But knowing "I need help" may not mean you know what kind of help you need. For example, do you need a "detox" program? Is an "inpatient" program best for you? Do you need 90 to 120 days of follow-up after-care once you leave treatment, or is attending NA or AA meetings daily enough to help you live without using? Of course, being a minor, you may not get to make all the decisions on which type of treatment you end up getting, but that doesn't mean you can't go into a program understanding a little about it. If you're able to have some say in the matter, the following information can help you make your choice so that it will be the best possible treatment to help you overcome your chemical dependency.

It's easy to wish the problem would just go away. But it can't be wished away; action needs to be taken. Treatment is part of that action, and experts agree that treatment can work (especially when it's followed by an ongoing twelve-step program).

Even though you may agree that help is needed, maybe you're having trouble understanding why a "treatment" program would work. Remember that it's difficult, if not impossible, to stop your addiction without working through specific symptoms of the disease. You can't stop using simply because you want to. Once again, just quitting isn't enough—you need to work on the things that led to your addiction so that you won't relapse. Here are three reasons to go into treatment:

1. **A treatment program gives you a "time out."** A treatment center is a safe place to face the physical and mental withdrawal of chemical dependency without knowing that the drug or alcohol is just a phone call away. When it's not so easy to get to the drugs or alcohol, your obsession doesn't have the same power to consume you as it does when you're in the same environment you were in when you were using. Having this distance gives you time to think more clearly and to see your behavior and your life from a more realistic point of view.

2. **A treatment program works because it educates you about the nature of addiction and helps you map out a road to recovery.** It's important to learn about the disease of addiction and alcoholism. Treatment provides this through lectures, discussion and reading material. Whenever someone

has a chronic illness, he or she needs to understand how the disease works and how to manage it. It's important to learn the facts about what has happened to your body and your life and what might happen if you don't stop using or drinking. You need to learn what it will take for you to restore your mental and physical health, and what you can do to put your life back together.

3. **A treatment program provides professional help in a supportive, respectful setting to begin to change your life.** The best treatment will provide for your physical, emotional, intellectual, spiritual and social well-being. It may also address things like grief, anger- and stress-management and low self-esteem.

Types of Treatment Programs: Choosing One That Is Best and Right for You

Following is a brief overview of different kinds of treatment programs that can help you learn to live drug-free. You'll notice that we've not provided the cost of programs. This is because the cost for treatment can vary greatly. If you find your treatment through a nonprofit program, which is funded by different grants, your treatment may be free if you meet certain eligibility requirements. Many programs offer payment on a sliding scale, which means your cost is calculated according to how much your family can afford to pay. On the other hand, if a program is private (or a nonprofit with limited funds) it can be quite expensive. Many times insurance will help pay part of the costs of some treatment programs, so you'll want to check to see if your parents have insurance that covers the cost of treatment (either through a health coverage plan through your school, their work, or if they have family health coverage). You'll need to check with each individual program in order to learn what they charge. You may want to go visit different treatment programs within your community before deciding which one is right for you. If you are "going away" for treatment outside of your area, be certain to send for brochures. Some "typical" kinds of treatment programs are:

Detox

What it is: Detox is a program aimed at weaning your body from its dependency on chemicals, which includes treating you through the phase of physical "withdrawal."

When and why you would choose this: You would choose this in order to get the support you need through the initial withdrawal. Since physical withdrawal is a medical matter, detox can provide medical support (although some detox programs only provide observation and emotional support without any medical supervision).

Basic length of stay: Varies—usually three to ten days.

General description: Detox provides a setting for "coming off" drugs and alcohol that may or may not include prescribed medication. It can be in a hospital setting or a residential (inpatient) treatment facility.

Inpatient

What it is: An inpatient treatment program—where you stay in a dormitory or hospital-like building—provides a structured program of recovery activities.

When and why you would choose this: You would choose this in order to learn about and work on the issues surrounding your addiction, and become accustomed to the principles of working an ongoing twelve-step program of recovery.

Basic length of stay: Varies—usually twenty-eight to thirty days.

General description: This treatment usually includes educational classes, individual and group counseling (often family counseling, too), and often teaches twelve-step tools and includes attendance at twelve-step meetings.

Intensive Outpatient

What it is: Outpatient can often come after going through an inpatient or residential stay as follow-up aftercare treatment; but there is also outpatient treatment that stands on its own. This usually consists of two to six hours of treatment two to five days a week (depending on the program and the client needs).

When and why you would choose this: You would choose this to strengthen the recovery you received in residential treatment, or else as your only treatment program, in order to get treatment while still living at home and going to school and/or work. It is sometimes opted for because it is usually less expensive than residential treatment.

Basic length of stay: Varies—usually ninety days to eighteen months.

General description: Outpatient offers educational classes, individual and group counseling, and often teaches twelve-step principles and tools and requires completing "step-work" and attending twelve-step meetings.

Residential Treatment (Extended Treatment)

What it is: Residential treatment is a home or facility where you live as you attend a structured schedule of treatment activities.

When and why you would choose this: You would choose residential treatment in order to get intensive, thorough, around-the-clock supervision in your recovery.

Basic length of stay: Varies—usually ninety days to one year.

General description: In this house or facility, you have a structured environment where you get educational classes and individual and group counseling. A good number of residential treatment programs include twelve-step program attendance and actually take residents to twelve-step meetings. Many programs make twelve-step "step work" part of their treatment assignments. There are also "therapeutic communities" and other treatment programs that use "behavior modification" methods and include a lot of confrontational or encounter groups.

Recovery Home

What it is: A recovery home is a house where sober people live, work or go to school, in addition to receiving support and supervision in their recovery.

When and why you would choose this: You would choose a recovery home if you wanted to receive daily supervision and support in your recovery and treatment that wasn't as intensive or structured as an inpatient or residential treatment program.

Basic length of stay: Varies—usually ninety days to one year.

General description: Recovery homes have some structure, rules and guidelines for the people who live there. Often, they have groups, individual counseling and required twelve-step meeting attendance as part of their program.

Aftercare

What it is: Aftercare follows an inpatient, residential or recovery home stay. It also sometimes follows intensive outpatient treatment (with attendance hours reduced from the intensive outpatient schedule). It provides ongoing treatment and support after an initial treatment period. This usually consists of one to two hours of treatment one to three days per week.

When and why you would choose this: You would choose this to strengthen the recovery you received in residential or intensive outpatient treatment.

Basic length of stay: Varies—usually ninety days to eighteen months.

General description: Aftercare offers relapse prevention classes, individual and group counseling, and often teaches twelve-step principles and tools and requires completing "step work" and attending twelve-step meetings.

Sober-Living Home

What it is: A sober-living home is a house in the community where all the residents agree to remain drug-free and sober. These homes are usually only available to you if you are over eighteen years old.

When and why you would choose this: You would choose to live in a sober-living home in order to live in a safe, drug- and alcohol-free environment, so that you could benefit from the support of others in recovery who were dedicated to both abstinence and strengthening their recovery.

Basic length of stay: Varies—ninety days to two years.

General description: A sober-living home provides no treatment (other than possible referral) and little structure, although there may be curfews and assigned sharing of chores, and they usually require attendance of twelve-step meetings and a weekly meeting to discuss house problems or issues. The goal of sober-living environments is to provide the safety, support and accountability of a drug- and alcohol-free home to people in the early stages of recovery.

How do you find the right treatment program for you? Begin by talking with your school nurse or counselor or someone you know who can help refer you to where you can find out more about what is available to you. There are many organizations, hotlines, referral and information services and treatment centers all over the country whose purpose is to help you begin your recovery. At the end of this chapter, you'll find a section with phone numbers and addresses of resources and organizations that are there to help you.

A great place to start would be to make some telephone calls to help you sort out what kind of help is available for you. If you're not sure where to begin, you might start by asking your school counselor who you should call. Or you can start by taking out the phone book and looking in the yellow pages under some of following possible sections or listings:

- Drug and Alcohol Treatment / Substance Abuse Treatment / Chemical Dependency
- Community Drug Hotlines
- Alcoholics Anonymous, Narcotics Anonymous, or Al-Anon / Alateen
- City / Local Health Departments
- Local Emergency Health Clinics or Community Treatment Services

You'll want to plan what questions you want to ask once you reach the right person at these numbers. Different facilities offer different services and have different requirements. You'll want to ask each program about the treatment it offers. Here's a list of considerations you'll want to keep in mind as you ask questions:

1. Does the program offer treatment for teens? (Are there age-appropriate services?)
2. Is the program residential, outpatient or a recovery home?
3. Where is the program located?
4. How much does it cost, and is treatment covered by insurance? If so, how much will your insurance pay? (Note: When you provide them with information on your insurance policy, an administrator will then call your insurance and find out this information for you.)
5. Is there a waiting list to get in? If so, how long is it?
6. How long does the program last?
7. Does the program offer counseling (individual or group)? What are the daily recovery activities (curriculum, classes, groups, twelve-step meetings)?
8. Can your parents visit you? (Can anyone else? How often and when?)
9. Can you send and receive mail? Can you make and receive phone calls?

10. Does the program offer family counseling and referrals to help your family understand and support you in your recovery? What other services does it include (such as a tutor and educational services)?

11. Is the program state-accredited or licensed and run by trained professionals?

12. Does the program offer medical services, psychological services and social services?

13. Is long-term aftercare support encouraged and offered? (Research shows that longer-term treatment gives you a better chance of success.)

14. What should you take with you (clothes, toiletries, bedding, food)? Can you bring any medications?

15. Once you're in treatment, can you leave for any reason (such as dental appointments) and return to treatment?

Treatment is a time for the healing that begins the process of recovery. And recovery is most successful when it continues after treatment with self-help groups, such as AA and other twelve-step programs. After you've finished residential treatment, you and your family may be so happy that you're no longer using that you may be tempted to think you're "cured." But successful recovery takes ongoing, rigorous self-examination, which means doing a lot of work to change all the old behaviors and dig up the pain you've been stuffing, and then sharing it honestly with others.

Remember, you can't do it alone—and when you're working a twelve-step program you never have to. In the next chapter, you'll learn much more about twelve-step programs and exactly how they work.

Referrals and Resources
to Find Help Near You

Following is a list of twelve-step recovery programs, as well as informational referrals and sources to help you find treatment programs in your area. Many of these national organizations have local chapters that are listed in your phone directory. You can also look under Drug or Alcohol Counseling to find a treatment center or other resources you can call in your area. (All 800, 888 and 877 numbers are toll-free.)

800-ALCOHOL
800-COCAINE
800-448-3000, Boystown

Al-Anon/Alateen Family Group Headquarters
(Twelve-step group for family members of alcoholics and teens who are living with an alcoholic parent.)
P. O. Box 862, Midtown Station
New York, NY 10018-0862
212-302-7240
800-356-9996 (Literature)
800-344-2666 (Meeting Referral)

Alcoholics Anonymous
(Twelve-step program for alcoholics of all ages.)
World Services, Inc.
475 Riverside Drive
New York, NY 10115
212-870-3400 (Literature)
212-647-1680 (Meeting Referral)

Center for Substance Abuse Treatment
National Drug and Alcohol Treatment Referral Service
(*National organization to help you locate treatment programs in your area and throughout the nation.*)
800-662-HELP (twenty-four-hour, toll-free service)
800-487-4889 (TDD)
877-767-8432 (Spanish)
www.findtreatment.samhsa.gov

Cocaine Anonymous
(*Twelve-step program for cocaine addicts; will provide information on where and when meetings are scheduled in your area.*)
World Service Office
3740 Overland Avenue, Ste. C
Los Angeles, CA 90034
800-347-8998

Families Anonymous
(*Twelve-step program for family members of chemically dependent people; will provide help for finding places to go, and send free litera-ture and information on their program and other programs that are there to help.*)
P. O. Box 35475
Culver City, CA 90231
800-736-9805

Marijuana Anonymous
(*Twelve-step program for marijuana addicts; they will tell you the times and locations of the meetings in your area.*)
World Services
P. O. Box 2912
Van Nuys, CA 91404
800-766-6779

Nar-Anon Family Group Headquarters
(*Twelve-step program for family members of chemically dependent people; provides information on meetings in your area that offer both support and literature on how to help your chemically dependent family member.*)
P. O. Box 2562
Palos Verdes Peninsula, CA 90274
310-547-5800

Narcotics Anonymous (NA)
(*Twelve-step program for all chemically dependent people.*)
World Service Office
P. O. Box 9999
Van Nuys, CA 91409
818-773-9999 (This number provides information on where and when there are NA meetings in your area.)
www.na.org (This Web site provides meeting information, recovery articles and literature, as well as links to other recovery Web sites.)

National Clearinghouse for Alcohol and Drug Information (NCADI)
(*Provides information on treatment programs [locations and services offered] throughout the nation. Asking whether you are looking for programs that are either free, funded by the state or paid for or covered by insurance, staff will give you a referral number for your state. When you call that number, their staff will give you the programs closest to your area.*)
P. O. Box 2345
Rockville, MD 20847-2345
301-468-2600
800-729-6686
800-487-4889 (TDD)

National Council on Alcoholism and Drug Dependence (NCADD)
(*Offers referrals and information on treatment programs, referring you to your local treatment information center to learn what treatment programs are available in your area.*)
20 Exchange Place, Ste. 2902
New York, NY 10005
212-269-7797
800-NCA-CALL
www.ncadd.org

Questions to Think About

♥ In finding help for yourself or your friend or family member, what three services would you call first?
♥ Why do you think you (or your friend or family member) would benefit (or not benefit) from residential treatment rather than outpatient treatment?
♥ What three things are most important to you personally when it comes to choosing a treatment program (for you or your family member)?

Unit IV

You're Clean and Sober: How to Stay That Way

*Forgiveness is the ability to release
the concept of a better past.*

—Source Unknown

It's never too late to be what you might have been.

—George Eliot

*I am not afraid of storms, for I am
learning how to sail my ship.*

—Louisa May Alcott

*Whoever wants to reach a distant goal
must take many small steps.*

—Helmut Schmidt

13

A Road to Recovery: Walking the Twelve-Step Program

"No Offense, But . . ."

When I was using, I was pulled over and charged with being "under the influence," as well as for possession (of marijuana) and for having drug paraphernalia on me. They put me in handcuffs, took me in a police car to the substation, took my picture and fingerprints and booked me—it was all pretty intense and very scary. Then my parents had to come and get me out—which was also pretty intense. After that, I had to go to court, and I was court-ordered to attend ten twelve-step meetings. I was relieved I didn't have to spend time in juvenile hall or anything like that, but I wasn't thrilled about going to these meetings either. But I'm not a big enough fool not to go and end up back in court, so I went to my first twelve-step meeting.

When I got to the meeting, some guy handed me a copy of something called "The Twelve Steps" and said, "There are a few readings that I hand out to be read at the beginning of every meeting, before we start our open discussion. You can read these when I call on you." I looked at the paper in my hands and thought, *Oh geez, it's going be worse than I thought: It's going to be like some sort of revival meeting!* On the sheet I was supposed to read, it actually had the twelve steps all written out:

The Twelve Steps

1. We admitted that we were powerless over our addiction, that our lives had become unmanageable.
2. We came to believe that a Power greater than ourselves could restore us to sanity.
3. We made a decision to turn our will and our lives over to the care of God *as we understood Him.*
4. We made a searching and fearless moral inventory of ourselves.
5. We admitted to God, to ourselves, and to another human being the exact nature of our wrongs.
6. We were entirely ready to have God remove all these defects of character.
7. We humbly asked Him to remove our shortcomings.
8. We made a list of all people we had harmed, and became willing to make amends to them all.
9. We made direct amends to such people wherever possible, except when to do so would injure them or others.
10. We continued to take personal inventory and when we were wrong promptly admitted it.
11. We sought through prayer and meditation to improve our conscious contact with God *as we understood Him,* praying only for knowledge of His will for us and the power to carry that out.
12. Having had a spiritual awakening as a result of these steps, we tried to carry this message to addicts, and to practice these principles in all our affairs.

I remember looking around the room, thinking, *I don't want to be here.* But I had to stay—or face jail—so I suffered through it, but I wasn't exactly overflowing with willingness or an open mind. I saw myself as way different and sitting with people who I had absolutely nothing in common with. It seemed to me that anyone who talked was either bragging, whining, being unrealistically optimistic or else a big phony. So, I wasn't convinced being here with "these people" was for me. But I was also absolutely sure I didn't want to use anymore, and I knew I needed help in quitting and staying drug-free. I had made such a mess of my life that I had to try something. And of course, like I said, I was mandated to go to the meetings, so I was stuck. I guess everyone could tell that I didn't want to be there, because as I was leaving they all said, "Keep coming back, then you'll see that it works— if you work it." Well, even with the advice, I knew that after I had my ten meetings signed off for the courts, I'd joyfully walk out of my tenth meeting convinced I'd never have to go back. Which is exactly the way it was—at first.

It wasn't long before I was "partying" again—and that meant I was using again. I got to using more and more, and needless to say, my life got worse and worse. I won't bother to tell you all the ways I managed to get in trouble—although this time, by sheer luck, there were no courts involved. And so this time I went back to the meetings on my own. I really wanted to stop using. I was tired of getting in trouble and always having my parents angry with me. This time, I really listened and wanted to be at the meetings. I even said "hi" to the people who said "hi" to me, and I smiled when they told me, "Keep coming back." So, this time I was all right with going to the meetings, but there were still a few things I wasn't going to do: I wasn't going to work those steps they talked about. I read them, and the ones I was okay with, well surely, reading them was enough. The ones I didn't like, well, no one would get me to "work" them. And, as far as I was concerned, there were a couple of them that just didn't apply to me (for example, I didn't have any "defects of character"). Another thing I wasn't going to do was to get a sponsor. I didn't need a sponsor. I had friends at school and a school counselor. And since I wasn't going to be working the steps, I didn't need a sponsor to show me how. But those things aside, I was now happy to go to the meetings. I was sure I had beaten my "using" habit.

Less than two months later I was at a party. Someone passed me a joint, and I just took it. After that, I was right back to where I'd been before I got clean. It only took a few weeks for me to be in trouble with my parents again and behind at school. So I went back to the meetings, determined to do *something* different again.

I decided I'd get a sponsor. There was this one woman who I really loved to listen to when she spoke at the meetings. She was almost thirty, but she'd been clean and sober for over twelve years, which meant she got clean when she was still in her teens! She always spoke about how the program worked in her life, and she was totally inspirational. Besides that, she was always so nice to me and to everyone, for that matter. She went out of her way to make each and every "newcomer" feel welcome. She'd given me her phone number and told me I could call her if I ever needed to talk to anyone. I just clicked with her, so I asked her to sponsor me, and she said she would.

She had me call her every day for the first thirty days, just to check-in and connect. Most of the time we didn't even talk much; it was really just a "check-in." She said it would help us get to know each other and get me in the habit of being comfortable with calling—so that I wouldn't hesitate to call if I needed her help. She also had me start some reading and writing assignments on my first step.

I'd just moved on to my second step when I made my first "help!" call to her. Melanie, an old using friend of mine, called me one Saturday and said she wanted to come by and pick me up so we could go to the mall. I found myself saying, "Yes," even though there was a part of me saying, "No! No! No!" Then I just freaked out when I hung up the phone. After all, I'd just written on my first step about how I was powerless over using drugs, and how every single relapse I'd ever had happened when I went along with someone who was using, thinking that I'd be okay—even though it was against my better judgment to go along in the first place. I knew my friend Melanie: She loved to cruise around, lighting up a joint to smoke as she headed for wherever—including the mall. What was I thinking? What could I do now? I'd already said yes. Well, maybe since I knew all this, it meant that I could handle hanging out with Melanie without using. My mind raced with thoughts, and I ended up calling my sponsor. I told her what had happened, and she said very calmly, "You need to call her back and tell her something else came up— and it has, because I'm coming over to take you to a meeting." And she did!

That was the first time having my sponsor to call saved me from doing something stupid or destructive, but it wasn't the last. She was also there for me when my parents got divorced, and it hurt so bad that I just wanted to get high to escape the pain. Every time I call her with a problem, she's there to give me the twelve-step program solution to it. She's the greatest. What's more, I'd never be able to thank her enough for guiding me through the steps. Even from that first incident with Melanie, I could see how important those steps were when it came to helping me not repeat my old mistakes.

I'm glad that I listened when they told me to "keep coming back"—and I'm glad that I finally became willing to work a complete twelve-step program to the best of my ability. Because my life is so much better than it used to be. Today, I have eighteen months clean and sober—and I'm proud of that. What people don't understand is what an accomplishment staying clean and sober is for those of us who struggle with addiction. When you've been chemically dependent, there are days you literally struggle every minute to stay clean. So for me, eighteen months is no small feat. But it is a huge step in the direction of my staying clean and sober for the rest of my life.

Alexis Johnson, 18

A Twelve-Step Program:
How It Works and How You Work It

As you may have noticed in the previous chapter, twelve-step programs or meetings often play a part in the recovery activities of inpatient and outpatient treatment programs. Chemical dependency professionals have discovered that combining treatment and twelve-step programs is a powerful advantage over using just one or the other by itself. One of the reasons is that when you go into a treatment program, you are only there for a certain length of time—whether twenty-eight days or even a year (or maybe you've chosen an outpatient program and only attend weekly meetings). Eventually, you will be back at home, and your time of treatment will be over. However, you will not be "cured" from your addiction, though it goes into "remission." It just gets arrested so that recovery is possible. In order to maintain recovery (living without the emotional and physical cravings that one experiences with chemical dependency), you have to continue to work on yourself and the thoughts, behaviors and issues that could lead you to use once again. This is one reason why working a twelve-step program is so important: It offers you the lifelong support and direction you need to continue to grow in your recovery and stay clean and sober.

Twelve-step programs are ongoing, and their doors are always open to anyone who has the "desire to stop" using drugs or drinking alcohol. They are located in numerous places with meetings scheduled at different times throughout each day, every day of the week. Everyone who attends the meetings is also in recovery (unless it is an open meeting and someone who is not an addict or an alcoholic is visiting). The value of one person in recovery helping another has proven to be effective.

Twelve-step programs are "anonymous programs"—this means each person's membership or attendance is meant to remain anonymous. (Anonymous means unidentified.) This is why only first names are used in the meetings. When members are outside the meetings they are not supposed to talk about who else was at the meeting or who said what during the meeting. These anonymous programs include Alcoholics Anonymous (AA), Narcotics Anonymous (NA), Marijuana Anonymous (MA), Cocaine Anonymous (CA) and many other "anonymous" twelve-step programs. In fact, there are twelve-step programs for family members of alcoholics and addicts, and there are twelve-step programs for people who are addicted to gambling, food and sex. They all share the same twelve steps, which were first created and used by Alcoholics Anonymous; the only difference in these steps is relatively minor adaptations in identifying the specific drug or addiction. (This is how they became labeled twelve-step programs.) Those steps were detailed earlier in this chapter in Alexis Johnson's story, and later in this chapter you will read more about them.

What Is a "Sponsor," and How Do You Get One?

When you are new in recovery, you are considered a "newcomer." All twelve-step programs teach that the newcomer is the most important person in the meeting. You should feel welcomed, without worrying about being the focus of attention. Making certain that you are warmly greeted, yet that any desire you have for space is respected, should be the goal of the other people attending the meeting.

In twelve-step programs, the newcomer chooses a sponsor. A sponsor's role is to guide you in working through the twelve steps and to provide you with twelve-step solutions and support. Your sponsor should be someone who has worked the steps herself and who has long-term "clean time" (or sobriety). It is strongly suggested that your sponsor also be someone who is the same sex as you—to assure that you are able to share openly. Besides, if you want advice on how to be a female living a good life in recovery, you should seek it from a female living a good life in recovery. If you want advice on how to be a male living a good life in recovery, you should seek it from a male living a good life in recovery. It is suggested that you find someone who has the kind of recovery that you would like to have. Of course, you can't always tell for certain whether or not a person has "good recovery." But if the person seems kind, honest, responsible and active in attending meetings, it can be an indication that she has "good recovery." It can also be important to feel like you connect with a person. If you are having trouble with being certain about who to ask and would rather not commit to anyone yet, but still want to get started on working your steps, you could ask someone to be your "temporary sponsor" until you find the right person to ask to be your permanent sponsor. You can also enlist the help of people you meet at the meetings by asking them who they think might make a good sponsor for you.

Once you've chosen who you would like to have as a sponsor, simply ask that person. So long as the person knows they have the time to give you the attention you deserve, she is certain to tell you it will be her honor to sponsor you. Sponsoring others in the program is not just an honor; it is part of what helps those who have significant lengths of sobriety remember where they have been. It strengthens their own recovery to give and be of service in this way. So don't be afraid to ask. You are not just asking something of this person; you are giving something to this person, as well.

Since a sponsor has been through early recovery herself, she knows the shame of having hurt herself and others when using. She has also gone through the same kinds of experiences with fears, anger and life problems that can be part of getting and staying clean. Therefore, she is able to understand and to listen without judgment and provide suggestions that worked for her in her own recovery.

What Happens at Twelve-Step Meetings— And What Can You Expect When You Attend?

Twelve-step programs encourage regular meeting attendance. You may have heard that ninety meetings are suggested in the first ninety days of recovery. Those meetings, held at various times and in various places, provide an opportunity for members to come together to share and strengthen each other's desire to live drug-free. (The only requirement for membership is a desire to quit drinking or using, and you are a member when you say you are a member. No one else monitors this.) The meetings are opened by a leader who invites everyone to join with him or her in saying the "Serenity Prayer." The Serenity Prayer goes as follows: "God grant me the serenity to accept the things that I cannot change, the courage to change the things that I can, and the wisdom to know the difference." For many years this prayer was thought to be anonymous, but has since been attributed to Dr. Reinhold Niebuhr.

Next the leader calls on a few different people to whom he has handed out short readings (a few paragraphs) from the twelve-step texts, and they introduce themselves, identifying themselves as an addict or alcoholic, and then read those few paragraphs. (These are just easy-to-understand excerpts from books put out by AA or NA.) The meetings, which are usually one hour to an hour-and-a-half long, then go on to follow their specific format depending on what type of meeting it is.

There are several different types of meetings. Following are the ones that are most often scheduled:

- Open discussion meetings, where members share on a specific topic or on what's going on in their lives that day.
- Speaker meetings, where a member, usually with significant "clean time" or sobriety, shares his story and his "experience, strength and hope."

- Book study meetings, where members read and share about a particular reading from the appropriate twelve-step text, discussing their understanding of the reading and how it applies to their lives.
- Step study meetings, where members read and share about one of the twelve steps, discussing their understanding of the step and how it works in their lives.

For a solid and strong program of recovery that makes certain to cover all bases, it is often suggested that you choose at least one "step" study meeting, one speaker meeting and one open discussion meeting per week.

Who Attends the Meetings?

These meetings are sometimes open to people who are not alcoholics or addicts, and they are sometimes closed to everyone but alcoholics or addicts. There are women's meetings, men's meetings and mixed meetings. There are "young people's" meetings and other meetings for people with different special interests or needs (such as gay and lesbian meetings, Spanish-speaking meetings and HIV/AIDS meetings).

How Is a Meeting Run?

When a person shares in a meeting, there is no "cross talk": This means everyone else listens without commenting or asking questions of the person about what he or she is sharing. A maximum length of sharing is usually requested (approximately five minutes). The meetings have a secretary, who is nominated and voted on by the group for the position. The secretary takes a commitment to keep the position for a specific length of time (usually six months). The secretary generally maintains the order of the meeting. The secretary chooses the leader of the meeting, who changes each week. The leader often selects the topic of the meeting, hands out the readings that open the meeting for other members to read, and is often (but not always) the person who calls on who will share.

When people share, they always introduce themselves by their first name only and then identify themselves as an alcoholic or an addict (depending on the twelve-step meeting they are attending) before they begin to share. In other words, John Doe would say, "My name is John, and I am an alcoholic," then he would talk about the topic of the meeting. The reason for identifying yourself as an alcoholic or an addict is to assure the other people present that you are there at the meeting to continue in your recovery and are just like them in that regard. It also reminds you of the reason that you are there. If you were to forget you were an addict or an alcoholic, your recovery would be in serious jeopardy—you might decide you could have "just one" drink or drug and control your use.

When you are a "newcomer" who is in his or her first thirty days of "clean time" or "sobriety," you will be invited to introduce yourself at the beginning of the meeting. This is so that the other people at the meeting can get to know you. You are not singled out for this; the leader just announces to the group something such as, "If there is anyone here in their first thirty days of sobriety (or clean time), we invite you to identify yourself so that we can get to know you better." All this introduction requires is the simple John Doe opening above: "My name is John, and I am an alcoholic (or addict)." Any people who are at the meeting for the first time are also often given the opportunity to introduce themselves in the same way.

Why Is It Called a "Spiritual" (Not Religious) Program?

In reading through the twelve steps, you can see the mention of "God" a number of times. The need to find a Higher Power is an important factor of twelve-step programs. However, some members choose to use the group as their Higher Power, especially until they "come to believe" in something more. The crux of the program is that each member is absolutely free to choose his own Higher Power—and establish a personal relationship with the God of his "understanding." The fact is that many agnostics and atheists successfully remain clean and sober through the twelve-step program—if they are willing to live and apply the spiritual principles of the program.

Members of twelve-step programs see themselves as joined by the common bond of a "shared disease" from which they seek a "daily reprieve" by practicing the spiritual principles of the twelve-step program. Twelve-step programs stress spiritual principles like honesty, willingness, open-mindedness, tolerance, unity, compassion, acceptance, surrender, forgiveness, trust, faith and perseverance. One way they actually live these principles is to agree that twelve-step programs are not for everybody. But members and recovery experts alike agree that the twelve steps, the support and the principles of the program can definitely work.

The Twelve Steps and What It Means to "Work" Them

You may wonder just how these twelve steps you're always hearing about work. What do you have to do to take these steps? Different treatment programs and different sponsors may have different ways to work each of the twelve steps. Your sponsor will probably direct you to work the steps in the same way her sponsor had her work them. There are also "step guides" and workbooks that have different questions to take a person through the steps. Sometimes, you may be able to buy a program's step guide at a meeting; other times you will need to go to a twelve-step or recovery bookstore to get them. There are often also other guides in regular bookstores under their "Recovery" or "Self-Help" sections. Again, all twelve-step programs use the same twelve steps with adaptations to fit the specific addiction they apply to.

Here are the twelve steps of Narcotics Anonymous and a brief, general description of how they are *usually* "worked" or "taken" with a sponsor:

1. **"We admitted that we were powerless over our addiction, that our lives had become unmanageable."** This first step is all-important. Perhaps one of the big reasons that twelve-step programs work is that they don't hide or give any false impressions on how addiction works. Twelve-step programs come right out and say the addict is powerless over alcohol and other drugs. To "work" or "take" this step your sponsor will most probably give you some sort of writing assignment that details the powerlessness, unmanageability and the progression of the disease in your life. Many times this assignment includes an auto-biography of your drug use. More than likely you will also be told to read specific literature on the step. You then need to go on to remember that you are powerless over drugs and alcohol and act accordingly in your daily life by abstaining from using them and doing what it takes to grow in your recovery.

2. **"We came to believe that a Power greater than ourselves could restore us to sanity."** To "work" or "take" this step your sponsor is likely to give you some sort of writing assignment that details the insanity of using drugs, as well as one that helps bring about some sort of belief in a Power greater than yourself. You will also probably be told to read specific literature on the step. As you progress in your recovery, your belief will also grow—as will your "sanity."

3. **"We made a decision to turn our will and our lives over to the care of God *as we understood Him.*"** To "work" or "take" this step your sponsor will probably give you some sort of writing assignment that details your understanding of your Higher Power. In most cases, you will say a "third-step prayer" with your sponsor. (This is a prayer where you "turn your will and your life over to the care of God.") More than likely you will also be told to read specific literature on the step. Living this step and applying it to your life should then become an ongoing, daily practice.

4. **"We made a searching and fearless moral inventory of ourselves."** To "work" or "take" this step your sponsor will most probably give you a writing assignment that inventories all your resentments, fears, relationships and those things you are ashamed of. Usually, you will be looking for "your part" and patterns in the things you are writing about. More than likely you will also be told to read specific literature on the step.

5. **"We admitted to God, to ourselves and to another human being the exact nature of our wrongs."** To "work" or "take" this step you will read your fourth step to another human being—usually your sponsor. More than likely you will also be told to read specific literature on the step. Sharing everything you've written in your fourth step helps take the power out of the shame, the anger and the fear.

6. **"We became entirely ready to have God remove all these defects of character."** To "work" or "take" this step your sponsor will probably give you some sort of writing assignment that involves listing your "character defects," shortcomings or weaknesses (many times you will also make a list of your strengths and assets). You will

probably read your list to your sponsor. More than likely you will also be told to read specific literature on the step. Once you've listed these "character defects" and written about how you act on them (such as manipulation, impatience, dishonesty, self-centeredness), it then becomes easier to see when you are acting on them in your daily life after that.

7. **"We humbly asked Him to remove our shortcomings."** To "work" or "take" this step it is likely that your sponsor will ask you to say a prayer asking God to remove those weaknesses you listed in your sixth step. More than likely you will also be told to read specific literature on the step. This step should become a regular practice in your life.

8. **"We made a list of all people we had harmed, and became willing to make amends to them all."** To "work" or "take" this step your sponsor will most probably give you some sort of writing assignment that lists everyone you hurt while you are using. You will read your list to your sponsor. More than likely you will also be told to read specific literature on the step.

9. **"We made direct amends to such people wherever possible, except when to do so would injure them or others."** To "work" or "take" this step your sponsor will most probably give you direction as you set about making "amends"— apologizing to the people you hurt and taking action to make "wrongs" right. This can include emotional amends and financial amends. You will probably also be told to read specific literature on the step.

10. **"We continued to take personal inventory and when we were wrong promptly admitted it."** To "work" or "take" this step your sponsor will more than likely give you some sort of writing assignment that involves looking at any

ways you may have acted out on character defects that day, how you may have hurt others, where you are in your relationship to your Higher Power and others. It includes then making amends where necessary, so that you don't create new "wreckage" in your life. More than likely you will also be told to read specific literature on the step. This step is meant to become a regular practice.

11. **"We sought through prayer and meditation to improve our conscious contact with God *as we understood Him,* praying only for knowledge of His will for us and the power to carry that out."** To "work" or "take" this step your sponsor may (or may not) give you a written assignment on prayer and meditation and improving your relationship with your Higher Power. The greater part of this step is the regular, daily, ongoing practice of it. More than likely you will also be told to read specific literature on the step.

12. **"Having had a spiritual awakening as a result of these steps, we tried to carry this message to addicts and to practice these principles in all our affairs."** To "work" or "take" this step your sponsor may give you a written assignment on "carrying the message" to others and how you practice the spiritual principles the twelve-step program teaches in your daily life (such as humility, service, unity, forgiveness). The greater part of this step is putting it into action in your daily life. More than likely you will also be told to read specific literature on the step.

If you'd like to find a twelve-step meeting in your area, you can look in the telephone book for the local hotlines. These will be listed under the specific anonymous program to which it applies (for example, Alcoholics Anonymous, Narcotics Anonymous). The person answering those lines will be able to tell you where and when meetings are held in your area.

Questions to Think About

- ♥ Where and when is there a "Step Study" meeting you could attend?
- ♥ Where and when is there an "Open Discussion" meeting you could attend?
- ♥ Where and when is there a "Speaker" meeting you could attend?
- ♥ What will you look for in a sponsor?
- ♥ Which of the twelve steps do you most (and least) look forward to working and why?

14

How to Get Out from Under the Jaws, Claws—And PAWS—Of Drugs

The Nudge from the Judge

I stood in line for the school dance wondering what the heck I was doing there. "I wonder where Julie is," my friend Warren commented, looking around for his girlfriend who was supposed to meet him there. "I'm sure she'll show up," I muttered—knowing there'd be no one showing up to meet me. I felt totally out of place. I glanced up at Warren whose eyes were still combing the crowd for Julie. He was an old friend, which is why I'd let him talk me into coming, but I just didn't belong at school dances anymore—and I really didn't have any business hanging out with Warren either.

Warren didn't use drugs and now that I did, our lives were as different as night and day—as this moment proved. He was looking for his girlfriend; I was waiting for my head to clear. I'd smoked some pot and some crystal right before I picked Warren up. Now I was kind of paranoid and a little "amped" out from the crystal, but mostly I was just really uncomfortable being with normal people at a normal event like a school dance. The whole thing made me feel sad, like homesick for the way things were before I started using.

I knew I wouldn't be dancing, and I'd just end up hanging out against some wall, waiting to go home. So when Julie finally got there, I asked, "Hey, Warren, do you think you could get a ride home with Julie? I'm not really up for this—I think I'm going to leave." Warren tried to talk me into staying, but with Julie there, it was just a token attempt. He could tell I was high and probably was as uncomfortable with me as I was with him.

While I was driving home, I couldn't stop thinking about how much my life had changed. There was nothing normal or fun about it anymore. While lost in thought, I didn't even see the stop sign—but the cop who pulled me over saw me run it. I was arrested for being "under the influence," had handcuffs put on and was taken to juvenile hall. So "with a nudge from the judge" I was put into a drug treatment program run by the city. I was there for nearly a month, and then went to a follow-up out-patient recovery program so that I could learn how to live life without using drugs or alcohol.

The first days that I was clean and sober were tough—I felt awful—but by the fifth day, I was feeling less wiped out. I really thought I had it licked. Oh, I knew I had to get serious and work a program of recovery—change my old behaviors and old think-ing—but I figured I was halfway there, since my withdrawals were a thing of the past. Then, a whole new set of problems set in. Suddenly, I couldn't sleep because I was having bizarre and frightening nightmares. I couldn't concentrate on any kind of schoolwork—even with the special tutor I'd been given going over everything with me one-on-one. Even if I thought I was concentrating, by the next day I'd forget what I'd studied. The trouble didn't end there. I was a nervous wreck—clumsy and jumpy—and I always felt edgy. I used to be a great hackey-sack player. Now—forget it—I was as nimble as a rhino.

My moods were unbearable—for everyone around me and for myself. I remember this one day, this guy in one of my classes was being a clown. He's always a clown, but suddenly it irritated me so bad. I leaped from my chair and snapped, "Hey dude, why don't you just stop trying to be so funny—because you're not!" I was right up in his face in the middle of the classroom. I don't know what made it such a big deal to me. Another time, we were talking about different animals that were becoming extinct in my science class, and I felt like I was going to start crying. It's not like I'm Mr. Wild Kingdom or something. I mean, sure, I like animals, but this reaction was totally not like me. I just got so emotional, and over something that wouldn't usually bother me.

And you should've seen me the day I misplaced my history book! I was a total wild man—running from one place to another—accusing everyone around me of having taken it and ripping everything out of my locker. I was just totally stressing out, which is not cool because when I stress out like this, I get this feeling like I want to get high and forget about it. So there I was nearly sixty days clean and sober, and I was a mess of stress, craving drugs!

Luckily, one night in my outpatient program they had a class on PAWS—post-acute withdrawal syndrome—which is basically your body still freaking out from the chemicals you've put into it, which have played havoc on your central nervous system. So the result is a whole list of symptoms you can expect, such as trouble concentrating, feeling anxious, being clumsy, having nightmares and problems with sleeping and stuff like that. I could see that I was having a classic case of it. They said that it's usually at its worst when you are at about six months clean and sober. So it was really a relief to know what was wrong with me, and to find out it would pass as long as I rode it out without using drugs or alcohol. The counselor talked about things we could do to help deal with the symptoms—things like making sure we were getting decent nutrition, managing our stress and getting the support we needed to make it through the times when PAWS attacked.

I've been clean and sober for a year now, and I'm glad to say I haven't used any alcohol or drugs in all that time. It's been over six months since I have had any symptoms of PAWS. They say the symptoms can return off and on for up to two years—but they don't have to. Hopefully, they're over for good for me. You can trust I'm doing my part to see that those symptoms don't return. My life is a hundred percent better today than it was when I was using, and I intend to keep it that way.

Sean Peck, 17

Why Is There "Withdrawal"?

"Kicking" drugs and alcohol can be rough. In the first three to five days, sometimes even longer, the withdrawal symptoms can be very uncomfortable, even painful. Those symptoms (and how bad they get) vary depending on the chemicals you used, as well as with the amount and length of time you used them.

Withdrawal is the term that describes the process of the body cleansing itself of the "toxins" or poisons of the drugs. Basically, here's what's going on: The body is always at work keeping things "functioning" in normal, healthy ways (this process is called "homeostasis"). If a drug (chemical) is taken to slow down that normal flow of things, the body gets to work to speed things up—trying as best it can to bring it back to normal. If a chemical is taken to speed up that flow, then the body works to slow down the flow, again trying to get the body back to its normal level of health and functioning.

But should you use alcohol or any other chemical all the time, the body gets used to constantly fighting to create this normal flow of healthy functions. Once you take the drug away, the body takes a while to "get it" that it doesn't have to keep on fighting. If you were taking a drug that was speeding up the flow, and your body is still fighting to slow itself to normal, you come "crashing" down. The result is that you end up with symptoms such as feeling unbearably tired, irritable and edgy. On the other hand, if you don't have a drug that once slowed down the flow and the body is still fighting to speed it up, you go into a state that is typically called *high anxiety*. This means you won't be able to sleep, your nerves will twitch and your stomach will be upset.

If you want to understand this principle better, try this experiment:

- Hold your hand out and ask a friend to push down on it.
- As your friend pushes down on your hand, try to keep your hand in the same place, fighting against the pressure your friend is applying to keep it where it is.
- Tell your friend to keep pushing down on your hand and then just pull his hand away without warning you ahead of time.

You'll find that once your friend pulls his hand away, your hand will shoot into the air with the force of trying to keep it in place against the pressure that had once been used to hold it down. When your body fights for homeostasis during drug withdrawal, it is like your hand shooting into the air because it's still fighting to keep things at a normal level, even when the pressure to keep it down has been removed.

While immediate drug withdrawal is usually over in four to six days, your body has yet other work to do in adjusting its "thermostat" and getting back to "normal." As your body tries to readjust, as it struggles to once again find its way to "normal," you can experience what experts in the field of chemical dependency refer to as PAWS, or Post-Acute Withdrawal Syndrome.

Watching Out for the Claws of PAWS (Post-Acute Withdrawal Syndrome)

After finally getting through those first miserable days, you feel relieved to think the "worst" is over. And it is, as far as physical pain and the power of the mental obsession goes. Remember how Sean Peck talked about feeling as if he were all set to get out in the world and live a drug-free life? Imagine his confusion and disappointment when a whole new set of symptoms appeared. As Sean told us, this is post-acute withdrawal syndrome (PAWS). This "syndrome" or "group of symptoms" was identified and written about by Terence T. Gorski, M.A., a well-known expert in the field of recovery—and relapse prevention, in particular.

Those symptoms can begin seven to fourteen days after you stop using (abstinence), and quite often return off and on for six months to two years. However, as Sean Peck's story mentions, the symptoms usually "peak" at about six months. Sometimes the symptoms are mild; sometimes they are more severe (although they are rarely as intense as the symptoms of early withdrawal). Sometimes these symptoms never appear at all. The most important thing to remember if you or someone you care about is going through PAWS is that to get over them you have to stay clean and sober.

Why does PAWS happen? *PAWS is caused by the damage that alcohol or drugs have done to the central nervous system.* How bad the PAWS symptoms get depends on how much the brain was harmed by the drug or alcohol abuse. It also depends on how much stress is going on in the recovering person's life—as well as his or her ability to cope with stress.

Here are some of the common symptoms—the "claws" of PAWS:

- **Difficulty remembering things.** "The teacher will ask the class something, and I'll know that I knew the answer to the question just a few days ago, but I just can't remember it!" seventeen-year-old Lindsey Rigotti describes. "I've not used for more than three months, but I still just seem to forget things." Lindsey is experiencing memory problems—a common symptom of PAWS. Sometimes there's even difficulty learning. The good news is that the damage that caused these symptoms isn't usually permanent. So long as you don't drink or use, the odds are you will be back to normal within two years.

- **Unable to concentrate or think clearly.** Not being able to concentrate can certainly be frustrating, as Shelsey Brown, a seventeen-year-old, experienced: "My brain seemed scrambled. I just couldn't seem to think straight, and I really couldn't concentrate. My mind was always running all over the place—or it would get stuck on one thing, and I couldn't let it go to think about anything else—even when I really needed to. It took me a while and some really focused work to improve my thinking skills. I was really surprised to find out that drugs had taken such a big toll—and I'm clean and sober. I can only imagine what my thinking was like while using!"

- **Emotional roller coaster.** Another very different symptom is either overreacting to situations or emotional "shut-down" (numbness). "I've been clean and sober for over a year, and I still have radical mood swings," seventeen-year-old Tyla Adams explained. "One minute I'm full of hope and excitement for my 'new' life. The next minute I feel like life totally sucks, and everything is just too hard to face. What's just as frustrating is that the emotions I'm feeling don't have anything to do with the situation I'm facing. I can get an A on the sociology test I've been cramming for and still feel like crying because I'm sad for no good reason!"

- **Trouble handling stress.** Keith Reiser, fifteen, describes his experience with PAWS this way: "I'd be fine, then suddenly out of nowhere I'd have this terrible feeling of nervousness and worry. When some problem came up—like finding out I only had two days to turn in a paper I'd forgotten about—I would work myself up to being totally anxious and scared. Sometimes, the problem I was stressing over would be so small that I didn't know what it was I was worrying about, but it would just consume me. Other times I'd be filled with this feeling like something awful was going to happen, and I'd be scared for no reason."

- **Sleep problems.** "It wasn't bad enough that I couldn't seem to fall asleep," fifteen-year-old Erin Wise explained, "but when I did finally fall asleep, I couldn't stay asleep. On top of that, I'd have these really weird dreams, and I'd wake up because they were so creepy. Then I'd have trouble falling back to sleep again." Erin is describing both the sleep problems associated with PAWS and the unusual dreams that Sean Peck talked about earlier.

- **Body out-of-sync.** Kylie Mienke, seventeen (whom you met in chapter 8), described her bout with PAWS this way: "The first year I was clean, my whole body was out of whack! I seemed to get a cold every month. On top of that, I was suddenly so clumsy. It was so bad that my friends started teasing me, calling me Grace." Not only can PAWS throw your immune system into a tailspin, but it can also cause dizziness, imbalance, slow reflexes, and aches and pains.

- **Craving drugs and alcohol.** Sixteen-year-old Cameron Ansler told us, "I'd be doing so great, and then some little crisis would come up in my life, and I'd have this irrational craving to just get high—one drink, one line, one anything—was all I wanted. But I didn't give in. The craving passed quickly if I just didn't let myself dwell on it. I tried to get busy and do other things. If I felt the cravings were really bad, I'd head out the door to an NA meeting or call my sponsor because I knew that the possibility of relapsing, for me, was very real. It's been over two years now, and I'm still clean and sober. I don't get those cravings the same way that I used to." (Though "intense," experts say cravings last approximately seven seconds.)

Six Ways to De-Claw PAWS

Those "claws" can seem pretty intimidating. So how do you de-claw PAWS? Besides waiting it out—knowing "this too shall pass" and there is every probability that eventually all the symptoms will disappear—how do you manage the symptoms? Here are six things you can do to cope with this stage and move beyond PAWS.

1. **Talk to someone.** Talk about what you are going through, as well as how you're feeling (your symptoms). This can help you make it through "the moment." You would also be well-advised to talk to your chemical dependency counselor. You might even ask your parents to help you schedule a visit to your family doctor and make certain to follow his directions for dealing with the symptoms and getting your health back on track. Go to your parents, your twelve-step sponsor and the members of your recovery "support group" and let them know what you are going through. Sometimes just talking this way makes you aware of things you wouldn't realize otherwise. It can also give you a more realistic view of what's going on.

2. **Journal.** Keep a journal about what is happening with you, and how you're feeling, day by day. How does it compare to other episodes? What are the similarities? What are the differences? Write about what changes you could make in how you're dealing with the symptoms. This is your own reference guide for dealing with future symptoms. Keeping

track of your feelings and behaviors allows you to see your progress, as well as to come up with coping strategies that work best for you. What's more, it gives you another opportunity to process all the emotions that are coming up. When you do this processing in writing, you are able to keep going until you come up with solutions.

3. **Learn how to manage stress in healthy ways.** When life seems particularly stressful, it's time to be extra good to yourself. Get adequate rest, eat properly and get the exercise your body needs to burn off tension. The important thing is that you work diligently at learning to cope effectively with stress and stressful times, so that you don't resort to chemicals to escape the pressure.

4. **Practice your relaxation skills.** Listen to soothing music, talk with your friends and hug your pet. Learn to laugh and play. Relaxing and having fun reduces stress. Relaxation can even produce stress-reducing hormones.

5. **Work on the spiritual aspects of your recovery.** Learn about and practice the spiritual principles of your twelve-step program. If you're not working the steps, take the time to find out what they are and how they work (more on this in chapter 13). You will find a copy of the twelve steps in the back of this book. Faith is a potent source of comfort in times of duress; whatever your faith, apply its doctrines and meaning to your life. This can help you persevere in tough times and give you the strength to stay committed to live drug-free.

6. **Vow to hang in there.** As each day passes, chances are you are getting closer to the day when your PAWS will fade away. There's no cure for the disease of addiction, but you can put it in "remission"—as long as you work on your recovery. Especially because you've used, it's important

that you act as your own taste berry. Encourage yourself to stay in recovery and face life one day at a time. Don't compare yourself with others. Yes, you probably have lost time in your studies and other parts of your life, but just stay focused on doing your best for today. Look at how far you've come in your recovery, and continue to stay clean and sober—one day at a time.

Questions to Think About

♥ What symptoms of PAWS have you experienced?
♥ What have you done to cope with PAWS?
♥ What do you do to overcome trouble concentrating?
♥ How are you "extra good to yourself"?
♥ What are your favorite techniques for "hanging in there" when you are faced with stress and emotional overwhelm?

15

Overcoming Shame: Have You Done Some *Awful* Things?

"Sick" Secrets

I'd always been such a "nice" girl. I got good grades in school, and I never had to work very hard for them. Learning always came easy to me. Most people would say I was smart—at least as far as they could see from my grades. People described me as "sweet," and I was "the quiet one" in my group of friends. For anyone who knew me, I was one of the last people they would think would get into drugs.

I'm not really sure why I started, but I guess it had something to do with the fact that I never really felt like I fit in. I felt so ordinary. So plain. So boring. It seemed to me that practically everyone at my school was so together, so with it, so "happening." I knew that some of the kids were "experimenting" with drugs—even the cool kids. So when I saw a couple of girls drawing in on a joint—and when, upon seeing that I'd seen them do this, they offered me some—I took them up on it. So that's how I started. I thought that maybe if some of the "in" kids saw me as someone who smokes a joint now and then, they'd accept me as one of their crowd. So I smoked when I could, which really meant whenever I was offered a hit. But you can't always be a mooch—pretty soon you've got to offer some back. So that's when I started buying a little from those who had it to sell. Hanging with this crowd led to smoking more often, and pretty soon I was one of the crowd—well, at least "that crowd."

I soon learned "that crowd" was smoking more than pot. The truth is, they were experimenting with a lot of different drugs. And soon I was, too. One thing led to another, and it wasn't long before I was also introduced to smoking heroin. After that, well, let's just say that I no longer had feelings of being "left out or boring." Little did I know that my using would take me deep into problems that far surpassed those of feeling ordinary, plain or boring.

Not only did heroin make me sneaky, but also a liar and a thief (along with other not-so-admirable things). I did things I never would've done if I weren't using. I changed so much—but when I was using, I didn't really notice. For example, when I was younger, I remember being with some friends one day after school. We'd gone to the store for some fingernail polish, and while we were there one of the girls suggested we make a game out of seeing who could shoplift the most lipstick. I thought I'd have heart failure! I never took a thing—not a lipstick, not a pack of gum, nothing in my whole life. I'll always remember how panicky I felt about being involved with something as terrible as stealing. Well, after I started using drugs, stealing didn't scare me nearly so much as the thought of not being able to get high. If my conscience started to object, it was quickly silenced by the overriding, overwhelming need to use. Stealing was simply a means to an end: to get the drugs I now "needed."

The first time I stole something in the name of drugs was from my locker mate. She had taken off her necklace and put it in her locker so she wouldn't lose it playing volleyball in physical education class. The necklace had been a gift from her grandmother. In my mind that necklace became no more than my next high. I took it and traded it over the noon hour for my heroin for the day. When my locker mate discovered the necklace missing, she was hysterical—and even indignant that someone could've gone into "our locker" and done such a thing. Of course I played surprised and dumb, just like I did when my mother began commenting on the money missing from her purse. I always felt bad about going into my mother's purse and taking her money. She didn't have much left over from her paycheck to spend on herself; there was always a bill that needed paying or one of us kids who needed something. But then I also needed something: drug money. So I'd steal from my own mother. Of course I told myself I would put the money back when I got some money. But on some level I must have known that I never had money because I didn't work or get an allowance, so unless I used my lunch money, I didn't have any. Even though I felt really bad about stealing from my mom, that didn't stop me from taking money from her purse again—and again. Of course, I lied when she asked me about it—I even suggested that my older brother's friend who always came over to our house was probably the one who took it. Soon my mother started hiding her purse.

I became like an opportunistic parasite—always looking for my chance to get something I could steal to trade for drugs, be it a jacket on the seat of a car with an open window, CDs I could slip into the pockets of my jacket, even tips left on restaurant tables. I stole whenever I could. As I needed more and more drugs, I stole more and more—anything that would get me drugs. Every material thing I saw was just measured into money to be traded for my drugs.

The ultimate came when a police officer showed up at the door of my class and escorted me to my locker where I had stored a couple of stolen items—a watch and ring from a woman who was our neighbor and a leather jacket from the coatrack at Denny's Restaurant near my house. I was arrested on the spot and taken to jail. Wouldn't you know the bell rang and everybody was in the halls on their way to their classes. So everyone in the world saw me being "escorted" away by the police. That was really embarrassing. But not as bad as the feeling I had when my parents showed up at the jail to bail me out. That was the most awful feeling. I mean, I was sick to my stomach.

Seeing the tears in my father's eyes was absolutely heartbreaking. I'd only seen him cry one other time, and that was at my grandpa's funeral. Seeing my parents—people who probably had never been in a jailhouse in their entire lives—there to bail out their daughter was a sickening feeling for me. I'd have to say it was the most terrible I'd ever felt about anything in my entire life. It was also sobering: I'd let them down. I'd let myself down. I'd let everyone down. I felt like the lowest form of life. Actually, I felt even worse than that. Because of my drug use, I coaxed others to use drugs as well. Some of those I encouraged had never used before. It was at my hands that some have now fallen to drugs—and become prisoners to chemical addiction. Can you imagine what I think of myself for not only hurting myself, but others, too? How had I fallen so low?

My parents took me to get help. I was placed in a twenty-eight-day inpatient treatment center, and after that, I went to a ninety-day outpatient "rehabilitation" center. At the treatment center I was told to go to twelve-step meetings. I started going to them regularly, and I'm still going to them today. Now I'm back in school, but it's a new school—where kids who have had problems with drugs are working on repairing their grades and trying to get their GEDs. Some are just working on getting back their study habits! I've learned drugs really can wreck your brain!

It's been over eleven months now since I've used. I'm working hard to get back on track. I still find it unbelievable that I became someone who did drugs. And I'm still haunted by all the terrible things I did to pay or trade for my drugs. When I think about my locker mate, I think about the special necklace her grandmother had given her. Knowing how precious the gift was to her, I just feel so sleazy about it. There are nights when I lay awake and try to think of a way to get it back—but I know it's long gone. And it's irreplaceable. It's terrible to know that you've done something to hurt someone that can never ever be repaired. I haven't actually told her I'm the one who took it, but I'm sure she knows. And I know one day I'm going to have to say those words—and apologize. I just want to have something to offer her besides an apology. Words seem so empty when your actions have been so hurtful. And while I've told my mother I'm really sorry for taking her money (and she said she forgave me entirely), still, sometimes I'll look at her and think of everything she's done for me and how she's always been there loving me. Then I'll just want to cry, because I'll feel so bad that I ripped her off so many times. My dad's tears still haunt me. I've told my parents how sorry I am. I'm offering them more than empty words by showing them all new actions. I try to make up for all that I've done to them by helping them out more at home and always remembering to be respectful, even when I'm feeling grouchy. How can I make up for hurting them the way I did? It's such a long way back when you've done awful and terrible things.

I feel like I really humiliated them. One more humiliation to add to my own for having been taken from class by the police. Whenever I think about them seeing me locked up by the police, I think of how embarrassing—and scary—that must have been for them. Even when I'm out in the community with my parents or at the mall with friends, I sometimes wonder how many of the kids from school are around, looking at me and thinking, or whispering to the person sitting next to them, "That's the girl who got arrested right out of her fourth-period class for being a druggy and a thief."

I'm getting better. For a long time, I was so depressed that I felt physically sick over it all. Then in a twelve-step meeting I learned that "we're only as sick as our secrets," and that an important step in getting well—in moving on, "recovering"—is to not keep our "secrets" in the dark, but rather, bring them to light—into the open. I learned that talking about your deep dark experiences—bringing your "secrets" out in the open—is the first step for getting beyond your feelings of being ashamed for all the things you've done. So I knew I wanted to take this step toward getting well. I was tired of the burden of my thoughts, so tired of being sorry, so tired of feeling helpless and just plain like a "bad" person. So I knew that I had to tell somebody about everything I'd done. Sure it was no big secret that I was a thief, but no one knew the extent of it. No one had heard it from me. And no one at treatment or the twelve-step meetings knew about my past. All they knew was that I wanted to stop using drugs.

At first, I thought I could just act like it had never happened, and I'd never have to talk about it—or else I would talk about it when I was good and ready. At the treatment center, and also at the meetings, that time had finally come. I began to talk about everything, from stealing to lying to the shame I felt over even using in the first place. I was surprised by the "freedom" I felt having shared it, and even more surprised that no one looked down on me or thought less of me—which was something I also worried about. Then I learned how the separation was "easy" because I did those things when I was using: I wasn't "a bad person trying to get good," I was "a sick person trying to get well." Everyone at the meetings had a "story" to tell—surprisingly, some were "worse" than mine.

When you work through the steps in a twelve-step program, you are supposed to find a sponsor to give you direction on how to work them, and your sponsor is supposed to "have what you want" so far as good recovery goes. Mine definitely has that kind of recovery. So when I was having such a hard time with my feelings of shame, I talked to my sponsor about it. She said I needed to give myself a break. She also told me that she had done things every bit as terrible when she was using drugs, and then she told me about some of them. Somehow seeing her and what a good life she is living and how kind and compassionate she is, and knowing she'd once done the same things I had done for drugs, made me feel better. It gave me hope. Sharing my secrets really did help.

When I get those feelings of shame now, I talk to my counselor or my sponsor. They both remind me I'm not doing those things today. I don't know if or how I can ever make it all right—to my mom and to all the other people I stole from. I can't ever get my locker mate's necklace back, but I have to find some way to make it up to her. My sponsor tells me I'm not on that step yet; she says to wait until I get there, and then I'll be able to figure out how to make amends. For now, she says I should work on being a good daughter and friend and helping the newcomer in the twelve-step program.

I don't even want to think about having to face people and make amends. And I guess I don't have to today. Although it's nowhere near as bad as it once was, I still feel guilt and shame. Still, the more I follow my sponsor's suggestion and try to be a good daughter and friend and to help the newcomer, the less painful it seems. Hopefully, one day I'll have it all behind me—but that day hasn't arrived yet.

Holly Nichols, 17

Have You Done Things
for Which You Are Truly Ashamed?

Holly felt remorse for having "become someone who did drugs" and for all of the things she did while using. It's understandable that she feels bad about the things she did and the pain her actions caused others. Twelve-step programs label the consequences of those actions "the wreckage of the past," and coping with the feelings of shame this causes is known to be part of "dealing with the *wreckage* of the past." How do we get well and move beyond the "wreckage" of the past? Bringing your "secrets" out into the open—disclosing what drugs you used and what you did in order to use—means the truth is no longer a secret. The shame you feel is let out of its dark cage, and now you are free to work on making amends—toward self and others—instead of simply dwelling in the pain of feeling ashamed.

A healthy amount of remorse or guilt shows an awareness of having done something that goes against your values. This can create positive change and keep your actions in line with your values. So it is good and productive. Shame, on the other hand, is counterproductive. It doesn't create positive change and, instead, it eats away at you, constantly reminding you that you are, in the words of thirteen-year-old Dayanna Karnes, "dirty." So "coming clean"—talking about those things that shame you—is an important step to removing the shame that keeps you from getting well.

This is true even for the shame you feel over things that aren't your "fault"—the shame that isn't about anything you've done. This shame happens when someone has been abused, either verbally, physically or sexually, or is made to feel they are not loved, special or worthy. Sixteen-year-old Martina Strickland understood this when she explained, "My father was an alcoholic, and ever since I was a little kid I was so embarrassed by the way he acted. He would come home drunk and call me all sorts of names. My mother couldn't really protect me; he was calling her names, too. I always hoped it would get dark before he got home, so none of the other kids in the neighborhood would see him. But there were days when he was home earlier, and they did see him. I thought that there must be something wrong with me to have a father like him, and of course there must be something wrong with me if he called me such awful names. My mother finally left him, but ironically, his going away didn't make the shame go away."

The kind of shame Martina is describing can be every bit as painful as shame for something you have actually done wrong. If it isn't dealt with, it can also lead a recovering person back to using to escape the painful feelings it creates. So, no matter what kind of shame you're feeling, it must not remain a secret—because all secrets need to be brought out in the open.

Ten Ways to Let Go of Shame—
And Get On with Your Life

So you've shared your secrets, but you find every now and then you're reminded of the past, and a wave of shame floods the moment, sometimes even haunting you for days. Now what? We have a friend, a counselor in the field of recovery, who is fond of telling the story about a man who was dealing with shame over his mistakes, so he went to a minister and begged, "Please tell me why I can't get over this." The minister took him to the window and pointed over to the bell tower of the church and said, "Do you see the bell tower? Each hour, our church custodian goes to that bell tower and pulls the rope. As long as he pulls the rope, the bell rings. But then, even when he stops pulling the rope, the bell continues its motion for awhile and it still rings." Have you ever felt that way—as if the shame is still there, even though you've "let go" of it?

Here are ten suggestions to help you stop pulling that rope and make certain that you've let it go. (Throughout this book, you will learn others ways to "let go of the rope.")

1. **Talk to someone about your shame.** Talking to someone (whether it be a professional counselor, your sponsor, your parents or someone else you trust with your feelings) about your recurring feelings of shame can continue to take the power out of the shame. Remember, that is how shame "dies"—making sure it doesn't remain a secret, you bring it

out of the dark and into the light of honesty. This way, its power is taken away, and you are freed to move on to other issues of learning to live life clean and sober. Sharing your shame can be very difficult. It may mean that you will need to let go of fear and learn new levels of honesty and humility—but doing so will "free" you in a way that will allow you to now live sober and clean. The important thing is to not feel that you have to go it alone. We urge you to talk with a professional, who can help determine how you can best deal with your issues and get well.

2. **Forgive yourself.** It's been said, "Forgiveness is the ability to release the concept of a better past." You can't change the things that you've done in your past. Forgiving yourself means accepting your past and learning from it—and then doing those things to get on with a better present. How do you go about forgiving yourself? You get busy creating a new reality—you stay busy doing positive things. And you draw upon your faith, asking your Higher Power to help you forgive yourself.

3. **Give yourself time.** Forgiving and forgetting takes time, so allow yourself the time to forgive yourself. Consider that the things you've done to feel shameful about are "wounds" on your heart. Like all wounds, they take time to heal. The bell continues its motion and rings for awhile after the rope is no longer being pulled. The same holds true when you're working with many painful feelings and memories in your life. It takes awhile for the energy of those painful feelings, such as shame, to disappear.

4. **Don't "beat yourself up" by dwelling on your mistakes.** Don't entertain those thoughts that "beat you up"—let go of the rope. If you're holding on to the rope, the shame is still there weighing you down. If you are holding on to

thoughts of how awful you are and what awful things you have done, you're still ringing that bell. It's not going to slow down on its swing while you're still giving it energy. If you want to clear away the shame, you have to free your mind. To do this you need to stop beating yourself up by replaying the past in your own mind—shaking that finger of blame at yourself and scolding "if only . . ." and "I should've . . ." Play a new tape, one that shows all the good things you are doing today. (More on this in the following suggestions.)

5. **Do a "memory exchange"—bring new thoughts to mind.** When you practice self-forgiveness, healing happens in your life. Self-forgiveness (as well as forgiveness of others) can be a memory exchange, meaning you replace the painful memory with a more positive one. Self-forgiveness means that you release your attachment to a negative memory. Changing the way you think about something is a good way to stop focusing on the painful memories and the "what ifs." Instead, choose to think about what you've done that is good. You can start by thinking about the change you are creating in your life. How do you do this? Whenever you start dwelling on those memories that cause you shame, visualize a bright yellow neon street sign glaring with huge red letters that are blinking "STOP!" at you. See it as your signal to stop thinking about the painful memories. Once you have it in an imaginary place, find a new memory to think about instead. As you find that memory, visualize the letters on the street sign as they switch to a bright green "GO!" Then think of all the new memories you're creating—and all the future memories you hope to create.

6. **Look for the positive lessons you have learned.** It can sound "ironic" to think that there have been positive

lessons, but probably you've learned a lot—and much of it is useful in terms of now wanting to get back on track and live your life free from alcohol and chemical use. Ask yourself: What have I learned? For example, have I learned to be a more compassionate, tolerant and understanding person? Have I learned a new respect for my mental and physical health? What have I learned about the cunning and deceptive effects of drugs, and how has this made me commit to my personal growth in recovery? The answer to any and all of these questions can show you a new way to view your past that can help put an end to your shame. You can be thankful for having learned—or solidified—these values. Thank yourself for "getting it" and moving on to better things, richer for the hard-won experience.

7. **When the time is right, make amends to those you have harmed.** As mentioned by Holly Nichols in this chapter's opening story, it takes more than empty words to show people you are sorry for having hurt them. A spoken apology is a good beginning, but you'll want to make it up to them with your actions. If you've hurt them financially or taken something of monetary value, you should make that right whenever possible by replacing the item or the value of the item. If this isn't possible, knowing you are willing to do so and being an honest, giving person is a step you can take until you are able to make financial amends. Remember, you have to wait for the right time to make amends. Don't rush out and try to fix everything right away. You need to be working on strengthening your recovery to make certain you don't create new "wreckage." Before making any serious amends it is important to check with an advisor, such as your counselor, sponsor or a parent. He or she can help you decide what kind of amend is appropriate and the best way to deliver it.

8. **Journal and highlight your new beginnings, new habits and new actions.** Journaling is a powerful tool to help you be more aware of all you've learned and how far you've come in life. Set aside a time each day to journal. It can also help you focus on the solution. You can write about your shame to help give you perspective and take the power out of your painful feelings. Writing about what your past has taught you and how it can benefit others will also ease the pain of shame. It's also important to write about all your new beginnings, all the new habits you are developing in your life, all the new actions you are taking. You can move past the "shameful" memories as you write about those new memories you are building—and all the positive change you are creating in your life. Each night, try to make the time to write about the things you have done in the day that make you feel good about yourself.

9. **Remind yourself of the goodness of being human.** One of the most effective ways to increase your self-respect and make you feel better about yourself is to do good things. Helping others is one way to do this. Doing positive things reminds us that we are good human beings after all. It also reminds you how good it feels to be human. Eighteen-year-old Lonnie Virgil tells us how this worked for him: "I felt ashamed of a lot of the things I did using. I was always stealing, always just looking out for myself. That really bothered me once I was clean. One day I heard that a hospital in my area needed volunteers to bring their pets to the hospital so children undergoing chemotherapy sessions could hold the animals while taking an injection of chemo. Holding a friendly animal helped ease the burning and pain of the treatment for the child. My dog is a real people-lover, and I thought it would be great to help out. So I volunteered to take my dog to the center. I wouldn't

trade those hours for anything. Now I do it on a weekly basis. When I see those little kids fighting for their lives it really touches me. Especially, when I think about how busy I used to be nearly killing myself. Helping others makes me feel more connected to life. It reminds me how important life is and how meaningful it can be. It's great for my sobriety and for me. I sure feel different about myself these days—I don't feel so ashamed of my past anymore. After all, the present is something I can be very proud of."

10. **Connect with your Higher Power.** Reminding ourselves that we are part of something far bigger and more grand than ourselves is a comforting feeling. Use your faith to comfort you in connecting with that Higher Power. Whether through reading, prayer or appreciating nature—nurture your faith. By this faith you can be lifted from your world into one that is so much greater and grander. There's little time for shame in this greater, grander space—and it is a great place to build new memories—memories that affirm the fact that you are worthy, there is a purpose for your existence, and of course, that you are not alone in coping with any painful feelings or problems that come up when living life without the use of drugs.

Seven Suggestions for Where to Safely Share Your Secrets

As you read in the previous section, one of the first and most basic steps in overcoming shame is letting go of the secrecy around it. Sharing your secrets is perhaps the most important step when it comes to moving past your shame. So find someone you can trust and get those secrets off your chest—out of the dark and into the light. Here are some suggestions for who you might go to for this:

1. **A trusted best friend.** Maybe you have a best friend with whom you've shared a lot, including your deepest, darkest secrets. If so, that's great. Having a friend who listens, understands and still cares about you can offer comfort that helps you move past your shame. What's more, if you're comfortable enough to be completely open, you can process your shame out loud and come to new insights about yourself and your mistakes. **A word of caution:** Don't let being able to talk to a friend stop you from getting professional help. Though a teen friend helps you feel accepted and as if your shame isn't the end of the world, your friend doesn't have the skills that a trained professional will have in being able to help you "go the distance" in moving through shame and on into the other phases of recovery—learning to live life free from alcohol and chemical use.

2. **Your mom or dad.** If you have a strong bond with your parents, you can go to them to share those things that cause you to feel ashamed. Of course, this will depend on the kind of relationship you have with your parents. They've known you all your life, and no doubt love you for better or for worse. Parents almost always put the well-being of their children first over their own fears and insecurities, and will do all they can to help you. So if you have the kind of relationship with your parents that assures that you will be received with compassion, you may want to share your feelings of shame with them.

3. **Your school counselor.** Many school counselors are trained to work with teen issues. Providing a safe ear to listen and sound direction to follow, your counselor may be a good source with whom to share your secrets. If she feels your

problems and concerns are beyond her training or expertise, your counselor will know where to refer you to someone else who can help.

4. **Treatment-program counselor.** If you have been through treatment or are considering it, your substance-abuse counselor is someone who is trained to work with people with addictions and is able to help you work through your feelings of shame.

5. **Therapists or other mental health care professionals.** Most licensed therapists have been trained to help you process and cope with matters such as shame. If you don't know how to find a therapist, your school counselor or community hotlines may be able to direct you.

6. **Minister or clergyperson.** Sometimes your minister or clergyperson can offer a forgiving and compassionate source of support as you share the reasons for your shame. He or she can also refer you to other sources of help and support in your desire to move past your shame in order to stay clean and sober.

7. **Your sponsor.** If you're active in a twelve-step program of recovery, you are already connected with a sponsor. Most sponsors are sponsors because they have chosen to be a part of another person's recovery. Giving back to others what was so freely given to them helps them in their own recovery. So don't hesitate to ask for your sponsor's help. Most sponsors who have long-term clean time or sobriety are working a diligent twelve-step program of recovery themselves. Providing they have already worked the twelve steps on their own shame, they can share their own "experience, strength and hope" and guide you through working the steps to help deal with your feelings of shame. Having dealt with the shame for their actions while using, they are able to be compassionate with you as you cope with your feelings.

No matter who you choose, remember that the important thing is to share with those who will be compassionate, nonjudgmental and able to help you forgive yourself. If you find yourself wanting to avoid this altogether, keep in mind that sharing your shame and the reasons that caused it is part of the "house cleaning" that it takes to stay clean and sober. By "housecleaning" we mean setting yourself, your thinking, your feelings, your behaviors and your life in order. It means sweeping away the shame and the old behaviors that don't serve you and replacing them with new ideas and new spiritual principles to base your actions on as you create positive new memories.

Never forget that each day is an opportunity to learn and grow—to be the best "you" that you can be. Choosing to live and look at life this way leaves far less time for crippling shame. Shame was part of the problem, and today you are living in the solution. Having fearlessly exposed your secrets, you are living in the light of a brighter present and future.

Questions to Think About

- ♥ Who are three people you can trust with any of your secrets? What is it about each of these people that makes you feel that you can trust them? Have you told any of these three any of your deepest fears and secrets, or about the things for which you feel shame? Why or why not?
- ♥ How have your mistakes helped you to be a better person? In what ways are you "better"?
- ♥ What have you done for which you've felt ashamed? Did you "forget" as well as forgive yourself?
- ♥ What is the difference between forgiving and forgetting?

Unit V

You've Relapsed—
Now What?

*If you always do what you've always done,
then you'll always get what you've always got.*

—Source Unknown

*We meet ourselves time and again
in a thousand disguises on the path of life.*

—Carl Jung

*You gain strength, courage and confidence by
every experience in which you really stop
to look fear in the face.*

—Eleanor Roosevelt

16

Relapse: How to Learn from Yours and Avoid a Repeat Performance

Lost Love x 2

"But we always have so much fun together, and the prom is just a month away, and I don't want to go with anyone but you—I don't know what else to say—I don't want us to break up, so please don't say you want to break up," I told Keith, who had been my boyfriend for over six months.

"I just need some space," he replied. "I'm sorry. You're really special and being with you has been great. I don't want to hurt you, but you know that my parents even said we were too young to be so serious, and well, maybe they're right. I think we should date other people for a while. And who knows, someday we might get back together. But for now, I need to break things off. Please don't be upset, and please don't be mad at me. I am sorry. . . ."

And with that, he backed off the steps of the porch in front of my house where the two of us had been sitting and walked away. Just like that, he walked out of my life.

I heard that he'd gone out with Tabitha Harris that Friday, but it was something I just wouldn't let myself believe. But then on Saturday, when my friend Annie talked me into going to our other friend LaToya's party, in walked Keith with Tabitha. My heart dropped, I could feel the blood drain from my face as my feet and fingers went all tingly—I felt sick to my stomach. He was really going out with her. They walked together hand-in-hand through the house and into the backyard where there was music playing and kids were dancing on the patio. I could feel people staring at me to see what my reaction was going to be. I wanted to run somewhere and curl up and cry—but I wasn't going to cry here in front of all these people. I felt so humiliated. I hated that I had really believed that Keith and I had something so special, when here he was with someone else—already. I told Annie I needed to leave and she said, "Sure." But I didn't want to go home and be all alone, so I said, "Let's go down to the beach." When we got there, we ran into some kids from our school who hang out down by the pier every weekend. They were drinking, as usual. I hadn't drunk in more than a year—I was in recovery and proud of it—but when they offered me a beer that night, I reached out and took it. Annie looked shocked, but she didn't say anything to stop me. I guzzled that first beer and a couple of others, too, blaming it on trying to drown out the pain of my lost love.

After that night, I didn't just feel awful about myself because Keith dumped me. I felt awful about myself for relapsing. So I kept on drinking for another few weeks, knowing that I was going to undo all that I'd put in place—and quite possibly sink to the low I'd worked so hard to get out from under.

Going back to that first AA meeting after my relapse wasn't easy. I felt so ashamed and embarrassed. I was a "newcomer" all over again—after having one year, two weeks and three days of recovery! I'd started drinking and suffered some terrible consequences. Some of my friends from the meetings had called me "the kid wonder" because I got sober and I stayed that way. I was the one who was always there for the new teens coming in to the program: the role model, the person who reached out to them and told them the program works even when you're young. But now I'd relapsed. I felt like my whole identity changed. How could this have happened to me?

But of course, I know how it happened—and it was all so predictable.

I had grown "complacent" in my recovery. I had Keith—an awesome guy who didn't drink or use and never had. I guess I thought I was "all that" and more, and I slowly started to let my recovery take a backseat to my social life. I had a very busy schedule of events each month besides school: dances, school games, trips to the mall, parties, hiking and the beach. There wasn't really time for meetings. There also wasn't time for step work, at least written step work. Who had time to write? My sponsor said there were things that were supposed to be done in writing, but I'd put her off.

Then I wasn't going to meetings, and I wasn't talking to my sponsor, either. But I didn't really see it as a problem. I had a full life. I reasoned that there was every chance that I'd outgrown my alcoholism. Besides I had Keith, a really great boyfriend, and he was all I needed out of life. The thing is I started to become more and more irritable—it was always someone else's fault, and I usually had to let the person know about it. Sometimes it was Keith's fault, and I felt it was my duty to let him know that. Well, soon enough, I obviously wasn't "all that" to him anymore— since he broke up with me. I was devastated. My heart felt like it had been broken to the point where it would never heal. I was sick to my stomach, and I couldn't sleep at night. But I held out hope for those first few days, thinking maybe he'd change his mind—until I saw him with Tabitha. Then I knew for sure that I had lost the perfect guy in the world for me. I was sure I'd never love again. I was also sure I'd never hurt this way before in my life, and I didn't want to keep hurting that way.

That's when I completely forgot that it was the very first drink that would bring me back to the utter devastation I'd known before I got sober. I forgot there was no such thing as one drink for me. I forgot that alcohol was never a solution to my pain—it always brought me more pain. I forgot how hard it had been to get sober in the first place. I forgot to ask my Higher Power for help—I forgot all the tools I'd once known so well. And I went to the pier and took the first drink that was offered to me and proceeded to get drunk. Fortunately, I felt so awful after just a few weeks of this that I called my sponsor. She came over to take me to a meeting.

So I'm back to doing my sobriety "one day at a time"—like they say, "We only have today." I have to put aside my ego and embarrassment and go to ninety meetings in ninety days. I know my relapse was predictable. I did all the wrong things. It didn't come out of nowhere. I quit going to meetings, calling my sponsor, working a program. I let my lost love with Keith lead to lost love for myself: I guess that makes my loss of love times two. I may lose other guys in the future, but now I'm committed to my love for myself—which means, always putting my recovery first.

Kathleen Griffin, 17

What Is Relapse?

Relapse means *a return to using or drinking after having a time of abstinence and recovery.* When you relapse, it's easy to feel terrible about yourself, just as Kathleen confessed to feeling. You may think you just can't get this recovery thing right. You may wonder how this could've happened to you. Take some comfort in being assured that while relapse doesn't ever have to be a part of recovery, it often is. What's more, a relapse can be that wake-up call that leads you to work more seriously and diligently on your recovery.

When you first get free of drugs and alcohol, there can be such a sense of sheer relief. You made it! You broke out from under the powerful jaws of being chemically dependent—and how it changed your life to make using your goal for the day and as a way to get through the day. Many people think that recovery is simply a matter of not using alcohol or drugs. They may think that long periods of abstinence mean you are no longer an addict. And so when a person uses again, relapse is not only a disappointment, but considered a sign of failure. These notions are far too simplistic.

As you read in chapter 11, recovery is the goal, not just abstinence. There may be times when a relapse can be the experience that helps you commit—once and for all—to live drug-free. In chapter 9 you read about "hitting bottom" and how it's possible to have an experience that convinces you it's time to give up using. But sometimes we forget how "awful" that bottom was, and in the face of our current problems and challenges, turn yet again to alcohol or drugs as a way of coping (or we use again thinking it will be "okay, just this once"). Relapse may be "just that one drink," or it may be a drug or alcohol binge of days or weeks or months—and some people never make it back from a relapse. Some may end up in jail or even die from an overdose.

While relapse is serious, it does not have to mean "failure." Relapse can be the hammer that hits you over the head and the turning point in your recovery. It can awaken you to the necessity for putting your recovery first and foremost in your life, knowing that if you don't, you may invite experiences that range from living the misery of a drug-addicted life to the loss of your life because of it. So relapse can be what triggers your true commitment to forever "work the steps" and walk the path of recovery. Of course, recovery always requires rigorous honesty, and this includes being honest about your relapse. Since admitting you've relapsed is the first step in returning to work on your personal program of recovery, it is crucial for you to be honest about your relapse. So don't let feelings of shame or embarrassment for having relapsed cause you to either be down on yourself or hide from those who can help you in your recovery. Instead, stand up, brush yourself off and get back to the work of recovery.

Seven Ways Relapse Begins Before You Use

Understanding how your relapse happened, when it started and what you could've done differently should help you not to suffer a "repeat performance" and relapse once again. Even so, you should know that relapse begins long before that first drug or drink. A relapse doesn't usually just happen out of nowhere— even if it felt that way to you. Relapse first starts with a change in the way you look at things, a change in attitude and actions. You return to that distorted thinking you had when you were using—probably not so out of focus as when you were in the midst of the chaos of your using, but out of focus, nonetheless. Your attitude—well, it becomes terrible! Your emotions are all over the place, and you can return to old "using behaviors." Three of the most common of those behaviors include:

- Dishonesty (you'll be back to rationalizing for your bad attitude and behavior).
- Arguing and expecting too much of other people.
- Complacency about your recovery and beginning to put less time and effort into it (fewer twelve-step meetings, less "step work" and less connecting with those who support sobriety).

Let's look at some of the relapse attitudes, thinking and behaviors that come before you actually return to "using." A word of caution: While it may be just an "off mood" to feel, think or act these ways on occasion, if the following list of "attitudes" keeps up or grows worse, it can indicate that you are in relapse mode (so you need to take it seriously, talk to a counselor, attend twelve-step meetings and "work your twelve-step program").

Each of the following can signal you are in relapse, even though you haven't used or taken a drink—yet:

1. **"Life is boring, boring, boring—and it sucks."** Life is boring and you've been feeling this way for some time now. You're not sure why—your teachers are fine, so is everything at home, but you're just never satisfied with life or with yourself. Nothing feels like it's quite right. You feel impatient with life, with yourself and everyone else. Nothing seems fun or interesting, and even when you find something that you think might be, you lose interest quickly. What's more, people who are having fun and seem happy with their lives may irritate you.

2. **"I'm way cool: I've got it going on—I'm on top of it all, and I've got the drug thing licked."** You tell everyone you feel great all the time, and your life is darn near perfect—in fact, you're darn near perfect, too. But most important, you know without a single doubt that you will never, ever drink or use drugs again—your problem with drugs and alcohol is a thing of the past.

3. **"What's the use? Nothing ever goes right for me."** You are filled with feelings of sadness—depression. You're not sleeping well and have started avoiding people, often preferring to be alone. Then you're disappointed in yourself. Growing more and more sad, you start to feel like everything is hopeless. You may even have thoughts of suicide, feeling as if you'd like to just end it all.

4. **"Everyone is such a loser—can't anyone get things right?"** First you feel out of sorts—grouchy—but then you become more and more irritable, until you snap and complain about any little thing. You are impatient—no one is doing things

the way you think they should; you feel the need to argue about even small things. You always have to be "right," and someone else has to be "wrong."

5. **"There's so much to do, and I have a zillion things I just have to tell you."** You are hyper, always on the go—way too overactive. Even the way you move is fast, and the way you talk is abrasive. You start to talk and talk and talk—compulsively—but you have absolutely no real interest in what you are saying, and chances are you're not even making any sense.

6. **"Just let me kick back, because I don't have any energy to do anything else."** You are so tired, just plain exhausted, and it's a feeling of being emotionally drained, too. Being that way makes you tense, but you try to cover it up by pretending you're just mellow and calm. When you wake up in the morning, it seems as though you're as tired as when you went to sleep. You may let people know you feel awful, but you become withdrawn. You want nothing to do with anyone or anything.

7. **"I've hurt everyone, and I deserve to be miserable and lonely."** You feel like you're a total loser who's failed at everything. Your feelings of loneliness and depression usually include remorse, guilt and self-pity. You may even feel rejected or abandoned. From one day to the next, you can go from feeling like nobody really cares about you, to feeling like you just have to make up to your friends and family for all the ways you hurt them. When you think about all those "wrongs"—all the pain you caused—you go further and further into feeling all alone because you think you really deserve to be alone. You feel like it is all so hopeless.

Did you see yourself in any of the descriptions above? Often it's a combination of the attitudes and behaviors that you'll be experiencing. For example, you can go from being irritable and grouchy to feeling terribly sorry for yourself. Whatever "relapse modes" you see yourself acting out, you to need start taking action to avoid a complete relapse.

It's very important to realize that just because you find yourself experiencing the feelings, thoughts and behaviors of relapse, it doesn't mean you have to relapse. It doesn't even mean you are going backwards—because each time you catch yourself and "work your program" on these feelings, thoughts and behaviors, you are growing stronger in your recovery. It is part of "growing up" in your recovery and becoming more emotionally mature. As time goes on, you will recognize these relapse modes earlier and earlier and deal with them right away. Those in recovery say that addiction is a "disease of forgetting"—that's what happens with a relapse:

- You forget that first drink or drug starts the vicious cycle of addiction all over again.
- You forget that you can't use in moderation or just use "less harmful" drugs.
- You forget that drugs aren't the solution to the way you feel—they are the problem.
- You forget all the painful consequences of using or drinking.
- You forget all the energy and work that you did to get clean and stay clean up until this point.
- You forget all the good, the beauty, the love, all you have to be grateful for in your life—and how you can lose all sight of it when you use.

Ten Ways to Prevent Relapse

1. **Make your recovery your priority.** Staying clean and sober always has to come first—without it you will have nothing to offer yourself or anyone else. This means you have to make time for twelve-step meetings or any other aftercare or support groups you attend. You need to make time to do the "footwork" involved in "working your program."

2. **Live a day at a time.** Tell yourself you won't use or drink today. Don't worry about whether or not you will tomorrow—it isn't here yet. Just work on getting through the day at hand. If you do this each day, and only for the day, no matter how strong your cravings to use, you will stay clean and sober. If you have to, just stay clean and sober for the hour or the minute. Your using thoughts and feelings will pass; they will not last forever.

3. **Allow others who are working a good program of recovery to share their experience, strength and hope with you.** Take time to listen with an open mind. Sometimes when you are in relapse mode, you are the last person to know it—let others share what they are seeing in you. If you feel like you want to use, call your sponsor right away (or someone who supports your sobriety—your mom or dad, or a counselor with whom you may be working). You have to forever give up the illusion that you can do it alone!

4. **Share with others.** Get a phone list if they have them at the meetings you attend (oftentimes they do). If not, ask for phone numbers of people you respect and connect with at the meetings and use them, most especially when you're in relapse mode. Stay in touch with the people in your support group and be honest with them about how you are feeling and what you are going through.

5. **Go to meetings every day.** Regular twelve-step meeting attendance cannot be overstressed. If you are in your first ninety days of recovery, you should be going to "ninety meetings in ninety days." If you have more than ninety days clean and sober but find you are in "relapse mode," it is time to reinstate that course of action. Whenever you're overcome with a desire to use, get to a meeting!

6. **Journal.** Write about your feelings, what relapse will lead to. You might even share it with your sponsor, your counselor or someone else you trust. The value of writing about what you're experiencing helps you sort things out and commit to healthy ways to cope.

7. **Read inspirational works.** There's a lot of literature written to inspire, strengthen, encourage and educate you. For example, reading the literature put out by twelve-step programs can help you feel less alone; their books include other chemically dependent people's stories and tell you how they made it through the same kind of feelings and challenges with which you are struggling. (Be sure to check out the Suggested Readings section at the back of this book.)

8. **Help others.** Reaching out to help others takes you out of yourself. Addiction is a disease of self-centeredness—so giving to others is an effective tool for combating it. If you look at the attitudes that represent being in a relapse mode, you can see how reaching out and helping others wouldn't leave much time for them. If you're truly giving of yourself to comfort another going through a hard time, there's little room for loneliness, irritability, remorse, boredom or depression.

9. **Pray and work on your connection to a Higher Power.** Sooner or later there comes a time in every recovering

person's life when their relationship and connection to a power greater than themselves is their only defense against relapse. Your Higher Power is always with you to help, guide, strengthen and protect. You may face a moment or circumstance where there is no meeting, you can't reach your sponsor or counselor, and the strength not to use or drink will depend on your spiritual condition. Taking time for prayer (talking to your Higher Power) and for meditation (listening to that Presence) on a regular basis will help prepare you spiritually to get through that moment clean and sober. In the moment of craving, you will know that you can ask your Higher Power to help you get beyond it.

10. **Practice being grateful.** When you remain grateful for being clean, your chances of relapse are nearly impossible. If you connect with that feeling of gratitude, you are not going to want to use in that moment. So the more you are able to stay in that place of gratitude, the more you will avoid relapse.

Questions to Think About

♥ Have you ever relapsed? If so, what do you feel led to your relapse? When exactly did your relapse begin?

♥ How do you catch yourself and change your behaviors when you find yourself in relapse mode?

♥ What area in your program of recovery do you need to strengthen the most in order to avoid relapse?

♥ Have you looked at someone and known they were in a relapse mode? How did you know?

17

Know Where the Monsters Sleep: What Triggers Your Using?

"Sooner or Later, You're Going to Get a Haircut"

I "used" for over a year. It all began when I'd drink and do a little pot mostly on the weekends with my friends. Then I started to use a little during the week, telling myself that I deserved a "hit" after such a long or hard day. Of course, the more I relied on this "excuse," the more I found most all of my days "long" and "hard." So I was probably using more than I'm even admitting. When it comes to that year, I can only say that those last six months I was worn out and worn down. I was always in "trouble" with someone—my parents and teachers for getting lower grades at school; at home for, well, you name it—everything from not ever picking up my room to not ever being in on time; with my friends for either not showing up when I said I would, or "borrowing" things and never returning them. It was like everyone had "had it" with me, and I wasn't surprised; I was pretty sick of myself. I'd tell myself I was going to do something, but I'd never get it done. Or I'd make a promise to do something or be somewhere on time and not be late, and I couldn't even live up to my own wants and needs. So while I hadn't gotten kicked out of school or been arrested or any of those kind of things, I was still able to see that my using was bringing me down.

One day, I decided enough was enough. I went to my parents and told them I'd been using, and that I was ready to stop. They helped me get into a ninety-day outpatient rehab program, where I attended meetings four evenings a week. When I got clean, I felt so relieved—it was like I was finally able to laugh and feel safe again.

Then, when I had just about two months clean and sober, one of my old friends called me and said a group of friends were all going out to the canyon that has this lake and these cool water-falls that Saturday. It was our old "stomping grounds"; we always partied there when the weather was good. We always had so much fun: You could play music as loud as you wanted, and no one for miles around could hear it. We'd dive off these incredible high rocks into the water—it was just the best. I said yes to the get-together in the old canyon.

We all went there the next Saturday. Then, because the weather was warming up, we went there for the next four Saturdays after that. It was the week of my fourth time at the canyon that I "used" again. It also marked the week I stopped attending my rehab.

It wasn't long before I was back to my old ways. The summer came and went, and by the time school began, I was a mess again. I was upset with myself, because it was clear even to me that my disease had crept up on me—then pounced like a fero-cious, merciless monster overtaking my life all over again.

I remember how these "old-timers" at the meetings say, "If you hang around the barbershop, sooner or later you're going to get a haircut." I always knew that it meant if you hang around where everyone's using and drinking, you're going to drink and use, too, but I guess I didn't really believe it. I believe it now—and I intend to stay out of the "barbershop" from now on. I know it won't be easy. But I know that I always need to do what a diabetic (or anyone else with a disease or health condition that needs to be monitored) does: Keep a close watch on the condition of my disease and my recovery every single day.

So I'm going to meetings again, and I've got 120 days clean and sober.

Adam Mason, 16

Four Relapse Triggers—
And How to Avoid Them

As Adam Mason admits, the chance of relapse always exists—unless the chemically dependent person continues to work on how he or she copes with life. When dealing with such a powerful disease, it's wise to know what those in the field of chemical dependency call your "triggers."

"Triggers" are those feelings, emotions, situations, people, places and things that "trigger" (or bring on) a craving, desire or decision to use drugs and alcohol again. This can trigger a response in you: Completely forgetting all the tough times your using brought on, you instead grow nostalgic for those times again. If you give in to those cravings, you face the heartbreak of relapse—of using again. And of course this starts your path of destruction all over again. Knowing your triggers is the first step in staying away from these "monster" lairs so that you don't relapse.

Triggers can be caused by things going on inside of you (feelings and emotions), or by stimuli from the outside (certain people, places and things). What sparks an urgent craving to use in one person might well create absolutely no desire to use in someone else. Regardless of the trigger, the important thing is to know how you can respond in a positive, proactive way once that craving is sparked. In other words, how to cope without giving in to the craving or desire.

Here are four areas where you are most likely to experience "triggers" and possible solutions for dealing with them.

1. **Trigger: Connecting certain scents, sights or sounds with using.** Have you ever heard a certain song or smelled something that reminded you of another time or place, or some person or event? You might literally smell something that makes you want to use, such as someone smoking a cigarette. Adam Mason experienced these feelings when he listened to the music from his partying days in the canyon. **Solution: Don't "romanticize" or "glamorize" your using and drinking.** When this sort of trigger hits, recall all the prices you paid and how hard you worked to get where you are today. Those in recovery have an expression for this: *"Play the tape all the way through."* This expression is considered a "tool" to remind you of all that can happen if you use "even this once." (Remember for the "recovering addict" there is no such thing as one drink or one high.) Be honest with yourself. Remember all the trouble and pain that your addiction can cause, has caused and will cause if you *choose* to release it all over again.

2. **Trigger: Experiencing painful feelings.** These triggers have to do with the "inner senses"—feelings and emotions—feeling sad, upset, angry, frustrated, impatient, confused, anxious, worried.
   Solution: Knowing those feelings that trigger a desire or craving to use drugs or alcohol can help you be prepared to deal with them. First, you need to know that emotions, even unpleasant ones, such as feeling sad, upset, frustrated or worried are a "normal" part of life. And experiencing them, "feeling them," can be a good thing in that they can serve as a siren, an alert telling you it's time for you to take care of yourself. You might want to consider learning skills

to effectively cope (for example, managing stress, frustration and anger). And you may need counseling to help you work to the other side of painful feelings. Maybe you need time to be with a trusted adult you can confide in, one who helps you feel "put back together" and leaves you feeling optimistic again. And avoid setting yourself up for what you know will only bring you heartache. For example, if you know that a former "special someone" is going to be at a party or gathering, and seeing that person still brings on painful reminders of a time together, make plans to do something else instead.

3. **Trigger: Hanging out at places, or with people, who use.** Putting yourself in places or contact with those who use is risky business because it makes using too tempting. Remember the expression, "If you hang around the barbershop, sooner or later you're going to get a haircut."
   Solution: Avoid the places, people and situations where you used. If you're trying to stay sober and clean, don't hang out with those who use or hang out in places where you know others are using. It can be hard to say good-bye to old friends, but your recovery and health have to come first. Just like Adam Mason in this chapter's opening story learned, there will be times when you have to say good-bye to the past and get on with your life.

4. **Trigger: Conflicts with people you can't avoid.** Sometimes, there will be people (family members or classmates or others) you can't avoid, even though they "trigger" a craving or desire to use or drink. Maybe they don't use, but nonetheless, it's the feelings and emotions they bring up for you that are a trigger.
   Solution: Be open to learning new skills, such as how to communicate in open, honest and assertive ways. You

can't avoid some people, some places and some situations, but you can learn to set boundaries for yourself on what you will and won't do. For example, if it's a stepparent, a sibling, your mom or dad, or a classmate who is the "trigger," you may not be able to "avoid" this trigger, and instead may need to learn skills to protect your sobriety in relation to them. If the "problem" is with family, strongly consider that your family might need to get into family counseling to help each member learn healthy ways to relate to each other, as well as to work through unresolved issues of hurt, pain and blame. If your "triggers" are school-related, remember that teachers, counselors and the principal consider it their job to first and foremost protect the emotional and physical well-being of all students—so don't hesitate to turn to these personnel when you feel you need support maintaining your goal of living drug-free.

As you continue to work on yourself and your recovery, you will learn and grow as a person. As you become strong enough in your recovery and in how you feel about yourself, arguments and conflicts with others won't have as much power over you. Experience and applying a twelve-step program of recovery are sure to teach you how to cope more successfully with these issues.

A Checklist to Identify Your Triggers

The best strategy is to be aware of what your "triggers" are so that you can develop a plan of action to cope with them when confronted. Here are some of the "triggers" that many teens list. As you read them over, think about which ones apply to you. Then, at the end of this list, add any others that are unique to you.

❑ Being around friends or other people who are using drugs or alcohol.

❑ Being in places where you once used drugs or alcohol.

❑ Remembering things that have hurt you in the past. (This can be anything you find painful, from the death of a loved one to being "dumped" by your boyfriend.)

❑ Feeling angry at someone else.

❑ Feeling angry at yourself.

❑ Feeling frustrated, or like you or your life are just hopeless.

❑ Feeling worried or anxious, whether justifiably or for no good reason.

❑ Feeling bored, like there's nothing fun to do, especially without drugs and alcohol.

❑ Feeling guilty and ashamed, either of the things you did while using or drinking, or because of other things in your life. (You might even feel just guilty and ashamed of who you are for some unfounded reason.)

❑ Feeling sad or depressed.

❑ Feeling tired or exhausted.

❑ Feeling lonely, whether being alone or in a crowd.

❑ Feeling overwhelmed either by problems or by day-to-day life.

❑ Feeling happy, good about yourself and your life.

❑ Feeling like you have a reason to celebrate—anything from getting an A on a test to having a birthday.

❑ Smelling something that reminds you of drinking alcohol or using drugs.

❑ Hearing a song that reminds you of drinking alcohol or using drugs.

❑ Seeing something or someone that reminds you of drinking alcohol or using drugs.

❏ Being somewhere or in some new situation where you feel like no one would ever know if you used drugs or drank alcohol (just once).

❏ Feeling totally stressed out—for reasons big or small, or for no apparent reason at all.

❏ Feeling sorry for yourself (self-pity).

❏ Putting on weight and feeling like using drugs could help you take it off.

❏ Being in totally new situations where you have to meet new people.

❏ Not going to twelve-step meetings, treatment or counseling sessions.

❏ Having fights, arguments, conflicts or trouble getting along with specific people (such as your parents, your friends or someone you are dating).

❏ Not having any friends who don't use drugs or alcohol.

❏ Feeling out of control in other areas of your life (such as shopping too much, eating too much, dieting too much, overworking yourself or acting impulsively).

❏ Feeling like the best way for you to get attention is to drink alcohol or use drugs.

What else would you add to this list?

❏ _____

❏ _____

❏ _____

The above list is in no way a complete list of possible triggers. We provide it to heighten your awareness in reminding you that you must be absolutely diligent in knowing what "pushes your buttons" and can therefore trigger a relapse for you. By knowing where your "monsters sleep," you can take steps to be certain you do not awaken them.

Six Things You Can Do
to Send Your Monsters Packing

Identifying your "monsters" is one thing, but keeping them at bay is another. You're going to need a find ways to deal with those monsters so they don't wake up your addiction and cause you to relapse. And you're going to need a plan of action for those times when the monsters wake and you are tempted to relapse.

Put simply, you're going to have to develop coping strategies to assure that you stay on the path of sobriety and remain drug-free. Here are some suggestions:

Reach out, get help, understand you don't have to go it alone. You don't have to "do it" on your own nor go it alone, nor should you. Don't feel that you have to always be strong or know what to do in all situations. Always protect your goal for sobriety and recovery from chemical dependency. When you're facing a tough time:

- Reach out and get help. Talk to someone about how you're feeling (your twelve-step sponsor, a friend, your mom or dad, your counselor).
- Go to a twelve-step meeting.
- Get any counseling and supportive services you might need. You can go to your school counselor for this. If she isn't able to help you, she can refer you to someone who has experience working with teens in the field of chemical dependency.
- Pray or meditate (talking or listening to your Higher Power).
- Get involved in volunteer work, service work, giving back.

Avoid temptation. When at all possible avoid dealing with the craving—or the trigger—altogether. If it never comes up, you don't have to cope with it:

- Stay away from places where everyone is drinking or using drugs.
- Hang around friends who don't drink or use.
- Don't hang around with friends who use and drink.
- Steer clear of painful or stressful situations that could lead to drinking or using drugs.

Manage your thoughts. In chapter 18, you'll meet teen Kyla Branson who talks about "the committee" in her head and how she sometimes had to "silence" all who were on the committee. As she learned, "the committee" in your head can get you in a lot of trouble—if you let it. There may be those times when you need to tell "the committee" how it's going to be. Be prepared to learn some skills on how to know when your thoughts are rational or not. There are skills to help you:

- Remember all the trouble using drugs and alcohol caused for you. ("Play the tape all the way through.")
- Use "affirmations"—positive "self-talk"—and say kind, uplifting things to and about yourself.
- Tell yourself "just for today" you won't use or drink.
- Think of all the positive things you've gained in recovery.
- Refuse to make excuses for yourself or your disease.

Find de-stressing activities. While not all stress is negative, it's important to keep your stress in check. So be diligent in doing those things, such as exercising, when your stress levels get high. It's very important to learn healthy ways to cope with your stress. If you're feeling all stressed out and like you just want to escape—even at the risk of your recovery—try healthier tension tamers:

- Take a walk to calm down.
- Listen to music that makes you feel better.

- Take up a new hobby, leisure or sport activity.
- Find a book you'd love to read (and start reading).
- Take a nice hot bubble bath to relax.
- Go watch a beautiful sunset.

Take care of your body. When you aren't feeling good physically, you aren't at your best emotionally or mentally to combat the cravings. Guard your health:

- Begin by making an appointment with your family doctor. See a doctor to determine the status of your health. You may very well need help and support in managing conditions such as severe depression, nutritional deficiencies or infections. Only your doctor will know if these conditions are present, and if they are, how they should be treated.
- Make certain you are eating healthy meals and getting all the nutrients your body needs to sustain your body's stage of growing, as well as to restore the nutrients you may have lost while you were using. Don't just make decisions about what this is. Talk to your school nurse, as well as your family doctor.
- Get the rest and relaxation that you need.
- Make sure to get the sleep you need at night.
- Drink plenty of water; it cleans your system of poisons and helps your body do its job.
- Get regular exercise (such as bicycling or dancing).

Put your thoughts in writing. Writing out your feelings, frustrations, angers, fears and hope for your recovery can be a positive way of managing stress, of coping with and working with and managing the distress signals of relapse. Journaling is a powerful tool to help you work through thoughts, feelings and problems. This means it is a great tool for making progress toward living drug- and alcohol-free. (It can even help you understand if you may need to find professional help in working through some of your feelings and emotions.) The final unit of this book will give you a great opportunity to journal, as it provides you with questions, prompts and space to journal on issues that are important to staying drug- and alcohol-free.

- Journal all about how you're thinking and feeling.
- Make a list of everything for which you are grateful.
- Make a list of all the ways you use denial and rationalization.
- Write about your goals and dreams.
- Write a letter to someone you'd like to thank or to ask forgiveness for a wrong you committed. Or write a letter to yourself. (You can thank yourself for staying clean or forgive yourself for the mistakes you've made.)
- Write a letter of "good-bye" to drugs and alcohol.

Questions to Think About

♥ Do you have a friend who wasn't "good for you"? Did you end your friendship with that person? Why or why not?

♥ What is the feeling or emotion that is hardest for you deal with?

♥ What is the single most important thing you can do to guard your recovery?

♥ What kinds of things do you like to do in order to de-stress?

18

Tools for Traveling the Road of Recovery

How I Silenced "the Committee"

Those first few months when I was clean were really rough. Some days it even seemed like I wrestled with thoughts of wanting to get high all day long. I remember in school one day when I had two big tests in two different classes; all I could think of was how many times before when I had this sort of stress and pressure, I'd just take a hit of pot to sort of mellow out—or at least in my mind I felt that pot helped make things not seem so "extreme." Then I started to think about how I might even have studied better when I was high (which I know isn't true).

I guess I'd used pot as a "crutch" for so long that now, in my moment of "crisis," it seemed to me that a tough spot was easier when I was using. Of course, I know now that's not so, because when I got "conscious," the problem was still there—and if anything, was worse because it had "grown" while I was "taking a break" from reality. Well anyway, I made it through the first test without using, but my thoughts immediately turned to how I could get high during lunch hour so I could face my second test "more relaxed." So I could feel myself fighting my old way of coping. In AA and NA meetings, they call those thoughts "the committee"—they're the voices in your head that tell you all the reasons why you should use. And wouldn't you know it—"the committee" also spends a lot of time telling you how hopeless you are, so there's a tendency to think, *Well, hey, if I'm such a useless hopeless nothin', who cares if I use?*—so you use.

When I got help for getting beyond my drug use, I went into a twenty-eight-day treatment program. Because I was living in a dormlike setting inside a treatment facility for the first twenty-eight days, it made not using easier—since I couldn't just go get drugs. So "the committee" didn't have as much power to persuade me to give up. But when I got out, well then "the committee" turned up the volume. I'm grateful I had twelve-step meetings to help drown out "the committee's" noise!

In Alcoholics Anonymous (AA), I listened to everyone tell how they managed to stay sober day-by-day. I remember a really impressive dude who came to an AA meeting I attended, telling us, "I've learned to take my recovery 'one day at a time.'" Then a teen, who had once been a good athlete and a good student but had really bottomed out by using, said that the same expression was the most important words he'd ever heard. This was followed by a soft-spoken girl who said, "I was running late, my boyfriend had come to pick me up for school, and he was totally stressing about getting me to school on time (because one more tardy and I was going to be tossed out of my first-period class). I tossed my purse on the seat of the car, and when he came to a quick stop, my lipstick rolled out of my purse and the lid came off—and trying to gather it up, it smeared on my new skirt. So there I was, late to class anyway, and with lipstick smeared all over the back of my cream-colored skirt. Because I was frustrated, I'd yelled at my boyfriend, and so he had stormed off mad at me—also because the seat of his car was smeared with lipstick, too. I just wanted to scream—or light up. But I told myself, *This too shall pass,* and I took a deep breath and went to the office to call home so I could change." Everyone, it seemed, always had a story that included how they used clichés to get through the moment clean and sober.

As I was about to learn, I would be doing the same. That's exactly what I did the day I had the tests at school: In the middle of the craving, I told myself, "One day at a time. You only have to get through this one day." Then I reminded myself, "This too shall pass." And it did. I think in those early days the saying that I used the most was: *One day at a time.* I'd remind myself of that every single day. Sometimes I'd remind myself of it many times a day—because if I tried to think about having to stay clean and sober forever, it was just too overwhelming. So when "the committee" started in on all the reasons it would be so great to get high and how I was never going to make it anyway and how everyone else in recovery were big losers, I'd tell myself, *Just for today I'll stay clean.* Then I'd remind myself I only have to do this thing *one day at a time.* Just remembering I only had to stay clean for the day—I didn't have to worry about tomorrow—made me feel like I could manage it. Knowing this would silence "the committee." Then when the next day came, I only had that day to worry about. For me, *one day at a time*— which is a lot like the saying *just for today*—is a great reminder to live in the present and not let myself get caught up in problems that haven't arrived.

Now, I use *one day at a time* in a lot of other ways. When I start worrying about whether or not I'm going to have a date for the prom next June, or when I'm ever going to finish my fourth step and go over it with my sponsor, or how I'm going to buy a used car next year, or whether I'm going to get into a good college, I tell myself: *one day at a time.* It helps me stop worrying about the future, and it still silences "the committee." Then, I just do the best I can, today.

Kyla Branson, 16

"Voice-Overs":
Three Tools for Staying Clean and Sober

If you should suddenly find yourself facing some sudden craving to drink or use—or even confronted with a painful situation you feel could put your recovery at risk—you'll need a "life-line" so you don't relapse. Chapters 16 and 17 were designed to help with just those types of situations, so if you haven't read them yet, do so. This chapter will give you three tools to help you make it through tough moments so that you can maintain your sobriety or "clean date."

1. More Than Clichés: Slogans That Can Help You Cope

Has your mom or dad (or maybe your grandparents or a friend) ever tried to encourage you when you were facing a big challenge by saying, "You can do it!" or "Where there's a will there's a way"? Or maybe after a setback, someone said, "If at first you don't succeed, try, try again." Has someone reminded you that "Rome wasn't built in a day" when you were getting impatient with reaching a goal? Have you ever been directed, "A place for everything and everything in its place"? Where did all those little "sayings" and clichés come from, and why have people been using them forever? Well, no doubt they came from any number of places and sources—and have been handed down from generation to generation. As for why people have been using them forever—you know the old cliché: "There's a reason it's a cliché." In other words, if they didn't work they wouldn't be used so often, nor for so long. They serve a pur-pose—either to encourage, inspire or direct you. They're a quick, easy-to-remember remedy for discouragement or confusion.

As Kyla Branson in this chapter's opening story learned, they are easy little reminders to get you back on track. Snippets of wisdom, they have proven to be effective truths in the lives of countless recovering addicts and alcoholics who have been open to applying them to their lives. Slogans make great tools for your recovery because:

- **They serve as a reminder.** When you need a reminder—and pronto—slogans serve as a reminder that you can make it through this moment without giving in to using.
- **They provide direction.** These simple words can be powerful tools when you're faced with a crisis or just need to know what to do in a given situation. They can provide sound direction at those moments when you're at a crossroads in your recovery.
- **They inspire and encourage you.** There are times when life can seem really tough, times when you could use some inspiration and encouragement. This is especially true in recovery, when you're learning how to live again without the use of drugs or alcohol. These recovery "proverbs" can boost your confidence, offer you hope and give you the lift you need to stay clean and sober for the day.

Here are some slogans that teens say are their most helpful favorites:

"Don't pick up no matter what!" (This is a reminder that if you don't pick up the drug or alcohol, then you won't drink or use drugs. It's as basic as it gets when it comes to staying drug- and alcohol-free!)

"No matter what I'm facing or what position I find myself in, if I'm up against any kind of temptation to use, I use the old 'bottom-line' slogan, 'Don't pick up no matter what!' It's gotten me through some gnarly moments for eighteen clean and sober months now."

Mark Gish, 17

"Keep it simple!" or **"Easy does it!"** (Both are reminders not to complicate or get unnecessarily overwhelmed by the situation at hand.)

"Sometimes I make a huge deal out of something that doesn't have to be a huge deal. It really makes my life complicated. That's when I remind myself, 'Keep it simple,' and take a step back and look at the best way to do what it is that I have to do."

Charles Prather, 17

"Think, think, think!" or **"Play the whole tape through!"** (Both are reminders to think before you act and to consider all the consequences of where your actions could lead you.)

"Sometimes I'll find myself jumping into something I shouldn't. Like I'll get mad and say something I regret; or I'll say I'll go somewhere, like to some party, where it really isn't safe for me to be. So I try to stop and tell myself, 'think, think, think' before I jump into doing something I shouldn't."

Josh Skylar, 15

"Let go and let God" or **"Turn it over."** (Both are reminders that after doing your best, you leave the results up to your Higher Power.)

"When I've done everything I can think of to solve some problem or crisis in my life, instead of driving myself nuts trying to force the solution that I think is perfect, I just remind myself to 'Let go and let God.' Then, knowing I've done my best, I trust things will work out the way they are supposed to work out."

Angelique Miranda, 16

"An addict alone is in bad company." (This is a reminder that one of symptoms of chemical dependency is isolation, and that it's time to stop being alone and spend time with others who are good for your recovery.)

"I'm one of those people who gets myself in trouble if I'm left to myself too long. If I sit around alone, doing nothing—pretty soon I'm apt to come up with some plan because I'm bored or feeling sorry for myself. It's those times when I'm alone like that when I start thinking it might be fun to get high. So whenever I feel myself start slipping into one of those trains of thought, I remind myself, 'An addict alone is in bad company.' Then I call a friend or go to a meeting!"

Blane Weston, 17

"What we can't do alone, we can do together." (This is a reminder that recovery takes the support of others!)

"I tried for months to stop drinking and using. Finally, I started going to twelve-step meetings, and now I'm clean and sober. When I'm having a hard time and want to drink or get high, I remember: 'What we can't do alone, we can do together.' And I get to a meeting, or call my sponsor or someone in my support group and share what's going on with me. It's great to know that other people have faced the same kind of problems and cravings as I have and walked through them clean and sober, and that they're there to help me do the same."

Nicole Shuman, 15

"This too shall pass." (This reminds you that your problems and feelings are going to change, so know that this feeling is momentary.)

"When I'm in a bad mood, or my feelings are hurt, or I'm frustrated or mad, I'll think I'm going to feel that way forever. But I've figured out that all my feelings and moods, even my good ones, are going to change. Sooner or later, I'll be feeling better—or different. And it's usually much sooner than I think it will be while I'm in the middle of feeling awful. If I can remember this, it helps me hold on to my recovery and move through the pain. So whenever I'm really upset or hurt or feeling overwhelmed, I remind myself 'This too shall pass'—and it always does."

Amanda Ansler, 15

"When you do the right things, for the right reasons, the right things happen." (This is a slogan for helping you to re-examine your motives and stay on track.)

"If I start to doubt myself and the things I'm doing, I love to remember the slogan, 'When you do the right things, for the right reasons, the right things happen.' It makes me check out my motives. Then it keeps me focused and helps me trust in my integrity and in my Higher Power."

Rianna Riley, 17

"Remember HALT." (This acronym for Hungry, Angry, Lonely and Tired is a recovery-treatment slogan, reminding you that each can make you feel irritable, restless and discontent—which can lead to relapse, and so you must take care of each of them as soon as you recognize them.)

"They told me to 'remember HALT' when I was in treatment. So whenever I'm hungry, angry, lonely or tired—I halt and take care of those needs!"

Destiny Rivers, 15

"Keep your own side of the street clean." (This is a reminder to concentrate on doing what is right and staying in integrity with your new values in recovery. It means not spending your energy judging others, when you can be applying it to improving yourself.)

"If I happen to get in an argument or some kind of disagreement with someone, and I'll really think they owe me an apology—or else I'll think I've been totally disrespected and I need to retaliate in some way—then I remind myself, 'Keep your own side of the street clean.' I don't have to worry about what they're doing wrong—I need to make sure what I'm doing is right. This means 'working my own program' and leaving others to work their own program, too."

Dana Emerson, 16

"If you always do what you've always done, then you'll always get what you've always got." (This reminds you that you need to change your thinking and behavior if you want to change your life and grow in your recovery.)

"When I feel like just quitting—giving up—running from my problems and getting high, I remind myself of the saying, 'If you always do what you've always done, then you'll always get what you've always got.' Using 'got' me lots of misery and trouble. I also remember that saying when I'm acting on 'old behavior' in other ways, too. Like when I'm tempted not to study, I remember that saying and how I always end up with bad grades; or if I get mad at some guy and want to punch him—which I would do when I was using—I remember that I end up in big trouble. Those words remind me that I have to be willing to change if I want to stay clean and have a good life."

Rafael Marquez, 15

2. Identifying Your Support Team

Another way to silence "the committee" is by getting in touch with your strongest, staunchest supporters in recovery. The calming, caring voice of your sponsor or someone else in your support group can often still the mindless chatter of "the committee." Being in recovery doesn't mean it will always be easy going. In fact, you may often need help and support getting through those perilous minutes of craving or those challenging situations that are dangerous to your recovery.

Staying clean and sober will not only mean finding ways to stay away from classmates who use, but also developing a strong support group. A *support group* is that network of friends who are there for you with your best interests always at heart, no matter what. During your days of early recovery, you may be coping with many new feelings of guilt and overwhelm—and you'll appreciate someone who genuinely understands your struggle. In the past, you may have sacrificed your well-being by using drugs or alcohol to feel as if you fit in with your friends. Today, you want a healthier support group to give you that sense of belonging. It can take effort to avoid those old friends who are still using, but the truth is your recovery depends on it. What's more, you'll have little in common with them now that staying clean and sober is your primary focus each day. Reaching out to other young people at twelve-step meetings and asking for their phone numbers, then using those numbers, can help you build a new support group. You're sure to find that when you honestly share who you are and what you're going through, you'll attract friends in recovery who are going through, or have been through, the very same things. They will admire your openness and desire to stay clean.

A positive support group—a network of clean and sober friends you can trust and turn to—is crucial to your recovery. In those moments of doubt, temptation or crises, when you really have a craving or are dealing with painful problems or feelings that could lead to relapse, a strong support group is one of the most powerful and effective tools you can possibly have.

When you find yourself overwhelmed by the desire to drink or use, having your support group in place can make the difference between whether or not you stay clean. So you'll want to have an "Emergency Support Slip"—this is your support group lifeline—the names and numbers of your twelve-step sponsor, friends in recovery who will be there for you to help you get through the emergency without using or drinking, and anyone else you know for certain will be there to help you through the crises (such as a counselor or your parents).

Many teens find the Emergency Support Slip (like the one below) a great tool for keeping those all-important numbers at hand in those moments of recovery crisis. (You'll find additional copies of the Emergency Support Slip in the back of this book. Fill in the blanks with those crucial numbers. Then cut it out and keep it in your wallet or purse or on the inside of your school folder—anywhere you can find it when you need it.)

EMERGENCY SUPPORT SLIP

	Name	Phone #1	Phone #2
Sponsor:			
Supporter:			
Supporter:			
Supporter:			
Supporter:			
Supporter:			

3. "Between the Ears" Sobriety Schedule

Picture the following scenario: You're walking through the mall feeling restless and irritable. You had an argument with a friend, your parents are upset with you because you got a parking ticket, you need to find something to wear to the dance—whether or not you make up with your boyfriend—and today of all days, absolutely nothing looks right on you. In short, you are not having a good day. Then right there in the middle of the mall you see two of your old using friends. They say "hi" and you can sure tell they are (high, that is). Funny thing is, it doesn't look so bad—not with the way you're feeling. They ask if you want to "hang out" with them, and you say "no thanks," pointing out that you have to get a dress for the dance. They let you know they're going to be at the pizza place in the mall for a while if you change your mind. When they walk away your mindless chatter turns up the volume—it would be so easy to join them . . . you know where that would lead. Yet, where it would lead doesn't seem like such a terrible idea. About this time you're thinking it would feel good. What to do? Get to a twelve-step meeting! But where is there a meeting? And what time does it start? Knowing the answers to these questions can make the difference between whether or not you get through the day clean and sober. So it's important that you have a Sobriety Success Schedule—take the time, ahead of time, to know where there are at least three meetings each day of the week! Of course, that doesn't mean you'll be going to three meetings every day; it means you are prepared every day of the week with a meeting you can go to if you need one. And you're prepared for this any time of the day.

You can get the schedule of meetings in your area by contacting the AA or NA hotlines nearest to you. You can also get schedules of all the meetings when you are at a meeting. So if you get to just one meeting, you are well on your way to knowing where all the rest of them are located and what times they are held.

If you don't have a car, you may need to get a bus schedule to figure out how to get to meetings when you need them. Once you go to a meeting, you will probably be able to learn who goes to that meeting regularly, and you can work out getting a ride with that person. This is another reason why it is so important to ask for phone numbers at the meetings. Oftentimes, meetings will offer a phone list with numbers of all the people who attend the meeting regularly. This is a great source if you are having trouble getting to a meeting. Again, remember that one of the main principles of twelve-step programs is the need for its members to help other alcoholics or addicts maintain sobriety. So don't be afraid to ask for help with getting to meetings.

Getting to a meeting and sharing "what is going on between your ears" (as they say in AA) can really help take the power out of the uncomfortable feelings and destructive thoughts. Listening to those who share a common bond of recovery talking about how they are staying clean and sober will give you voice-overs in stereo to silence the mindless chatter coaxing you toward relapse. Once you have a schedule, use the form on the next page to plan the three meetings each day that you can go to in case of a "recovery emergency."

Of course, you'll want to have meetings that you attend regularly whether or not there is an emergency. Reminder: Carry your sobriety schedule in your backpack, purse or wallet at all times. You will find another copy of this schedule in the back of the book; make copies as you need them.

Sobriety Success Schedule

	Location	Time		Location	Time
Monday			**Tuesday**		
Morning:	_____	_____	Morning:	_____	_____
Daytime:	_____	_____	Daytime:	_____	_____
Evening:	_____	_____	Evening:	_____	_____
Wednesday			**Thursday**		
Morning:	_____	_____	Morning:	_____	_____
Daytime:	_____	_____	Daytime:	_____	_____
Evening:	_____	_____	Evening:	_____	_____
Friday			**Saturday**		
Morning:	_____	_____	Morning:	_____	_____
Daytime:	_____	_____	Daytime:	_____	_____
Evening:	_____	_____	Evening:	_____	_____
Sunday					
Morning:	_____	_____			
Daytime:	_____	_____			
Evening:	_____	_____			

Questions to Think About

♥ What are your favorite recovery slogans or clichés? What do they mean to you? How have you used them in your life?

♥ If you were to write a recovery slogan for your life—a reminder that was there to help you when you needed it most—what would that slogan be?

♥ Who is in your support group? How has your support group helped you cope with hard times? How have they helped you avoid relapse? What did your friends do to help you get through without using or drinking?

♥ What do you look for in a friend who you want as part of your support group? What qualities does he or she have? How do you find friends for your support group?

Surviving Feelings and Problems— Staying Clean and Sober

California Sunshine

The minute I walked into the house after school, I knew something was terribly wrong. My mother's eyes were all red and puffy; she'd obviously been crying. When she saw me, she swallowed and tried not to sob as she said, "Your grandmother passed away." I'll never forget the feeling—it was as if someone robbed me of all the air in my lungs. My limbs felt weak. It felt surreal. "Grandma?" I repeated, confused. "Grandma's not sick," I insisted. She hadn't been, either.

"It was a massive stroke," my mother explained, trying to explain things—and calm us, too. "Your father's coming home from work to take us to the hospital to meet your Aunt Katherine. Do you want to come with us?" I said I wanted to go along, not even knowing why. I just didn't want to be alone, and I wanted to feel like I was doing something. My grandmother was dead. I couldn't believe it. My grandmother who I spent summers with when she lived in Oregon, before she moved to where we lived in California to be closer to us. My grandmother who held me and told me I was her "California Sunshine" when I was a little girl. My grandmother who always loved me no matter what, who always believed the very best of me, who never gave up on me—even when I was at the very worst of my chemical dependency. But my beloved grandma was gone. Out of my life forever. It felt like all the joy in life was over—as if I'd never laugh again. I was totally shattered.

I'm sure that I had never hurt more than the day I learned my grandma died. The pain I felt was so bad that I hurt from the top of my head to my toes. I just felt empty. Not even crying relieved the pain. I was so completely "beside myself."

I'd only been clean and sober for eight months. I'd worked so hard, but now, all I wanted to do was escape the way I was feeling, so much so that I was actually thinking I was better off just using.

Luckily, I didn't. And the sole reason I didn't was because I kept telling myself to "think this through; think this through; think this through" because I knew getting high wasn't the solution. There was no hope in running from what I was feeling—and "using" wasn't going to bring my grandmother back to me. If I used I was sure to have more problems than I already had. I was sure to lose my new friends. I was sure to make my parents' suffering all the worse and end up at odds with them again. I was sure to be miserable and feel awful when I came down. And my body was free and clear of all the chemicals—and it had taken a long time to make that happen. No, I didn't want my cells clogged with chemicals again. If I did that, if I used, then everything good that I'd worked so hard to gain would be lost. No, using wasn't the solution.

Knowing that I needed a "lifeline" for the "crisis" I was facing, I called my sponsor and listened really hard as she assured me "this too shall pass." Then, I went to see my counselor who helped me "process" my feelings. And I went to my twelve-step meetings before school in the morning, and most days I found a meeting to go to at night, too. When I got home at night, I wrote in my journal, tears dropping on the page. I did *everything* that had been suggested for me to do when I was in treatment. I shared, I prayed, I wrote, I reached out, I tried to help others to get out of myself—everything.

So I made it through that rough time in my life without using. I'd lived the big bottom line: "Don't use or drink no matter what." Just like everyone tells you, with time my pain eased and I was able to get through it without creating a whole new set of problems for myself. Now I have the experience of having walked through the pain without using or drinking. It was a "test," and I passed it. Knowing that I've succeeded in making it through this painful time without using will help me when I'm faced with other challenges that make me want to "escape" by using. It's also an experience I can share with someone else who is going through her own heartache and wanting to use or drink: It's true what my sponsor said, *"This too shall pass."*

It's been almost a year since my grandmother's death. I'll always miss her—and at times, her passing is still "raw" for me. On holidays, her birthday and other special occasions when we used to gather at her house—all are especially painful. I am so thankful that she saw me break free of my addiction. I find comfort in believing that she knew how good I was doing in my recovery; as she said, "My California Sunshine is back!"

Being clean there are so many feelings to experience. Not all of them are painful. Now I'm seeing someone special, Nicholas—and I'm feeling happy, fun, romantic feelings for him. But I know that as great as those feelings are, my recovery has to come first—before any "feelings," good or bad—and I've learned through hard-won experience how to put my recovery first.

Melissa Miranda, 18

Three Tools for "Surviving" Your Feelings

As teens say, getting through their hectic schedule is the "easy part"; the more difficult challenge is "to survive" one's feelings. Melissa's story proves that this is true enough. It's the work of life—and "surviving" those feelings clean and sober is the work of recovery.

We all need to learn how to face challenges and problems in life. No one's life is without them, certainly not the teen years where your schedule is hectic, and where so many things are new and first-time experiences. But consider that the following difficult times happen to all of us:

- Disappointments
- Conflicts with other people
- Heartbreak
- Stress
- Success
- Failure
- Loss
- Grief

If you are new in recovery facing painful feelings, problems and challenges can be even more difficult for a number of reasons:

1. **You may lack experience—and skills—for knowing how to cope with the problems.** While using drugs or alcohol, you are a whole lot less likely to be facing your problems, so now that you are sober, you may be facing them for the first time.

2. **"Run and hide" is usually a chemically dependent person's first response.** Often having years of experience in how to run and hide from problems, your first reaction to pain is "escape"—now!

3. **Chemically dependent people can be especially sensitive to discomfort.** Addicts and alcoholics are very often hypersensitive to emotional pain.

4. **You may have a backlog of problems.** Not only were you not solving everyday problems as they came your way, but this "avoidance" may mean that you now have a huge mountain of problems. And, of course, your addiction has no doubt also created a multitude of new problems (most probably in every area of your life).

As you go over these reasons, you might find yourself wondering, "Do I stand a chance of learning how to face my problems and cope with my feelings?" You can rest assured, thousands upon thousands of recovering people who have gone before you have learned how to cope effectively with their problems and challenges, big and small. In fact, some would say they've been given an edge when it comes to problem-solving: Since their recovery and their life can depend on it, they have greater motivation to learn how to cope in healthy ways. Here are some "tools" teens say are important for continuing to work through the pains of life in effective—and healthy—ways.

The A + B = C Test
for Clear Thinking

If you are new in recovery, you, like Melissa, no doubt remember when your automatic response to any and every problem and challenge was "run!" Today, you don't have that option. You have to think the whole thing through, decide on the best course of action and then follow through with it. Your recovery depends on it. When you are faced with problems, painful feelings, challenges and just the day-to-day obstacles of life, you should practice the A + B = C Test for Clear Thinking. Translated, this means that you apply this "equation" to seeing if your thinking is clear and rational: A (*your thinking*) + B (*your behavior*) = C (*the probable outcome of the situation*).

This is a "slow down, let's think about what's happening" basic thinking skill. When you remember the recovery cliché "think, think, think," you can bring this skill into play. It will help you look squarely at what's going on, and then choose a response that's going to produce the best results. This way, you're better able to stay calm and cool under pressure and work your way out of the challenge that you're faced with—before it snowballs into a relapse.

Let's look at how this worked for Melissa:

A: Melissa's Thinking: "I hurt and I don't want to feel this way. Think this through—where will you end up if you use? Getting high isn't the solution. I need a lifeline—help."

+B: Melissa's Behavior: Melissa called her sponsor and followed all her sponsor's suggestions. She saw her counselor, went to meetings and journaled.

=C: Outcome: Melissa made it through the crisis without using.

Understanding and Reaching Resolution

Looking at all the ways you failed at problem-solving when you were drinking and using can be scary. The last thing you want to do is act on "old behavior" and run from your problems and painful feelings—especially if that running means relapse. With your past experience, you also know that if you happen to act impulsively or make a rash decision, chances are not only that you will fail to solve the problem, but you'll also make it worse. So you need new, effective ways to solve your problems.

Here's a simple but very effective five-step process to help you develop an organized approach to problem-solving, one that involves asking yourself the following questions:

1. **"What is the problem?"** Sometimes the problem isn't always readily apparent. At first Melissa might have said, "My problem is that my grandmother has passed away." But when she examined it more closely, she concluded, "My problem is that I feel devastated because I've lost my grandmother." Then, upon looking yet further, "My problem is I don't want to feel the way I'm feeling." Going on, she would say, "I want to escape my feelings." If the problem you are trying to solve is complex, just keep asking yourself, "What else is the problem?"

2. **"How can I solve my problem?"** Here you should come up with as many possible ways as you can think of to solve the problem. Basically, this means asking, "What healthy actions can I take to cope with the problem or the pain?" Melissa could have decided that the solution to wanting to escape her feelings was to use drugs, but she knew this was not a "healthy action." So instead she looked for healthy actions to cope with the pain: She went to twelve-step meetings, wrote in her journal, called her sponsor and her friends, met with her counselor—and didn't "drink or use no matter what."

3. **"What are the consequences?"** Not all solutions work equally well. After you've generated as many possible solutions to the problem as you can, assess the potential outcome of each proposed action by asking, "If I do that, what would happen?" Remember, thinking through potential outcomes can save you from experiencing even more problems. Melissa weighed the outcome of using to escape the painful feelings and realized the consequences weren't worth it. She then practiced the "healthy" actions she had come up with as solutions to her problem.

4. **"What is my plan?"** After considering all the consequences and which ones you are prepared to accept responsibility for, decide what you are going to do. Then, make a plan to do just that, and commit to the plan—just as we saw that Melissa did in following all the suggestions that had been given to her. When you take the time and effort to weigh the consequences and come up with a plan to solve your problems, you're far more likely to succeed at getting through your problems without hurting yourself with the disaster of a relapse.

5. **"How did I do?"** After you've followed through with your decision, evaluate how you did and make some value judgment about it. Was your decision a good one? What were the consequences of your decision? Melissa came out stronger in her recovery because of the decision she made to stay clean and sober no matter what. What's more, she was able to believe that her grandmother knew how well she was doing and was proud of her. Be certain to praise yourself for staying drug-free! Even if there were other areas where your decision had flaws, if you walked through the challenge clean and sober, you deserve to be praised for that victory.

It's amazing how many solutions you can come up with when you take the time to think things through. And it's a great way to keep yourself from being thrown off course on your journey of recovery.

Applying "One Day at a Time"

When faced with problems or when you're going through feelings that are "all over the map," it's important to realize, as Melissa learned, that in time, those feelings are sure to pass. No one wants to feel pain. It's human nature to want to feel good, and to feel good now rather than to have to wait for it. But the person who has "addictive thinking" doesn't want to delay feeling good or having rewards—even when both come at a cost. When caught up in this kind of thinking, even the recovering addict with a significant length of "clean time" loses a realistic view of time and the degree to which they can tolerate their feelings. That's one reason why twelve-step programs suggest "one day at a time" and stress that each person live "just for today."

Here are five great reasons to "live one day at a time":

1. **One day *is* manageable.** Trying to stay clean and sober for one day is a more manageable thought than "never, ever using again." Having to face the stress and pain of a problem for just one day is much easier to handle than the thought of having to face it forever—which is what many problems become in the mind of the recovering addict or alcoholic.

2. **You can't change the past.** There can be a host of painful memories in the past—especially for most recovering people. A lot of shame and regrets may come with thinking about the past, as well as an unrealistic longing to go back and change it all. Spending time and energy worrying about the past isn't going to change it.

3. **You don't know what the future holds.** The future is a place of uncertainties—who knows what could happen—so it can bring with it new insecurities and fears. Hours are wasted on the "what ifs"—thinking, fretting, puzzling. You can write out whole scripts and screenplays of what's going to happen—all in your own head. You write your lines, their lines, the whole story—none of which will necessarily happen, either for good or for bad. Spending time and energy worrying about the future won't change it either. But you can choose to live your day doing the footwork that helps create a future filled with good—sometimes that can

be as basic as "don't pick up a drug or drink no matter what" and just get through the day "clean and sober."

4. **The grace to face your problems comes a day at a time.** Day-to-day there may be painful feelings, challenges and problems to face. And day-to-day, as the principles of your recovery are applied, the grace to overcome those feelings, to face those challenges and conquer those problems will be given. Taking on the problems that aren't here yet—or the ones that are gone with yesterday—amounts to trying to cope with them on today's grace. Today's grace is just enough for today.

5. **The present moment is the safest place to live.** In the present moment is the power of change, the power of good, the promise of hope. In the present moment is where life lives— it happens in the now.

So if you are in recovery, remember that by maintaining your recovery right here in this day you steer clear of creating problems for your future. You only have today. Learning how to stay in the now can take a lot of practice. Even with practice there will always be times when you'll have to stretch to get to that place of "in the here and now." The mind is full of endless thoughts and admonitions—of countless "what ifs" and "if onlys."

Here are some simple tips for staying in today:

- Make a conscious decision to live in the now.
- Redirect your focus to the now when you find you're off-track. Each time you realize that you're off in thoughts of the past or the future, bring the present back into focus.
- If past regrets plague you, live a life of integrity and kindness today—that is the truest start toward making up for past mistakes.
- If future fears lurk in your mind, work on living a responsible

life of integrity and kindness and know that in so doing your fears will have little chance of coming to pass.

• Faith can help you live in the day. Through developing a relationship with a Higher Power and working on spiritual principles, you can find strength in surrendering to living life one day at a time.

The toughest times call for the fiercest determination. Making a decision to stick to "living in the solution" and staying clean and sober—rather than seeking the false comfort of using drugs or alcohol to get the immediate gratification of escape—is a requirement to achieving the long-term satisfaction of a full, happy drug-free life.

The goal is to live a drug-free life and grow in recovery no matter what feelings and emotions life throws your way. To do this, it's important to understand and cope with all your feelings and emotions—whether they are good or bad. Here are three ways to cope as you go through those feelings and emotions:

1. **Choose new solutions.** Choosing recovery means choosing new solutions—solutions that will bring you long-term satisfaction. It means choosing solutions that are best for your genuine well-being, rather than those that are self-destructive. This is what recovery is all about.

2. **Take action as you wait out the pain or problem.** Life's challenges don't always come in a neat little package with instant solutions. More times than not, overcoming challenges takes waiting things out, doing some footwork and taking the necessary action to create the change.

3. **Face your fears.** Sometimes getting through to the other side of problems, challenges and heartaches takes a "no matter what" kind of drive, like Melissa talked about in the beginning of this chapter. Oftentimes it takes true courage. When someone has courage, it doesn't mean they don't have

fear. It means they walk through their fears—seeking the solution, rather than hiding or running from the problem.

Facing those fears and remaining determined will not be easy, but you will gain confidence and strength of character to keep moving forward on the road of recovery. Here are some ways to survive your feelings and problems, choosing recovery rather than a self-destructive instant "solution" of using to escape:

- Use your support group (your sponsor, your friends, your counselor). Talk to someone else about what you're going through and how you're feeling.
- Journal about your feelings and challenges and how you're facing them. Always list and explore possible solutions.
- When tempted to go for "instant gratification," "play the whole tape through"—ask, "What will the end results be?" Just a reminder: There are consequences to every action.
- When faced with challenges, be flexible and keep an open mind when looking at solutions.
- Remember, pain can motivate you toward positive change. Ask yourself, "What needs to change?"
- Practice courage in the day. Even though you're scared, choose to do what is best for you and your recovery.

Questions to Think About

- ♥ What painful feelings do you find most difficult to "survive"? Which make you want to "run" or "escape"? How do you cope with these feelings in healthy ways?
- ♥ When have you chosen "instant gratification" over "long-term satisfaction"? What were the circumstances? What were the consequences? What price did you pay?
- ♥ When have you found yourself living in the day or in the moment? What were you doing? How did you feel?

♥ What painful feelings or problems do you face today? What are some of the "new solutions" you have found to work for coping with your challenges?

Unit VI

Your Personal— And Private— Journal

We are spiritual beings having a human experience.
—Source Unknown

It's not accident or time or fortune that keeps you from the things you want, but rather your own thinking.
—Lillian Hellman

Try viewing everyone who comes into your life as a teacher.
—Wayne Dyer

Yesterday is history. Tomorrow is a mystery. Today is a gift.
—Source Unknown

How Journaling Can Help You Survive Your Feelings

Why Should You Journal?

This unit is your very own journal, a private diary where you can write about your experiences and thoughts on a topic that is central to your wellness—your plans for living your life drug-free. Here we've provided you with questions, prompts and space to journal on many issues central to living your life without using.

Journaling is a powerful tool that can help you work through thoughts, feelings and problems. Writing things out is helpful because:

- It gets your thoughts out of your head and down on paper where it is easier to see how you are feeling about things. This can help you organize your thoughts and come to a clearer perspective on what's going on.
- It allows you to safely express feelings like anger, frustration and stress, as well as to express and get in touch with feelings like gratitude, love, satisfaction and excitement. Sometimes we are unaware of these feelings until we write about them.
- It gives you an opportunity to "process" your feelings, to

281

evaluate or reevaluate your problems so that you can sort things out and decide what is the next best thing to do. For example, you may decide that you can work through a particular problem on your own, or that you need to ask your parents or a counselor for help and support to work things through.

- It is your own reference guide for dealing with future challenges and obstacles. Because you have a "diary" of your feelings and behaviors, you can see your progress and which coping strategies have worked best—or least—for you and why.
- It gives you a means to express your hopes and fears, goals and aspirations so you're able to focus on what's important and worth attaining. It can support your efforts to live drug-free.

When Is the Best Time to Journal?

Journal whenever it is best for you. While some teens do this first thing in the morning, many like to do it just before going to bed because then you have an overview of the day. The important thing is that you take the time to listen to your feelings and express them. This is especially crucial when you are faced with challenges or an event that triggers a lot of emotion or stress. When something like this comes up, you want to take the time to journal as soon as possible, no matter what time of the day it is. The closer you are to the experience the better. When you write about something when you are in the middle of it, you get the benefit of seeing how a certain experience affected you, as well as your plans for working through your feelings and sorting out solutions right then and there (which may be different than how you may deal with the same incident or situation days or weeks, even months later).

How to Use This Journal

We encourage you to read and give careful thought to each question in this journal section, but even so, it's okay to skip around to those questions that attract you and prompt those feelings and thoughts you'd most like to explore.

You'll want to date each entry in your journal to make it easier to track your feelings and progress. That way, when you look back at where you were even a month ago, you can see how far you've come. So be sure to take the time to go back and review all of your entries. When you do so, ask yourself: Do I still feel that way? Why or why not? How have I changed?

You can respond to the journal's questions as they are in the book, remembering they are only here to prompt you and are not necessarily the only things you want to write about. Your journal is for you to write about any and all those things that are important to you. You will notice that at the end of the journal there are four blank pages for you to journal on your own. You can use these pages to write more about what's on your mind and heart, and how you are facing your challenges, and setting and achieving goals for your future. Always remember to explore possible solutions and attempt to finish your entry with an effective—and healthy—solution. We suggest you get a tablet or binder to give yourself more space to journal about those things that require additional pages of your written thought or attention. You can also use these pages to write about what you want out of life, what you are feeling each day, all your new beginnings and all the positive change you are creating in your life. While you're using your journal, write your new goals and how you plan to reach them.

And don't forget to make the time to write about the things you have done that make you feel good about yourself. The more positive you feel about yourself and your life, the more you'll feel "worthy" of living your life drug-free.

My Thoughts on . . . Living Drug-Free

♥ When did you discover that you were totally committed to staying drug-free? Describe the incident, situation or "moment" when you made your decision. Did someone help you come to this decision, or was it a choice you made on your own?

_____

_____

_____

_____

_____

_____

❀ How does being drug-free make you feel about yourself?

_____

_____

_____

_____

_____

_____

❦ How does being drug-free help you to be in an _authentic_ (honest) relationship with yourself?

_____

_____

_____

_____

_____

_____

★ How does being drug-free give you a better chance to "show up" for your life?

_____

_____

_____

_____

_____

_____

➡ What "rewards" for staying drug-free do you value most? List two.

❤_____

_____

_____

❤_____

_____

_____

❋ How does being drug-free help you do your best in school?

_____

_____

_____

_____

_____

_____

✦ How does being drug-free help you be your best in your relationships with family members?

Mom: _____

_____

_____

Dad: _____

_____

_____

Brothers/sisters: _____

_____

_____

✔ How does being drug-free help you be your best in your relationships with your teachers?

_____

_____

_____

_____

_____

_____

✎ What does being drug-free mean in your relationships with your friends?

_____

_____

_____

_____

_____

✮ How does being drug-free give you a better chance to discover your "true" identity?

_____

_____

_____

_____

✳ Have you ever been pressured (or enticed) to use? If so, when? What happened? How did you feel about it? What did the person (or persons) ask you to "try" (use)? How did you feel about yourself when you stood by your decision when being pressured to use?

_____

_____

_____

_____

_____

_____

_____

✪ What do you do or say in situations where others try to convince you to use—in other words, what is your "comeback"? Do you have a "pat" answer, or does it depend upon the situation? Explain.

_____

_____

_____

_____

✪ Do the friends you hang out with also value staying drug-free? How do you know?

_____

_____

_____

_____

_____

_____

_____

✓ Do you and your friends discuss the importance of not using alcohol or drugs? How does the subject of not using come up?

_____

_____

_____

_____

_____

_____

✎ If you heard about or saw a friend using, or being tempted to use, what would you say to that friend?

_____

_____

_____

_____

_____

_____

✤ Who, more than anyone else, was the person who influenced you to make the choice to remain drug-free? How did this person "convince" you of the importance of not using drugs?

_____

_____

_____

_____

_____

_____

▶ Is it easy for you to stay committed to being drug-free? Do you feel cool to cope, or do you feel like a "nerd" or "geek," or that it takes a lot of perseverance to not use? Explain.

_____

_____

_____

_____

_____

_____

✞ What do you do (or could you do) to make sure your friends know that you really don't want to use drugs or alcohol?

_____

_____

_____

_____

_____

_____

My Thoughts on . . . Using

○ Are you using? When did you start? What have you used, and how often do you use? How do you feel about being a person who uses?

_____

_____

_____

_____

_____

❖ Are you, or is someone you know, addicted to drugs or alcohol? When did you (or your friend/family member) cross the line from "using" to addiction? Write about how and when it became clear that the drug or alcohol use was a problem.

_____

_____

_____

_____

_____

_____

➢ What are some of the prices either you personally or someone you care about has paid for using "just a little bit" of drugs or alcohol?

_____

_____

_____

_____

_____

➥ Professionals in the field of chemical dependency say that an addict's chemical dependency "progresses," which means it takes more and more of the substance to satisfy the craving. How have you seen your drug or alcohol use (or someone else's) grow worse? How does experiencing (or witnessing) this loss of control make you feel?

_____

_____

_____

_____

_____

_____

❀ Chemical dependency creates an *obsession* with using the drug. This means the chemically dependent person cannot stop thinking about "getting high." Has there ever been something you could not stop thinking about (whether drugs, alcohol or something else—even a person)? What was it, and when did you feel this way? What did being unable to control your thoughts feel like?

_____

_____

_____

_____

_____

_____

♦ Using can lead to becoming "chemically dependent"—
which means that a person may use even against his or her "free
will." Have you ever felt as if you've lost your free will to drugs
or in any other way? If so, describe when and how.

_____

_____

_____

_____

_____

_____

☆ A person's conscience can become "shut down" by addiction. How do you value your conscience most? Describe a time
when your conscience "talked" to you. What was it telling you?

_____

_____

_____

_____

_____

➻ What have you learned from even your most painful feelings? What are the feelings you have experienced in just this one
day, and why were you experiencing them?

_____

_____

_____

_____

_____

❧ Drugs are chemicals that affect both the mind and body. What do you consider the most "frightening" risk of using, and why?

_____

_____

_____

_____

_____

_____

♠ Do you drink or use drugs? How does this affect your family? Or, how does your family member's using or drinking affect you and the rest of your family?

_____

_____

_____

_____

_____

_____

❀ Have you ever pretended you were feeling something you weren't? What were you hiding or pretending and why? How did it make you feel to be less than honest and open in this way?

_____

_____

_____

_____

_____

_____

✉ Write someone you know who is using a letter telling that person about your concern—without placing blame or accusing him or her of being a "bad" person.

Dear _____,

_____

_____

_____

_____

_____

_____

_____

_____

_____

_____

_____

✗ Chemical dependency has the power to erode relationships. Write about a relationship you personally have witnessed being destroyed because of someone using.

_____

_____

_____

_____

_____

_____

_____

✉ Who are you upset with, or who do you feel needs to change some sort of hurtful behavior (whether using, drinking, being rude or something else)? It is important to be able to express your feelings in a healthy way, which means without accusing or belittling the other person, while honestly sharing how you feel. Write three "I feel" messages telling this person how you feel about his or her behavior:

Name of person: _____

I feel: _____

_____

_____

_____

_____

I feel: _____

_____

_____

_____

_____

I feel: _____

_____

_____

_____

_____

✝ What do you feel is the best way to handle a situation where someone is hurting himself, herself or someone else? Have you ever dealt with such a situation and, if so, how did you actually handle it? What changes would you make if you were to deal with the situation again?

_____

_____

_____

_____

_____

_____

_____

_____

✳ Have you ever held somebody's secret when it wasn't wise to do so? If so, who was the person, and what was the secret? What happened as a result?

_____

_____

_____

_____

_____

♦ Have you ever tried to protect someone from consequences he or she would suffer because of his or her own actions or behavior? Who? What were the actions or behavior? What would the consequences be, and how did you protect the person from them? What happened as a result?

_____

_____

_____

_____

_____

_____

_____

✦ Have you ever practiced the "tough love" of letting someone face their consequences without getting in the way to protect them? Who was the person with whom you practiced this?
How did you let this person face his or her consequences, and
what was the result? What do you do to find the strength to do
this, and how do you cope with all the feelings it brings up for
you?

_____

_____

_____

_____

_____

_____

_____

_____

_____

_____

_____

_____

My Thoughts on . . .
Making the Decision to STOP Using

♥ How long have you used? What are you using?

_____

_____

_____

_____

_____

_____

❧ When were you first aware that your using was a "problem"? What feeling, event or series of events made you aware of this?

_____

_____

_____

_____

_____

_____

❀ When did you decide to quit using? Have you tried to quit before?

_____

_____

_____

_____

_____

_____

★ How many times have you tried to quit using or cut down on drugs and alcohol? What happened with each past attempt? How long were you successful at staying drug- and alcohol-free? What happened to lead you back to using again?

_____

_____

_____

_____

_____

_____

_____

_____

_____

_____

➡ When was the last time you told a lie so that you could continue to use? What was the lie? Did you know at the time that you were telling a lie? Why did you feel like you had to lie?

_____

_____

_____

_____

_____

_____

_____

_____

❇ How would you explain "hitting bottom" to someone who has never heard the term?

✦ Have you (ever) hit bottom? Explain the consequences that you consider being your "bottom" (or that you would consider to be enough to make you hit bottom)?

✱ What prices did you pay for using? Which of these prices were most painful to you? How big a part did each of these prices play in your "hitting bottom"? If you've never used, how has seeing a friend or family member pay these kind of prices helped you understand what it means to "hit bottom"?

☆ Has someone ever "interfered" or stopped you from hitting bottom? When and how did this person interfere? What was the end result of the interference?

_____

_____

_____

_____

_____

_____

✪ Have you interfered with someone else's hitting bottom? What consequences have you "softened" for them? Is that person still using?

_____

_____

_____

_____

_____

✒ How do you "take responsibility" for your own life? What things do you do on a regular basis that are part of being responsible for yourself? How do you feel taking responsibility for yourself relates to your decision to stop using drugs?

_____

_____

_____

_____

_____

_____

☞ When have you blamed someone or something else for something that was your responsibility? Who did you blame? When did you figure out that it was you who was responsible, and not the person (you used as a "scapegoat")? Did you go back and apologize? Explain.

_____

_____

_____

_____

_____

_____

▶ When did you decide it was time to stop blaming others and simply change your own life? How did you do that?

_____

_____

_____

_____

_____

_____

✓ What changes have you seen in your life because you took responsibility to "make change"?

_____

_____

_____

_____

_____

_____

❖ Since you are responsible for your behaviors, both good and bad, what are some of the good behaviors for which you can rightfully claim responsibility?

- _____
- _____
- _____
- _____
- _____

✎ Chapter 11 discusses the illusions of those who use. Some include: "I can't have fun unless I use," or "I can use just this once," or "Using makes me cool," or "Drugs help me relax (or give me energy)." What illusions did using make you believe in? What illusions have you "let go" for the sake of your recovery?

Illusion:_____

Illusion:_____

Illusion:_____

Illusion:_____

➡ Name two areas you need to work on changing most in order to be successful in your desire to quit using drugs and alcohol (or remain drug- and alcohol-free). For example, do you need to work on not feeling sorry for yourself, being honest or dealing with anger? What are some healthy ways to work on these changes?

_____

_____

_____

❤_____

_____

_____

♠ After reading information about treatment in chapter 12, what do you think would be the very best course of treatment for you, and why do you feel this would be the most effective?

_____

_____

_____

_____

_____

_____

_____

�֍ How are you working on repairing the problems your using has created? What are the problems, and what are you doing to correct them?

◗ Problem: _____

_____

What I'm doing to "correct it":_____

_____

◗ Problem: _____

_____

What I'm doing to "correct it":_____

_____

◗ Problem: _____

_____

What I'm doing to "correct it":_____

_____

My Thoughts on . . .
Staying Clean and Sober

☆ Have you gone to a twelve-step meeting yet? If so, what was your first meeting like? How did you feel? What did you learn? What happened at the meeting? What were the other people at the meeting like?

_____

_____

_____

_____

_____

_____

_____

⇒ Do you have a sponsor? If you do not, what will you (or would you) look for in a sponsor? If you have a sponsor, describe your sponsor and how you "enjoy" your relationship. In what ways does your sponsor "help" you stay clean and sober?

_____

_____

_____

_____

_____

_____

_____

✪ Are you working a twelve-step program of recovery? If so, do you plan on working the steps with your sponsor?

_____

_____

_____

_____

_____

_____

➦ How has your twelve-step program helped you come to believe a Higher Power could help you stay clean and sober? How would you describe your Higher Power?

_____

_____

_____

_____

_____

_____

✟ What is your spiritual faith, and how do you live it in your daily life? How do you feel your spiritual faith helps you in your recovery?

_____

_____

_____

_____

_____

✗ PAWS (post-acute withdrawal syndrome) are symptoms that happen when your body is "detoxing" from chemical use. What symptoms of PAWS have you experienced? How often do you have these kind of symptoms?

_____

_____

_____

_____

_____

_____

_____

_____

➥ What does it mean to you to be "extra good to yourself"? How are you "extra good to yourself"? What kind of things can you do to be "extra good to yourself"?

_____

_____

_____

_____

_____

❀ What "relaxation skills" do you practice?

_____

_____

_____

_____

◊ What are your favorite techniques for "hanging in there" when you are faced with stress and emotional overwhelm?

_____

_____

_____

_____

_____

_____

_____

✣ When was the last time you felt shame over something you've done? How did you free yourself from the shame?

_____

_____

_____

_____

_____

_____

_____

★ What have you learned about the cunning and deceptive effects of drugs, and how has this made you commit to your personal growth in recovery?

_____

_____

_____

_____

_____

_____

_____

_____

_____

_____

_____

_____

☛ When you practice self-forgiveness, healing happens in your life. Self-forgiveness can be a memory exchange, meaning you replace the painful or shameful memory with a more positive one. What great new memories have you created in the past?

_____

_____

_____

_____

_____

_____

_____

_____

_____

_____

My Thoughts on . . .
Relapse and Prevention

❋ Have you ever relapsed? If so, what do you feel led to your relapse? Have you told anyone? Why or why not?

_____

_____

_____

_____

_____

_____

❋ When exactly did your relapse really begin? What were you thinking and feeling, and how were you acting before you actually took that first drug or drink?

_____

_____

_____

_____

✔ When you find yourself acting in ways that indicate you're heading toward relapse, what do you do to _change_ your behaviors so as to prevent relapsing?

_____

_____

_____

_____

_____

✎ What are your relapse triggers, and what action can you take to avoid using when you are faced with each?

✦ Trigger:_____

_____

_____

Action: _____

_____

_____

✦ Trigger:_____

_____

_____

Action: _____

_____

_____

✦ Trigger:_____

_____

_____

Action: _____

_____

_____

✦ Trigger:_____

_____

_____

Action: _____

_____

_____

✦ The definition of "recovery" means more than just not using drugs and alcohol. It means changing the thinking, attitudes and behaviors that lead to using drugs and alcohol. In other words, recovery is about making changes. One of these changes is learning to face problems and uncomfortable feelings. What kind of feelings or emotions make you want to drink or use most? Which ones are hardest for you to deal with in your recovery? How have you learned to cope with them without drugs or alcohol?

_____

_____

_____

_____

_____

_____

_____

_____

_____

_____

❀ What are your favorite slogans or clichés, and how do these sayings or clichés either motivate or inspire you to stay clean and sober?

Favorite slogan:_____

How it inspires me to stay clean and sober: _____

_____

Favorite slogan:_____

_____

How it inspires me to stay clean and sober: _____

_____

✗ If you were to write a slogan for your life—a reminder to help you when you needed it most—what would it be?

_____

_____

_____

_____

_____

➥ Since you've been clean and sober, what "eye-opening" facts have you noticed about the friends you had when you were using? How did your friendships change when you were using?

_____

_____

_____

_____

_____

❈ Are your friends supportive of your recovery efforts, or do they pretty much not want to hear about it? Did the support of your friends (or lack of it) surprise you? Why or why not?

_____

_____

_____

_____

_____

★ How does being a part of your support group make some-one more than just a friend? What does the role include that friendship alone might not?

_____

_____

_____

_____

_____

_____

♠ What are you doing to develop healthy and supportive (and non-using) friendships? What actions do you take (how do you reach out) to find friends for your support group?

_____

_____

_____

_____

_____

_____

⇒ How has your support group helped you cope with hard times? How did support make you feel? What did your friends do to help you stay drug-free?

_____

_____

_____

_____

_____

_____

❋ How do you plan to use your support group to help you avoid relapse?

_____

_____

_____

_____

_____

◆ Have you ever "been there" to support a friend or family member so as to avoid relapse? Who was the person, and what did you do to be supportive?

_____

_____

_____

_____

_____

✟ Have you ever used a twelve-step meeting as your lifeline when your recovery was in danger? Why or why not? What was the recovery-threatening situation? What did you learn from the experience?

_____

_____

_____

_____

_____

_____

_____

Write about a recent success you experienced dealing with a problem (whether a disappointment, conflict, heartbreak, stress, failure, loss or grief). What was the situation, and how did you respond to it? How does it feel to know you came through it without using or drinking?

❖ What painful feelings do you find most difficult to survive without using or drinking—which feelings make you want to "run" or "escape"? How do you cope with these feelings in healthy ways?

❖ Do you have a "backlog of problems" built up from the days when you were using? What are they, and how are you coping with them today?

⇨ Problem:_____

_____

How I'm coping with/handling it: _____

_____

_____

⇨ Problem:_____

_____

How I'm coping with/handling it: _____

_____

_____

⇨ Problem:_____

_____

How I'm coping with/handling it: _____

_____

_____

◆ Staying clean and sober means having the courage to face your fears even when you would rather run from them. When have you practiced courage to face your fears? What was the situation, and how did you walk through it with courage? What did you learn from the experience?

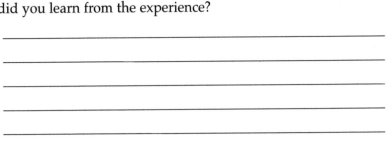

➻ Chapter 19 discusses how important living "one day at a time" can be to your recovery. How do you personally feel that it is important to your own recovery? When have you found yourself living in the day—being in the moment? What were you doing? How did you feel?

_____

_____

_____

_____

_____

_____

_____

☆ What are some of the obstacles and challenges that you face today? What are the "new solutions" you will use to effectively cope with them?

❧ Challenge: _____

_____

_____

✓ My plans for coping: _____

_____

_____

❧ Challenge: _____

_____

_____

✓ My plans for coping: _____

_____

_____

My Thoughts . . .

Date: _____   Time: _____

Subject:_____

_____

_____

_____

_____

_____

_____

_____

_____

_____

_____

_____

_____

_____

_____

_____

_____

_____

_____

_____

_____

_____

_____

_____

My Thoughts . . .

Date: _____ Time: _____

Subject:_____

_____

_____

_____

_____

_____

_____

_____

_____

_____

_____

_____

_____

_____

_____

_____

_____

_____

_____

_____

My Thoughts . . .

Date: _____   Time: _____

Subject:_____

_____

_____

_____

_____

_____

_____

_____

_____

_____

_____

_____

_____

_____

_____

_____

_____

_____

_____

_____

_____

_____

My Thoughts . . .

Date: _____   Time: _____

Subject: _____

_____

_____

_____

_____

_____

_____

_____

_____

_____

_____

_____

_____

_____

_____

_____

_____

_____

_____

_____

_____

_____

_____

_____

Epilogue

It has been our honor to write this book. We work with teens across the nation, and know of the struggles and challenges you face as you look to find your place in the world. While you seek to fit in and be a part of the crowd, you also want to stand apart and find your own voice. Becoming your own person, gaining independence, doing "adult things"—all are a part of the passage of going from teen to adult. It's important to remember that while you're trying to show the world that you are growing more and more capable of standing on your own two feet—and therefore desire and deserve more "space" and independence—you must never feel that you have to conquer the world—your life—alone. Know that as you strive to project an image of cool confidence and can-do, you don't have to go it alone, nor face challenges alone. We remind you of a simple little story that bears out not only the benefit of supporting others, but of letting others support you, as well:

A young boy and his father were out for a walk and came across a huge boulder on the side of the road. The curious boy looked up at his father and asked, "Dad, do you think I can move that big boulder?" To this, his father answered, "If you use all your strength, I know you can." So he ran over and, straining and groaning, tried to move the huge rock—but of course, could not. Discouraged, he looked up at his father and said, "You're wrong, Dad. I can't do it." Looking at his son, the father replied, "Oh, but you didn't use all your strength. You didn't ask me to help you."

As the boy found out, asking for help is a source of strength—even a way to "double" your strength. Never is this idea more important than in making it through the teen years. Especially if

your challenge is breaking out of the grips of chemical
dependency—as well as *staying* on a path of recovery—you will
need the support—the "strength"—from every taste berry you
can find to succeed in this most harrowing of challenges. Allow
others to be there for you.

Using "all your strength" may mean reaching deep within
yourself to find the courage to say no to drugs, especially if you
are someone who is trying to overcome an addiction, or trying to
"stay clean" or maintain sobriety. It may mean turning to those
who love and care about you, admitting that you have a problem
and then asking for help and support in getting through it. Or it
may mean turning to professional help—such as a counselor or
someone trained in the field of chemical dependency—and getting the counseling and treatment you need.

It can mean turning to your Higher Power for solace and
guidance to strengthen your will power and desire to live a
drug-free existence. At twelve-step meetings, it's not unusual to
hear the reminder that we are "spiritual beings having a human
experience." Almost everyone in long-term recovery—especially
those who are active in twelve-step programs—as well as many
experts in the field, agree that there will come a time when your
spiritual condition will mean the difference between holding
onto your recovery or relapsing. No one else can "nurture" your
spirit for you—but you can readily do it for yourself. One way is
to "eavesdrop" on the way the universe breathes its wonders
into life. Whether watching a spectacular sunset; sensing the
intricate interdependence of Mother Nature's creatures; or,
observing the joy felt by those who love each other as they
express their love, know that all are evidence of a Higher Power
at work in our lives. Whatever your faith, reach out for this connection, and you'll see the results of faith, hope and love at work
in your life: It can help you live your life drug-free.

We know there is much more to the topic of living your life
without succumbing to the pressures to drink and use drugs.

Getting through the teen years with a sense of feeling whole is a big job, but you can do it! Teens everywhere are living exciting and fun-filled lives with can-do "go for it!" ambition—without using drugs or alcohol. You can "survive" the full spectrum of feelings and experiences—the joys and sorrows, the triumphs and setbacks, even defeats—without using. And you can do all this without feeling overwhelmed by your feelings. And so as we have done in our books in the *Taste Berries for Teens* series, we will continue to address aspects of this subject in upcoming books and share with you how other teens your age are coping with challenges in positive ways. So please take the time to write us. We'd like to know how you found this book helpful and the ways it made a difference to you—or to the friends or family members you gave it to. And we'd also like to know how others served as a taste berry to you—helping, supporting, assisting, showing you the way, making your life better and sweeter—as well as how you've been a taste berry to someone else.

Wishing you all the rewards of a drug-free life!

Bettie, Jennifer and Tina

Our Web site is:

www.tasteberriesforteens.com

You can write to us at:

Taste Berries for Teens
3060 Racetrack View Drive
Del Mar, CA 92014

Appendix

Following are copies of the Emergency Support Slip that you read about in chapter 17. Many teens find these a great tool for keeping those all-important support group numbers at hand in those moments of recovery crisis. Fill in its blanks, then cut it out and keep it in your wallet, purse or on the inside of your school folder—anywhere you can find it when you need it. You may want to place an extra copy on your refrigerator or bulletin board at home, or in the glove compartment of your car, or maybe even tape it inside your locker door at school. The important thing is to be able to reach it when you are in need of support.

EMERGENCY SUPPORT SLIP

	Name	Phone #1	Phone #2
Sponsor:			
Supporter:			
Supporter:			
Supporter:			
Supporter:			

EMERGENCY SUPPORT SLIP

	Name	Phone #1	Phone #2
Sponsor:			
Supporter:			
Supporter:			
Supporter:			
Supporter:			

Use a twelve-step meeting schedule to complete the form below and plan for three meetings each day that you can go to in case of a "recovery emergency," as well as those you can attend regularly even when there is not an emergency. Reminder: Carry your sobriety schedule in your backpack, purse or wallet at all times.

Sobriety Success Schedule

	Location	Time		Location	Time
Monday			**Tuesday**		
Morning:	_____	_____	Morning:	_____	_____
Daytime:	_____	_____	Daytime:	_____	_____
Evening:	_____	_____	Evening:	_____	_____
Wednesday			**Thursday**		
Morning:	_____	_____	Morning:	_____	_____
Daytime:	_____	_____	Daytime:	_____	_____
Evening:	_____	_____	Evening:	_____	_____
Friday			**Saturday**		
Morning:	_____	_____	Morning:	_____	_____
Daytime:	_____	_____	Daytime:	_____	_____
Evening:	_____	_____	Evening:	_____	_____
Sunday					
Morning:	_____	_____			
Daytime:	_____	_____			
Evening:	_____	_____			

The Twelve Steps

1. We admitted that we were powerless over our addiction, that our lives had become unmanageable.
2. We came to believe that a Power greater than ourselves could restore us to sanity.
3. We made a decision to turn our will and our lives over to the care of God *as we understood Him.*
4. We made a searching and fearless moral inventory of ourselves.
5. We admitted to God, to ourselves, and to another human being the exact nature of our wrongs.
6. We were entirely ready to have God remove all these defects of character.
7. We humbly asked Him to remove our shortcomings.
8. We made a list of all people we had harmed, and became willing to make amends to them all.
9. We made direct amends to such people wherever possible, except when to do so would injure them or others.
10. We continued to take personal inventory and when we were wrong promptly admitted it.
11. We sought through prayer and meditation to improve our conscious contact with God *as we understood Him,* praying only for knowledge of His will for us and the power to carry that out.
12. Having had a spiritual awakening as a result of these steps, we tried to carry this message to addicts, and to practice these principles in all our affairs.

Resources and Referrals

800-ALCOHOL
800-COCAINE
800-448-3000, Boystown

Al-Anon/Alateen Family Group Headquarters
(Twelve-step group for family members of alcoholics and teens who are living with an alcoholic parent.)
P. O. Box 862, Midtown Station
New York, NY 10018-0862
212-302-7240
800-356-9996 (Literature)
800-344-2666 (Meeting Referral)

Alcoholics Anonymous
(Twelve-step program for alcoholics of all ages.)
World Services, Inc.
475 Riverside Drive
New York, NY 10115
212-870-3400 (Literature)
212-647-1680 (Meeting Referral)

CDC National AIDS Hotline
800-342-AIDS
800-344-SIDA (Spanish)
800-AIDS-TTY (TDD)

Center for Substance Abuse Treatment
National Drug and Alcohol Treatment Referral Service
(National organization to help you locate treatment programs in your area and throughout the nation.)
800-662-HELP (twenty-four-hour, toll-free service)
800-487-4889 (TDD)
877-767-8432 (Spanish)
www.findtreatment.samhsa.gov

Children of Alcoholics
(Publishes information, but doesn't hold groups.)
555 Madison Ave., 4th Floor
New York, NY 10022
212-754-0656 or 800-359-COAF

Cocaine Anonymous
(Twelve-step program for cocaine addicts; will provide information on where and when meetings are scheduled in your area.)
World Service Office
3740 Overland Avenue, Ste. C
Los Angeles, CA 90034
800-347-8998

Families Anonymous
(Twelve-step program for family members of chemically dependent people; will provide help for finding places to go, and send free literature and information on their program and other programs that are there to help.)
P. O. Box 35475
Culver City, CA 90231
800-736-9805

Marijuana Anonymous
(Twelve-step program for marijuana addicts; they will tell you the times and locations of the meetings in your area.)
World Services
P. O. Box 2912
Van Nuys, CA 91404
800-766-6779

Nar-Anon Family Group Headquarters
(Twelve-step program for family members of chemically dependent people; provides information on meetings in your area that offer both support and literature on how to help your chemically dependent family member.)
P. O. Box 2562
Palos Verdes Peninsula, CA 90274
310-547-5800

Narcotics Anonymous (NA)
(Twelve-step program for all chemically dependent people.)
World Service Office
P. O. Box 9999
Van Nuys, CA 91409
818-773-9999
www.na.org

National Clearinghouse for Alcohol and Drug Information (NCADI)
(Provides information on treatment programs [locations and services offered] throughout the nation. Asking whether you are looking for programs that are either free, funded by the state or paid for or covered by insurance, staff will give you a referral number for your state. When you call that number, their staff will give you the programs closest to your area.)

P. O. Box 2345
Rockville, MD 20847-2345
301-468-2600
800-729-6686
800-487-4889 (TDD)

National Council on Alcoholism and Drug Dependence (NCADD)
(Offers referrals and information on treatment programs, referring you to your local treatment information center to learn what treatment programs are available in your area.)
20 Exchange Place, Ste. 2902
New York, NY 10005
212-269-7797
800-NCA-CALL
www.ncadd.org

National Organization of Student Assistance Programs and Partners
4760 Walnut St., #106
Boulder, CO 80301
800-972-4636